BRITISH FAIRY ORIGINS

LEWIS SPENCE

Facsimile Edition.

Lewis Spence. *British Fairy Origins*
First published in 1946.

ISBN: 978-2-925611-28-8
Printed in the USA.

www.ultimatumeditions.com

BRITISH FAIRY ORIGINS

BY

LEWIS SPENCE

Author of *The Gods of Mexico, An Introduction to Mythology*, etc.

LONDON:

WATTS & CO.,

5 & 6 JOHNSON'S COURT, FLEET STREET, E.C.4

INTRODUCTORY

FEW relics of tradition have aroused so much interest in the minds of lettered and unlettered alike as that body of superstitious belief which relates to the existence of fairy spirits. Only within the lifetime of many who still survive has it been partly resigned by the peasantry of this island. At the end of last century, and in the early years of this, it received the enthusiastic consideration of some of the most distinguished minds of the period, as the roll of its recorders and their critics reveals. In Europe its research has been productive of one of the most extensive and accomplished literatures known to modern culture. Debate as to its lore and origins has aroused controversies as vehemently eloquent as any known to the spheres of philosophy, religion, or politics. Yet a seemingly indefatigable and highly distinguished scholarship has lavished its utmost powers upon its investigation, with results which cannot be described as more than partially successful.

How are we to account for this seemingly egregious solicitude on the part of so many eminent and gifted scholars and writers for a theme so apparently trivial? I have tried to analyse the reasons for my own profound and life-long absorption in the legend of Faerie, although I may not compare myself with its more notable exponents. A large collection of fairy tales inherited from a romantic grandfather, acting upon a mind naturally receptive of the marvellous, though still oddly sceptical of it, inspired me at an early age with a powerful preference for the fairy theme. At a more adult stage the critical faculty naturally cast about for explanations concerning the origins of what now appeared as fabulous, and I gradually embarked upon the serious study of fairy tales as folk-lore.

This very simple and natural process fully explains, I believe, the circumstances in which most students have embraced and pursued the problem of Faerie. It is not the mere enchantment of its *fabliaux* alone which intrigues the mature mind. It is the supreme difficulty experienced in accounting for the origins of the fairy superstition, in finding a formula which shall express its original nature, which has inspired so many brilliant men and women to ransack the records of elfin tradition. Here indeed is a problem which might satisfy the most exacting seeker after hidden things. It challenges one's intellectual vanity, it excites one's curiosity. The best proof of its complexity is the existence of the very numerous theories which seek, or pretend, to account for it. Scores of other vexed questions in tradition and in the greater fields of science have been laid at rest; yet this remains unsolved and seemingly insoluble. Since the first decade of this century the pursuit of its secret has been engaged in only fitfully by an exhausted and depleted corps of interpreters. It has become the philosopher's stone of traditional science. Concerning the origins of the fairy belief, students of folk-lore have agreed to differ, and to-day even the most knowledgeable among them allude to it in the phrase of compromise.

Towards the end of last century, as we shall see, the controversy on fairy origins was waged with a vigour and ingenuity truly remarkable. Men whose names were household words in respect of their achievements in the sphere of tradition debated the numerous ancillary questions which relate to it with a fervour and a display of erudition which won for the study a popular interest it has never succeeded in regaining. With the passing of the more distinguished among its exponents—Alfred Nutt, Andrew Lang, Sir John Rhys, E. S. Hartland, Sir Laurence Gomme, Edward Clodd, Marian Roalfe Cox, Grant Allen, S. Baring-Gould, J. G. Campbell, A. C. Haddon, and others—the study of Faerie languished, and was indeed diverted into the larger channel of animistic speculation which the researches of Sir James Frazer so greatly augmented. Still, several well-known students of fairy lore have continued to pursue its problems solely because of the anthropological interest and value they possess, and not because they were inspired to do so by a sentimental adolescent " hangover."

The case for the origins of British Faerie has not so far been dealt with historically. No published work dealing exclusively with the subject has adequately summarized the several important theories which seek to explain these beginnings, as I hope to be enabled to do in the pages which follow. But to summarize them alone, without adding one's own point of view, would be unfair both to those who conceived them as well as to the theme. Perhaps more than sixty years of sojourn in fairy precincts has given me the right to advance an opinion of my own concerning the nature of their primitive foundations. But it would be more than absurd to hope for complete success where so many of my superiors have failed.

In my view the study of fairy origins assumes a greater degree of importance than popular opinion is wont to concede to it. Indeed, the ideas associated with it strike at the very roots of human belief and primitive methods of reasoning. It is scarcely to be questioned that the explanation of fairy origins is of the utmost value to the better comprehension of primitive religion. Later it will be made clear that, for the writer at least, the whole tradition of Faerie reveals quite numerous and excellent proofs of its former existence as a primitive and separate cult and faith, more particularly as regards its appearance and tradition in these islands. At times I have drawn upon foreign examples of tale and rite to illustrate my contentions; but the main body of proof as represented in this book is almost entirely associated with the content of British fairy tradition. Had it embraced the whole range of elfin lore and literature at home and abroad, it would inevitably have greatly surpassed the limits of such a work as the present.

L. S.

CONTENTS

CHAPTER I

THE FAIRY SUPERSTITION

ANY adequate review of those theories which seek to account for the origin of the fairy superstition must necessarily be prefaced by a general description of the beliefs which compose that tradition. For this reason I have devoted the first two chapters of this book to a fairly generous summary of the data associated with British fairy belief. The material in question is by no means of a uniform character as regards its period and authenticity, nor is it drawn from one part of the British area alone. Its examples are occasionally as remote in time, one from another, as is the fifth century of our era from the day-before-yesterday. Portions of it may possibly be derived from the notions of aboriginal British tribes whose very names have been forgotten save by a specialist minority; or they may represent fantastic ideas which have gained popularity from the writings of Elizabethan or Jacobean poets. The possibility that any example or legend respecting fairy belief or practice may be the result of late invention—either of a literary nature, or arising out of local hearsay—must also be steadily kept in view.

The derivation of the word " fairy " has aroused the polemical instincts of etymologists, but here I must deal with it briefly and practically. The generally accepted opinion is that it was distantly derived from the Latin *fatum*, or " fate," describing those goddesses or supernaturals who presided over human fortunes. This term gave rise to the early Italian form *fata*, which, through Roman provincial influence, appeared in Spain as *hada*. It seems as though the Celtic population of Gaul may have slurred or elided the " t," so that it came to have in early French the sound of *fa'a*, with a plural *fa'ae*. My own impression is that this term, through the medium of Norman–French influence, introduced to the English tongue the word " fay." There is, however, the alternative possibility that from *fatum* was derived a mediaeval form *fatare*, meaning " to enchant," with a past participle *fáe*, which resolved itself into *fée*. This again was productive of a noun, *fairie*, or *féerie*, signifying " enchantment," or the state of illusion. It would seem to have been adopted into English as implying both the region of Fairyland, the spirits who dwelt there, and, through later usage, an individual fay, or, as we now say, a

" fairy." [1] The word is certainly not derived from the Persian *peri* or *pari*, as was formerly believed in some quarters, Professor R. A. Nicholson having indicated the virtual impossibility of such a derivation. [2]

The appropriate word in English for an individual of this class of spirit is " fay," not " fairy," which is the objective form, although the latter is accepted so generally that it would be pedantic to insist upon the older usage. The Anglo-Saxon equivalent is *aelf*, our modern " elf." Chaucer and other Old English writers employ " faerie " principally as meaning " enchantment " or " illusion," and only rarely as describing a member of the elfin race. In old Scottish poems and ballads we seldom find " fairy " in the singular, the term " elf," or some substitute-name or cant term, being usually employed, while Fairyland is known as " Elfame," which recalls the Norse *Elf-heim*. Later we find such Scottish plurals as " fairy-folk " or " fair-folk," which reminds one of the Welsh *Tylwyth teg*, " the fair clan, or family." The name " fairy," at least in the singular number, is an acceptance of comparatively recent introduction into Scotland, and does not appear to have been much in use before the end of the sixteenth century, although prior to that time we find the expression " the Fary " used in speaking or writing of Fairyland.

One thing is certain: in old British usage the term faerie, or fairy, more frequently implies " enchantment," " sorcery," or " illusion " than a spirit of the elfin class, and quite overshadows the use of the word in this latter sense. It may perhaps have been a synonym or translation of a genuine Anglo-Saxon noun, *sidsa*, associated with the second part of the term *aelf-siden*, meaning " fairy art or power." [3]

In the older England and Scotland the folk invented a large variety of substitute names for the fairies, as it was considered most unlucky to speak of them directly. The free use of the genuine names of supernaturals was believed to offend them and tempt their vengeance, for, according to savage belief, if you know the name of a person or spirit, you have power over him. So we

---

[1] F. Delattre, *English Fairy Poetry*, p. 25, note 1; J. Grimm, *Teutonic Mythology* (trans. J. S. Stallybrass), I, p. 410; J. A. MacCulloch in Hastings's *Encyclopedia of Religion and Ethics*, I, pp. 678 ff.

[2] R. A. Nicholson, *Folk-Lore*, XLI, p. 355.

[3] M. S. Sergeantson, " Vocabulary of Folk-Lore in Old and Middle English," *Folk-Lore*, XLVII, p. 62.

encounter the use of such expressions as " good folk," " wee folk," " seely (happy or blessed) folk," " the good neighbours," and the like.   In Scotland the elves, or a section of them, were at one time known as " pechs," a word which seems to mean " dwarf," or " goblin."   This expression has been confused in the popular mind with the racial term " Pict," with somewhat vexatious results to research in folk-lore.   In the West of England we find " pixie," and in Old English " pook," meaning " a spirit," both of which are possibly of the same origin as " pech."

Among the Celtic peoples of the Scottish Highlands and Ireland the fairies were known as *sidhe* (pron. shee), meaning " hill-folk " ; that is, dwellers within the hills or mounds.   In modern Ireland such sobriquets as " the Danes " and " the Gentry " are still used in speaking of the elfin race.   Irish antiquaries have not yet made up their minds whether the first of these is a recollection of Scandinavian invaders or of the Tuatha Dé Danann, the gods of Irish mythology.   That it was reminiscent of the latter there is, I think, little question.

The fairies of Britain belong to several dissimilar though scarcely well-defined groups, and these may represent various strata of fairy belief which have grown up at intervals from aboriginal times onward.   We seem, for example, to recognize a very primitive type in certain forms which are described as rough and hirsute in appearance.   We catch glimpses of these in English literature.   Ben Jonson, Shakespeare's great contemporary, speaks in one of his plays of " the coarse and country fairy," while Milton, in his " L'Allegro," alludes to " the lubber fiend " who stretches his " hairy strength " upon the hearth.   He was occasionally known as " Lob-lie-by-the-fire."   He threshed the corn and churned the butter, after which he cast himself down by the hearth, as Ritson says, " like a great rough hurgin (urchin ?) bear."   Puck is universally described as shaggy and primitive in appearance. J. F. Campbell, in his *Popular Tales of the West Highlands*, alludes to various " supernaturals " mentioned in old Gaelic stories as being " bald and crop-eared " and rough of hide.

Similar descriptions are afforded of the brownie of Lowland Scotland and the North of England, a dwarfish and aboriginal-seeming type, of rugged and hirsute exterior.   He undertook odd jobs about farms, receiving milk and food for his services.   That he was one and the same in appearance and habit with Puck is clear from the description of Burton, in his *Anatomie of Melancholy,* who, writing of fairies, says: " A bigger kind there is of them, called with Hobgoblins and Robin Good-fellowes, that would in these superstitious times, grinde corne for a messe of milke, cut wood, or do any kind of drudgery.work."   In the Isle of Man we find the *fynoderee*, another hairy sprite who undertakes agricultural tasks; while in Ireland we encounter the *leprechaun*, whose name links him with the old English lubberkin.

In the Scottish Highlands the *gruagach*, or " hairy one," is a variety of the brownie.   The *urisk*, also, resembles both and undertakes tasks, while the *brollachan*, or *fuath*, is also pictured as rough or hirsute.   " Writers immediately before Shakespeare's time," remarks Alfred Nutt, " regarded the fairies as rude, coarse, and earthy."[1]   A fairy monarch who appeared to the ancient British king, Herla, is pictured as having a large head and a fiery face, while the lower part of his hairy body ended in goat's shanks and hoofs. Hirsute fairies mentioned by St. Augustine were also known in ancient Gaul as *pilosi* (hairy) and *dusii* (devilkins,) [2] and Jacob Grimm equated these with the Scottish brownie.   The pechs of Scotland, whom I have mentioned, were described as " short, wee men, wi' red hair and long arms, but unco' strang," a striking illustration of the primitive " rough " fairy.

In fact nothing could less resemble the delicate and diaphanous fairies of later literary imagination than do these early primitive forms, which appear to have an affinity with the satyrs or fauns of classical myth.   But one characteristic of the " rough " fairy should especially be noted—his almost inevitable association with a certain agricultural family and steading, and more particularly with the household hearth, which he persistently haunts.   This indicates the relationship of the brownie, Puck, the *fynoderee*, and the rest of the hirsute elves, with a well-established European type associated with the hearth and home, and which finds its earliest known exemplar in the *lar* or domestic genius of the Romans, although it is also widely distributed from Britain to Russia and from Scandinavia to the Mediterranean.   The *lar* was a house-spirit; his shrine was the hearth, and it is believed that his cultus was associated with the primitive burial of the family dead beneath the hearthstone.   He is usually represented as clad in the skins of dogs, the animal associated with the dead.   Libations of milk were made to him, as offerings of it were made to

---

[1] A. Nutt, *Folk-Lore*, XXXII, Presidential Address, *passim*.
[2] Augustine, *The City of God*, Bk. XV, c. 23.

brownie.[1] Were the early Roman dead wrapped in dog-skins, as some other Mediterranean corpses were in goat-skins, and did this practice give rise, partly or wholly, to a belief in hirsute ghosts or spirits? It is to be noted, too, that the Highland *gruagach* was in the habit of attending to the domestic cattle. Unless nightly offerings of milk were made to him, the best cow might be found dead in the morning. All through the West Highlands hollow stones are found in which milk-offerings to the *gruagach* were poured, and these are still popularly known as " gruagach stones." [2]

Also ancestral in character are those fairy spirits of the *banshee* type, known in Ireland, the Highlands of Scotland, and Wales, and not altogether unfamiliar to England, as " white ladies." These forms (*banshee* in Ireland, *banshee, glaistig*, and *bean-nighe* in Scotland, *cyhiraeth* in Wales) are usually attached to ancient native families, usually of distinction, and thus differ from the brownie class, who are associated with the humbler folk of the soil —farmers and yeomen. They lament the death of their kindred by terrifying outbursts of grief. The name *banshee* simply means " fairy-woman," but the type is by no means exclusively Celtic, and is known all over Europe. The *glaistig* (water-sprite), a form of the *banshee*, was sometimes believed to be the spirit of a deceased woman of the family, under fairy enchantment.[3] But the *banshee* may be the later representative of a Celtic goddess of death.

To this summary of British fairy classifications must be added some account of the more generalized idea of the British elf of later popular acceptance. Seemingly standing apart from such solitary and non-gregarious types as have already been briefly described is that species of elfin being who dwells in communities. These, the " standard " fairies of folk-lore, are known throughout Britain, from Cornwall to the Shetlands, and tales concerning them vary only slightly in the several British areas. They dwell in mounds, hills, or wild places. Definite objective statements concerning their general appearance are few and vague. They are given to magical practices, possess neighbourly qualities, yet are frequently resentful of human interference and are somewhat treacherous. They are prone to the kidnapping of mortals and their children, and in some cases exact a tithe or tax of corn and

[1] Juvenal, *Satires*, 9. 12.
[2] J. G. Campbell, *Superstitions of the Highlands and Islands of Scotland*, p. 185.
[3] J. G. Campbell, *op. cit.*, p. 45.

milk from their human neighbours. Every seventh year they must pay a tribute of one of their number to Satan. They are governed by a king and queen, marry and bring forth children, and die at an advanced age. The chase appears to be their favourite amusement. They are often the jealous guardians of treasure. The craft of the leech is usually assigned to them, and they possess great skill in the preparation of herbs for medicinal purposes. Occasionally they borrow goods and articles of household use from their mortal neighbours, but invariably repay their debts in full, often adding some gift or boon. Sometimes they inflict injury on human beings by shooting at them with a fairy dart or arrow, or merely by dealing them a buffet. They possess the gift of prophecy. Very frequently they call upon mortal midwives to assist in the delivery of their children. If a mortal penetrate to their subterranean dwellings he can be released from their toils only by the agency of certain spell-breaking rites at certain fixed seasons. In short, their entire economy constitutes what may be described as a definite culture-complex which marks them out as a class of being or spirit not only distinct from man, although in many ways closely resembling him, but also from other spiritual beings.

It has been divulged by the late Alfred Nutt, one of the most precise exponents of British fairy lore, that the British fairy culture-complex, as revealed in the folk-lore of England and Scotland, is to a great extent paralleled by that of modern Ireland. But the process of fairy development in Ireland is much more capable of explanation by virtue of the existence of an associated literature of very considerable antiquity. Some modern Irish fairies descend in an unbroken line from the ancient pantheon of the Irish gods, the Tuatha Dé Danann. In tales possibly a thousand years old they are described by the same name as the Irish peasant describes them to-day—that is, *aes sidhe*, " the folk of the fairy hillocks." We find the self-same fairy characteristics in the personnel of the fairies of Arthurian lore, and to some extent in those of modern British fairy lore.[1]

I will not dwell upon Nutt's theory here, at any length, as its fuller consideration will be necessary at a later stage ; but I may conveniently state that I believe it to be generally sound, and that much of what is posited of the fairy lore of Ireland may also be accepted concerning that of England and Scotland. This being so, it provides us with something in the nature of a horizon or background. But

[1] A. Nutt, *Folk-Lore*, XXXII, Presidential Address.

we must nevertheless encourage a scientific nervousness of a hypo-thesis so very broad. In certain instances and localities the resemblances it suggests appear to hold good. Such tales as that associated with the Scottish minstrel Thomas the Rhymer, for example, and the general circumstances of elfin existence as described in certain early Anglo-Norman romances, as well as in some " modern instances " of British fairy lore, lend colour to it; but numerous exceptions leap to recollection, and it is obvious that in certain localities and cases either an extraordinary degree of degeneration must have taken place in such a tradition, or there has never been any affinity with it. The nature of the English fairies is rightly described by Shakespeare as having a relationship with the concerns of agricultural life. The Scottish elves are similarly interested in agricultural growth and management. All this recalls so closely the tendencies and propensities of the Irish Tuatha Dé Danann and their modern Irish representatives that the resemblance pleads for the most careful consideration of Nutt's general conclusions. Oddly enough, his thesis breaks down precisely in that very area where it might have been thought the circumstances of its Irish association would most naturally have justified its very definite appearance—the Highlands of Scotland. In that region, if we except tales and incidents obviously of Irish importation, we encounter a complex of ideas greatly more primitive and seemingly aboriginal. This notwithstanding, the general picture of elfin life in the Highlands exhibits a superficial resemblance to Irish fairy economy which must almost certainly have been derived in both cases from a much more ancient and common primitive tradition than that associated even with early Irish literature and belief.

The records of English fairy typology in early times may cast some light upon the development of the fairy idea as it existed within this, the most extensive British area. Here, of course, they can only be summarized; but even so, a useful précis may assist the classification of British fairy types.

Roman altars found in Britain provide hints of sylvan spirits and of *deas*, or " mothers," who may be native fairy spirits in a semi-classical guise, although we possess no definite data to justify the acceptance of such a theory. If we depend on Welsh folk-lore and literature, as reflecting an earlier picture of ancient British fairy life, we find that it reveals forms closely resembling the Irish Tuatha Dé Danann—that is, communities of fairy

B

spirits dwelling in mounds and seemingly possessed of a higher culture and more advanced attributes than do the elves of England or Lowland Scotland, who, on occasion, appear as almost startlingly barbarous, thus probably revealing an admixture with aboriginal traditions. But we have no actual justification for the supposition that Welsh folk-lore *does* portray the circumstances of ancient British fairy life in other than a very general way. Regarding the fairy lore of the Anglo-Saxons we know little or nothing, unless from a few vestigial spells and recipes. But we may rest assured that it had the closest affinities with Teutonic. elfin belief, which, when all is said, differs in none of its essentials from Celtic fairy lore, both deriving from a common European traditional stock, as Nutt is careful to indicate.

When we reach the period of the Anglo-Norman writers we find Gervase of Tilbury (d. 1235) describing certain " demons " called by the English " portunes," who, though very diminutive, undertake the same offices as brownies, and indeed the names give the impression of having been derived from the same root.[1] Elsewhere in the same work Gervase speaks of "*follets*," who haunt the houses of the rustics and pelt them with stones and billets,[2] annoying them in much the same manner as did the brownies the folk of Berwickshire, as John Major assures us.[3] Walter Map, who flourished towards the close of the twelfth century, introduces us to a species of fairy later to be more intimately known in romance. He tells us that an English rebel against Norman authority known as Wild Edric beheld a number of strange women amusing themselves in an inn in the Forest of Dean. They were very tall and handsome, and becoming instantly enamoured of one of them, Edric rushed into the house, secured her, and made her captive. He married her and even presented her at Court, but she warned him that he must not reproach her with her supernatural origin. One day, however, he did so, when, incontinently, she vanished.[4]

William of Newbridge and Ralph of Coggeshall, Map's contemporaries, write of the capture in their time of a boy and girl in Suffolk who had penetrated to the upper world from a subterranean country. Their flesh was green in hue. Otherwise they had the appearance of ordinary mortals. The fairies seen by the

[1] Gervase of Tilbury, *Otia Imperialia*, D. 3, c. 61.
[2] Gervase of Tilbury, *op. cit.*, D. 1, c. 18.
[3] John Major, *Exposition of St. Matthew*, fol. xlviii.
[4] Walter Map, *De Nugis Curialium*, II, c. 12.

hero in the fourteenth-century English poem of *Orfeo and Heurodys* closely resemble the tall and dignified folk of the Irish Tuatha Dé Danann, or Map's Forest of Dean fairy ladies, although it is well to keep in mind that the *Orfeo* was a translation from a Breton *lai*. Chaucer's fairy ladies appear to have been of mortal height.

In the fairy types here enumerated we find forms so dissimilar as give us to believe that there must have been a considerable degree of culture-mixing. By the end of the twelfth century three distinct species of fairy had come to be recognized in England—a diminutive type, a dwarfish goblinesque spirit of the brownie type, and a taller and somewhat stately fairy damsel. The rather extraordinary thing is that in few of these stories are the supernatural beings of whom they are related designated by the class-name of " fairy," or by any name at all. There are also exceptions in the satyr-like creature encountered by King Herla, and the " green children " of Suffolk—the one approximating to an early Mediterranean form of wood-spirit, obviously adapted from Classical tale; the other to the elfin mound-dwellers of more general or standardized British superstition. That this latter species was well known in England in the twelfth century is made clear by a story of William of Newbridge, which tells of a community of mound-dwellers in Yorkshire from whom a peasant purloined a fairy cup.[1]

The fairies of Wales fall readily into several classes, and thus reveal the admixture of several cultures. The *pwccas* represent the Puck type of goblin-fairy. The *Gwragedd Annwn* are female fairies of the lakes and streams, of the water-nymph type. The fierce and barbarous mountain fays are known as the *Gwyllion*. The *bwbachod* resembles the brownie, and the *coblynau*, or gnomes of the mines, have their European congeners in those mine-spirits who gave their names to the goblins. The *Ellyllon* are will-o'-the-wisps. The *Tylwyth teg*, or " fair family," whom I have already mentioned, are of human stature, and the tales concerning them remind one of those recounted of the Irish Tuatha Dé Danann.

The question of the height, sex, and general appearance of British fairies demands considerable attention, as these attributes are by no means unimportant in arriving at conclusions about their type and origin. As regards the height of English fairies, we have already seen that it varies with type. In the romance of *Huon of Bordeaux*, an early sixteenth-century English trans-

---

[1] William of Newbridge, *Historia*, I, 27.

lation from the French, it is written of Oberon, the King of the Fairies, that " he is of heyght but III fote and crokyd shulderyd." The portunes of Gervase are only the size of one's thumb. Map's fairy ladies are above the mortal stature; the " green children " of average juvenile height. In later English folk-tales the fairies in the Cornish story of *Cherry of Zennor* are diminutive, but can alter their proportions as they list, while a fairy caught at Zennor is described as being " not more than a foot long." Others, mentioned by Bovet as seen at Taunton in the seventeenth century, were " of a stature near the smaller size of men," and fairies encountered by a Hampshire farmer were " the most diminutive that could be imagined." An elf who played with a boy at Rothley, in Northumberland, was " about the size of a child's doll." According to Hunt there are five varieties of the fairy family in Cornwall, all of whom are more or less diminutive, although some approach near to the lesser standards of human stature.

Scottish fairies vary in size. J. G. Campbell, a knowledgeable authority, wrote that " the true belief is that the Fairies are a small race: the men about four feet or so in height, and the women in many cases not taller than a little girl. Being called little, the exaggeration which popular imagination loves, had diminished them until they appear as elves of different kinds." [1] Grant Stewart speaks of Scottish fairies as being generally low in stature, and Hugh Miller describes them as stunted, misgrown, ugly, creatures with unkempt locks. [2] In a tale from Lochaber they are said to be " big, old, grey-haired men " [3] The ballad of *The Wee Wee Man*, I gather from a careful estimate, describes him as about fifteen inches in height, and he measures three spans between the shoulders. He consorts with fairy ladies who are " jimp and sma'." Mr. Wimberley, an American writer on the subject, holds that " the Fairies of British balladry are, as a rule, of human stature," like the Fairies of romance. [4] Donald MacMichael, who was tried at Inverary in 1677 for sorcery, said the Fairy King with whom he had associated, was like " ane large tall corporal Gardman, and ruddie." The Faerie Queen in the romance of *Thomas the Rhymer* reminds one of the ladies of the Tuatha Dé Danann,

---

[1] J. G. Campbell, *op. cit.*, p. 10.
[2] H. Miller, *The Old Red Sandstone*, p. 251.
[3] J. MacDougal and G. Calder, *Folk-Tales and Fairy Lore*, p. 281.
[4] L. C. Wimberley, *Folk-Lore in the English and Scottish Ballads*, pp. 171-3.

and is of mortal height.   In Galloway the fairies of folk-lore are small, but well proportioned.

The *sidhe* of Ireland, in ancient Irish saga, are scarcely to be distinguished from mortals, save by their beauty.   W. B. Yeats has assured us that " Fairies in Ireland are sometimes as big as we are, sometimes bigger, and sometimes, as I have been told, about three feet high."   Shape-shifting by magic may, he thought, partly explain the variation of their height.   Miss E. Andrews says that in Ulster the fairies were usually about the height of a well-grown boy or girl, though some are diminutive.[1]

The fairies of Shakespeare are, judging from their own descriptions, diminutive; yet they were represented on the stage as mostly of human height.   In *The Merry Wives of Windsor* we find both adults and children disguising themselves as the " fairies " who are to vex Falstaff.   The general notion appears to be that of spirits who can assume at will different degrees of stature, as well as animal and other shapes.   Nutt believed that Shakespeare was thinking of Teutonic fays alone when he envisaged his elves as diminutive.   In all likelihood fairies of larger stature were ancient gods in a state of decay, while their diminutive congeners were the swarming spirits of primitive imagination.

All three of the English types I have mentioned can, I think, be accounted for as the results of the presence of different cultures, existing side by side in the country, and who were the creation of the folk in ages distantly removed one from another.   In a word, they represent specific " strata " of folk-imagination.   The most diminutive of all are very probably to be associated with a New Stone Age conception of spirits which haunted burial-mounds and rude stone monuments.   We find such tiny spirits haunting the great stone circles of Brittany.   The " Small People," or diminutive fairies of Cornwall, says Hunt, are believed to be " the spirits of people who inhabited Cornwall many thousands of years ago."   The spriggans, of the same area, are a minute and hirsute family of fairies " found only about the cairns, cromlechs, barrows, or detached stones, with which it is unlucky to meddle."   Of these, the tiny fairies of Shakespeare, Drayton, and the Elizabethans appear to me to be the later representatives.   *The latter are certainly not the creation of seventeenth-century poets, as has been stated, but of the aboriginal folk of Britain.*

Some writers on fairy lore have insisted that fairies were of the

[1] E. Andrews, *Ulster Folk-Lore*, p. 2.

female sex alone, and that such tales as speak of male fairies are inspired by more modern and corrupt ideas. The late Sir John Rhys was at least a protagonist of this very lame hypothesis, which is set forth in his *Celtic Folklore, Welsh and Manx.* Yet in the first volume of that work I find not less than fourteen references to fairy *men* in Welsh tradition! It is true that in Wales fairy women figure more prominently than in Scottish folk-lore. But, setting modern fairy lore aside altogether, we find fairies of the masculine gender so continually alluded to in old Irish saga as to substantiate the existence of the male elfin beyond all doubt. Scottish ballads of an antiquity more than " respectable " contain many allusions to male fairies. An entire fairy caste such as the brownies—who are not exclusively male, by the way—which is obviously very ancient could scarcely have been imagined had it been a law of folk-lore that elves could not be otherwise than female. The Highland *gruagach* is likewise known to be of both sexes. The evidence of Scottish witch trials is full of allusions to fairy men. In England Puck is recognizably masculine, and Chaucer, in his " Wife of Bath's Tale," alludes to the dread of the country woman for the male fairy.

In old France, it is true, the female fairy was supreme. This eminence of the female in Gallic romance and the allusion to " islands of women " in ancient Irish saga, no less than the preponderance of the female elements in Balkan and modern Greek fairy lore, induced the notion in some writers of limited experience that the fairies were exclusively feminine. Nutt clarified the situation by remarking, with his usual acumen, that in Irish fairy tales the women stood out more clearly than the men " because the mortal hero was the centre of attraction, and to glorify the fairy woman is to heighten his glory." [1] Such an array of evidence, indeed, could be brought, were it necessary, against this lopsided argument that it would collapse under the sheer weight of adverse proof. That the existence of female classical forms resembling fairies (*Matres, Moirai, Fatae*) gave an impetus to the theory cannot be questioned. But these were goddesses who, through the possession of magical and other fairy traits, came to be drawn at a later time into the elfin aggregate and tradition, and who have little in common with the aboriginal idea of the fairy spirit, which was certainly of both sexes, as the whole record of early British fairy lore triumphantly reveals.

[1] A. Nutt, *Folk-Lore*, XXXII, Presidential Address.

Fairies appear to have had certain distinguishing marks. Shakespeare employs the expression " elfish-marked." In *Romeo and Juliet* he refers to elf-locks as having been " baked " by Queen Mab. Thomas Lodge, in his *Wit's Miserere* (1596), says of a person that " his haires are curl'd al f.ll of Elves locks." Elsewhere the elf-lock is described as " a hard matted or clotted lock of hair in the neck." We also hear of an elvish cast of eye, as witnessing to the fairy paternity of an infant.[1] Puck is frequently depicted with grotesquely pointed ears, resembling those of an animal.

The question of fairy costume is of almost equal importance. British fairies, as a general rule, are addicted to " the wearin' o' the green." There are notable exceptions, however. The plausibly classical elf encountered by King Herla was garbed in a spotted fawn-skin. The fairy ladies seen in Shropshire by Wild Edric were draped in graceful linen garments. Shakespeare, in *The Merry Wives of Windsor*, alludes to black, grey, green, and white fairies, and this may refer to the colour of their garments. ·Fairies who held a fair near Taunton were garbed in red, blue, and green, " according to the old way of country garb, with high-crowned hats." [2] The elves of the south-west of England wore green for the most part, with a red or blue cap and a feather.[3]

In North Wales, the *Tylwyth Teg*, or " Fair Family," wore blue petticoats. The elves of Pembrokeshire were garbed in scarlet, with feathered caps. Some modern Welsh fays appear to be dressed exclusively in white.[4] Others display striped garments. In the Isle of Man, *loaghtyn*, a woollen fabric occasionally undyed, but sometimes coloured green or blue, is the more regular elfin wear.[5]

In Ireland the ancient Tuatha Dé Danann appear to have been garbed in the elaborate costume of the upper classes, gorgeous in the extreme.[6] Green, however, seems to have entered into the general scheme.[7] Some of the fairies of later Irish folk-lore, like their Scottish congeners, occasionally wear tartan with plaids and bonnets.[8] They have also been described as wearing

<hr>

[1] E. S. Hartland, *The Science of Fairy Tales*, p. 60.
[2] T. Keightley, *The Fairy Mythology*, p. 294.
[3] R. Hunt, *Popular Romances of the West of England*, p. 120.
[4] Wirt Sikes, *British Goblins*, pp. 112–13.
[5] G. Waldron, *A Description of the Isle of Man*, p. 104.
[6] A. Nutt, *The Voyage of Bran*, I, pp. 131, 180.
[7] E. Hull, *Folk-Lore*, XXXVIII, p. 211.
[8] D. Hyde, quoted by W. B. Yeats in *Fairy and Folk-Tales of the Irish Peasantry*, p. 324.

" bracket " clothes and caps—that is, of speckled cloth (Gaelic *breacan*, or tartan.) [1]   In Antrim they occasionally dress in green or in tartan, although red is the more usual colour-scheme.

In Lowland Scotland the fairies, says Cromek, appear in " mantles of green cloth inlaid with wild flowers " and reaching to the middle.   They sport " green pantaloons buttoned with bobs of silk, and sandals of silver."   Their " long fleeces of yellow hair " are caught up with golden combs.   This is obviously a late and " literary " description.[2]   But an old woman of Nithsdale described the fairies to the same authority who made it as " wee fowk."   And he speaks of other fairies of the Galloway area as " small, beautiful, and cleanly," while others are of the height of " little boys."   Thome Reid, a fairy man seen by Bessie Dunlop, a Scottish witch, wore the costume of a Lowland small farmer. Other fairies encountered by this woman were dressed " like gentlemen," while their female companions wore plaids.[3]   A fairy queen, with whom a witch, one Isobel Goudie, had dealings near Nairn, was clad in white linen and brown cloth.[4]   The elves mentioned by Hugh Miller were habited in antique jerkins of plaid, long grey cloaks, and red caps.[5]   In the ballad of *Tam Lin* the hero is dressed in " elfin gray."   In that of *The Wee Wee Man* the fairy ladies are attired " in glistening green."

The attire of the Highland fairies is more constant.   The Rev. Robert Kirk, who lived at Aberfoyle, near " the Highland Line," at the end of the seventeenth century, tells us that " their Apparell and Speech is like that of the people and country under which they live, so are they seen to wear Plaids and variegated Garments in the Highlands of Scotland and Suanochs (coarse mantles) in Ireland."[6]   J. F. Campbell, in one of his West Highland tales, describes them as dressed in green kilts and green conical caps.[7] Scott tells us that the fairies of the moors " were sometimes clad in heath-brown or lichen-dyed garments," while Grant Stewart, a careful authority, declares that they were garbed in plain worsted green.[8]   J. G. Campbell avers that in Skye the fairy women dress

<hr>

[1] Lady Gregory, *Visions and Beliefs in the West of Ireland,* p. 107.
[2] R. H. Cromek, *Remains of Nithsdale and Galloway Song,* p. 237.
[3] W. Scott, *Letters on Demonology and Witchcraft,* pp. 145–6.
[4] W. Scott, *op. cit.,* p. 160.
[5] H. Miller, *op. cit.,* p. 251.
[6] R. Kirk, *The Secret Commonwealth of Elves, Fauns, and Fairies,* p. 73.
[7] J. F. Campbell, *Popular Tales of the West Highlands,* IV, p. 343.
[8] W. Grant Stewart, *The Popular Superstitions of the Highlands of Scotland,* p. 64.

in green, while the men " wear clothes of any colour, like their human neighbours," although these are occasionally dyed with crotal, a reddish-brown dye, extracted from lichen. The women dress in shaggy or ruffled coats and wrinkled caps, while the men have blue bonnets.[1]

Some discussion of the nature and temperament of the fairies is necessary in view of its possible bearing on their origin. J. G. Campbell tells us that in the Highlands of Scotland they were regarded as " the counterparts of mankind, but substantial and unreal, outwardly invisible." [2] They differ from mortals in the possession of magical power, but are strangely dependent in many ways on man. They are generally considered by the folk at large as of a nature between spirits and men. " They are," says Wentz, " a distinct race between our own and that of spirits." [3] Robert Kirk, who was inclined to be mystical in his views, says of them : " These *siths*, or Fairies, are said to be of a middle Nature betuixt Man and Angel, as were Daemons said to be of old; of intelligent, studious Spirits and light changeable Bodies (lyke those called Astral) somewhat of the nature of a condensed Cloud, and best seen in twilight." He adds that their chief vices are " Envy, Spite, Hypocracie, Lieing, and Dissimulation." [4]

Quite a number of writers comment on the decidedly human character of the fairies, but it must be obvious that practically all supernaturals partake of human traits, more usually unpleasant ones, being as they are the projections of man's fear and imagination and created by him, psychologically, in his own image. Fairies are frequently described as being peevish, irritable, and revengeful to a degree. Grant Stewart says rather unmercifully of the Scottish fairies that " their appetites are as keen as their inclinations are corrupt and wicked "!

So far as fairy polity and government are concerned, we find the British fairies generally thought of as governed by royalty. In England the old poets are rather lavish of their references to fairy kings and queens, and later, in the period of Spenser and the Elizabethan writers, this notion is even more clearly established. The name of Shakespeare's Oberon is a borrowing from the French, Oberon being merely the German dwarf-king Alberich (*Albe rich* —" elf-king ") in a Gallic dress : while his queen, Titania, is a late

<hr>

[1] J. G. Campbell, *op. cit.*, p. 14.   [2] J. G. Campbell, *op. cit.*, p. 2.
[3] W. Y. E. Wentz, *The Fairy Faith in Celtic Countries*, p. 47.
[4] R. Kirk, *op. cit.*, pp. 67, 81.

emanation from that second and Greek-Latin Diana, a sorceress-fairy associated with the moon and childbirth, who was regarded as the patroness of the Italian witches so lately as half a century ago. She possesses few of the traits of her more ancient mythological namesake.   In some French romances King Arthur is alluded to as the heir presumptive of Oberon to the fairy throne, but it seems unlikely that this idea was natively English.   In Elizabethan times the fairy queen was regarded as a species of sorceress capable of foretelling the future and guiding people to fame and fortune, as passages relating to her in Ben Jonson's play *The Alchemist*, and other writings of the period, make plain.

In many Scottish fairy tales allusions are made to kings and queens of Faerie, nearly all of which come from Lowland sources. Thomas the Rhymer, the thirteenth-century poet and seer, meets the Queen of Faerie on Huntly Banks and is introduced to her court.   Montgomerie, in his *Flyting*, or exchange of repartee, with Polwart (*ca.* 1515), speaks of " the King of Pharie and his court, with the Elf-queen."   Bessie Dunlop, an Ayrshire woman, in her trial for witchcraft in 1576, alleged that the Fairy Queen paid her a visit.   She was " a stout woman," who sat down and " asked a drink at her." [1]   James I and VI remarks, in his *Demono- logie* (1597), that a popular tradition of his time asserted " how there was a King and Queene of Phairie, of such a jolly court and train as they had," and he adds that many mortals were in the habit of visiting these royalties.[2]   Andro Man, who was tried at Aberdeen for sorcery, in 1597, declared that he had been the husband of the Fairy Queen for many years and had had children by her.[3] The Scottish witch trials of the sixteenth and seventeenth centuries are heavy with reference to fairy royalty.

In the Scottish ballad of *Tam Lin* a fairy queen is alluded to who is followed in her night-riding by three separate courts, these several bands being in keeping with the rank or station of the riders, for the elfin economy appears to have been the reverse of democratic.   Jamieson's collected ballad, or conte-fable, of *Childe Rowland* speaks of a " King of Ferrie," whose gorgeous surroundings recall those of the mortal monarchs of West Highland folk-lore.

It is an odd circumstance that, although the fairy monarchs of

---

[1] R. Pitcairn, *Criminal Trials in Scotland*, I, pt. ii, pp. 52–3.
[2] King James I and VI, *Demonologie*, p. 74.
[3] *Spalding Club Miscellany*, I, pp. 120, 127.

Lowland Scottish tradition bear a close resemblance to those of the Irish Tuatha Dé Danann, Highland fairy lore has very little to say of fairy royalties, though the reverse might have been expected, judging from its alleged Hibernian affinities—surely an added proof that, apart from local Irish literary influence in the West Highlands, the fairy tradition in Northern Scotland owes more to native and probably aboriginal tendency than to imported belief. This may account for the fact that Robert Kirk entitled his book on the northern fays *The Secret* Commonwealth *of Elves, Fauns, and Fairies*. In later Lowland legend the Fairy Queen appears as " a kind of feudatory sovereign under Satan," as Aytoun has it; this notion, of course, being due to the harsh and unimaginative attitude of the Church.

Irish fairy saga and tale abound in references to elfin kings and queens from its earliest records onward. In more modern times Fiachra ruled in Co. Mayo, while in Galway the famous Finvarra held sway. In Co. Limerick Donn Firinne, and in Co. Clare Donn Dumhach, led the fairy hosts. These are either ancient gods or heroes metamorphosed into elfin kings, " the gentry," who hunted, wined, and dined with the all-too-jovial Irish squireens of the early nineteenth century, who probably beheld them through the tinted glasses of Bacchus. " There is a king, a queen, and a fool (jester) in each house of them," Lady Gregory was informed.[1] " A map of fairy Ireland," wrote Alfred Nutt, " could without much difficulty be drawn, showing with almost political exactness the various kingdoms of the ' *Sidhe*,' and thus revealing their strong resemblance to human beings. We note that their territory and interests seem at times to tally with those of the great septs which represent the tribal organization of ancient Ireland." [2] " It is of those they steal away they make queens for as long as they live, or that they are satisfied with them," said an Irish peasant to Lady Gregory—a statement which appears as reminiscent of the ancient cult of the sacred queen.[3] The king of the Welsh fairies is Gwynn ap Nudd, who was also ruler over the goblin tribe in general and lord of the dead.[4]

As is the case with most spiritual beings, the creations of man's fancy, fairies are closely identified with the powers of magic and illusion. Magical skill would appear to vest in the fairy race, who

---

[1] Lady Gregory, *op. cit.*, p. 108.
[2] A. Nutt, *The Fairy Mythology of Shakespeare*, p. 14.
[3] Lady Gregory, *op. cit.*, p. 99.　　[4] J. Rhys, *Hibbert Lectures*, p. 84.

inherit it naturally, while mankind only acquires it. The form of sorcery most intimately connected with the elfin folk is that of enchantment, illusion, or, to employ its eloquent Scottish equivalent, " glamourie." By means of this art, or power, the fairies were able so to transform places and objects that they assumed a totally different appearance from that which they naturally possessed. What might appear to the night-bound wayfarer as a lordly castle or a magnificent palace, was found, in the light of morning, to be a noisome ditch or a barren rock. Or, in the twinkling of an eye, the whole fairy scene might vanish, giving place to moor or wilderness. Rags took on the semblance of the richest attire, while leaves or beans assumed the appearance of golden coin. In J. F. Campbell's tale from the West Highlands, *The Daughter of King Underwaves*, a castle vanishes overnight, appearing by daylight as a moss-hole.[1] Tales of this kind are so numerous in British fairy lore, and so familiar, that to quote a number of these as illustrating the superstition in question seems as unnecessary as reciting nursery rhymes to a gathering of adults. And, incidentally, I may say that, though I believe adequate legendary or primitive anecdotal illustration to be essential to the appropriate explication of major folk-lore problems, where the topic is of the nature of a household word, I am by no means convinced of its necessity. The late Sir James Frazer set a bad example of the long-winded collection of endless illustrations. I should be among the last to deny the practical results of his endeavours; but the world of tradition would have been all the richer had he given more space to the precise solution of its larger problems and less to the heaping-up of " illustrations," which in many cases amount to mere cataloguing, and can scarcely be denominated as of the nature of scholarly research.

Occasionally the fairies initiated certain favoured mortals into their arts, as we shall see when we come to discuss the question of Faerie as a cultus. Among these powers one of the most salient was the assumption of invisibility. Fairies everywhere possess the ability to disappear as suddenly as an office-boy when he is most wanted. In the ballad of *The Wee Wee Man* the elfin dwarf and his dwelling vanish in the twinkling of an eye, or, as the clumsy peasant rhyme has it:

> " But before ye could hae said ' What was that? '
> The house and wee manie was awa."

---

[1] J. F. Campbell, *op. cit.*, III, p. 421.

Hind Etin, in the ballad which recounts the kidnapping of his mortal bride, cast a fairy mist around himself and his captive so that none might behold their exit. Certain elves appear to be permanently invisible unless one possesses a talisman by which they can be descried. To others belongs some article of dress which renders them invisible—a hat or a cloak.[1] In British lore such vehicles of invisibility are rare, though one recalls the magic mantles of Arthur and Manannan and the ring of Luned.[2] In England fern-seed was the prime recipe for fairy invisibility, though it could also confer this on human folk. It must be gathered between twelve and one on Midsummer Night.[3] A good list of references to recipes for invisibility will be found in Miss M. R. Cox's masterpiece *Cinderella* (Notes, par. 67, pp. 517–18). To strike a fairy was to render him viewless.

> " 'Tis Robin, or some spirit walkes about.
> Strike him, quoth he, and it will turn to aire.
> Cross yourselves thrice and strike him." [4]

In the Highlands of Scotland we find the subject of fairy invisibility associated with the belief in what was known as "*fith-fath*" or "*fath-fith.*" This was an incantation or "word-spell" in rhyme (for that is what the term implies) originating in the idea that words held magical power.[5] It could either render the speaker invisible or transform a person or object into another form. Thus it was capable of changing human beings into animals.[6] It was also familiarly known in Ireland, and is employed by the gods of Irish mythology in many tales, either to effect physical changes in these deities themselves or to enchant mortals into shapes other than their own.

In many countries the fairies were supposed to possess an ointment or salve which conferred upon mortals the power of beholding them and their environment, and which, indeed, may have been regarded as the source of their own supernatural powers of vision. A tale common to many lands describes how a woman who nursed a fairy child was given a certain unguent to

[1] J. Grimm, *Teutonic Mythology* (English trans, Stallybrass), p. 462.
[2] Lady C. Guest, *Mabinogion*, p. 286.
[3] J. G. Frazer, *The Golden Bough*, II, p. 287.
[4] R. Corbet, *Iter Boreale.*
[5] G. Henderson, *Norse Influence on Scotland*, p. 73.
[6] A. Carmichael, *Carmina Gadelica*, p. 22   E. Hull, *Folk-Lore*, XXI, p. 442; W. MacKenzie, *Gaelic Incantations*, pp. 45 f.; O'Curry, *Atlantis*, III, pp. 386–8, note 15; D'Arbois de Jubainville, *The Irish Mythological Cycle* (trans. R. I. Best), pp. 156–8; J. Rhys, *op. cit.*, pp. 276, note 3.

rub on its eyes.   By accident or intention, she smeared the ointment over one of her own eyes, and was thus enabled to see the
elves at any time or place.   But when the fairies discovered how
she had overreached them, they deprived her of the sight of the
enchanted member.[1]

Shape-shifting was another prime attribute of fairy sorcery.
This applies more particularly to the protean method by which the
elves could assume any form they chose for purposes of illusion.
In English fairy lore we find Robin Goodfellow famous for such
metamorphoses.   In an old pamphlet which deals with his birth
and history we read of his father, the Fairy King, adjuring him to :—

> " change when thou wilt thine elfish shape
>   to horse or hog or dog or ape."

Ben Jonson, in his ballad of *Robin Goodfellow*, also alludes to
his hero's power of transforming himself :—

> " Sometimes I meet them like a man,
>   Sometimes an ox, sometimes a hound,
> And to a horse I turn me can
>   To trip and trot them round about."

In the ballad of *Tam Lin* the hero who has been changed into
a fairy youth must undergo many alterations of form before he is
finally released by the constancy of his sweetheart—an adder, a
snake, a red-hot iron, a fox, and an eel.   These may represent the
forms he was capable of assuming while he partook of the elfin
nature.   They seem to have no connection with initiation into the
fairy mystery and estate, as some authorities have suggested.   In
the Scottish Highlands most tales concerning shape-shifting are
associated with fairy women who take the form of deer.   If
these be shot at, the result is usually fatal to the hunter.   In Wales
a farmer's daughter beheld a troop of fairies assume the forms of
a flock of birds, sheep, swine, and infants within a short time.[2]
Some foreign fairies were prone to such transformations; the
famous Melusine, for example, partially assuming the form of a
serpent every Saturday.   Such notions may not arise out of
animistic doctrine, but may be due to a primitive belief in the fluid
or protean nature of spirit, which, it is universally thought, can
readily assume any form.   Sea-gods, particularly, are prone to such
metamorphoses, and this idea probably reflects the ever-changing

---

[1] E. S. Hartland, *op. cit.*, pp. 59 ff.
[2] Wirt Sikes, *op. cit.*, pp. 108–9.

character of their environment. Alternatively, and especially in the case of the enchantment of fleshly mortals by fairies into animal or other shapes, it may be the result of an overpowering belief in the potency of magic to effect any alteration—so ready is savage, and sometimes " civilized," man to give credence to the marvellous!

The elfin race were thought of as wreaking woe upon mankind by discharging at them magical flint darts or arrows, the wounds from which brought about partial or entire paralysis, the languor which followed enabling the elves to carry off their victims to Fairyland. Resembling this was " the fairy stroke "—a supernatural injury inflicted occultly, causing epilepsy or paralysis, which in some cases involved the hypothecation of the victim's soul. The former, in Scotland, was almost invariably fatal in its results. To be struck by a fairy whirlwind or blast also produced a similar effect of physical helplessness; but its results would yield to appropriate treatment by a " fairy doctor "—that is, a person who specialized in curing complaints induced by fairy agency. In some parts of Ireland the " stroke " induced a death-like trance, in which the real body was borne off by the fairies, a log of wood being substituted for it; and this, by magic, assumed the afflicted person's image. In other parts of Ireland the soul was spirited away and the body left. The idea probably originated in the superstition that certain planets or heavenly bodies discharged fatal " influences " disastrous to man. In ancient Mexico, for example, the gods, in planetary forms, were thought of as discharging malignant rays which caused paralysis and seizures.[1] This belief appears to have been transferred to the fairies as aerial spirits.

Prophecy—the foretelling of events and the future of children, as well as their endowment with certain gifts or qualities—was regarded elsewhere as a salient fairy characteristic; but this belief is scarcely very evident in British fairy tradition, though instances of it are by no means unheard of. Here I should like to mention my own conviction that, in Scotland, what was known as " the Second Sight " was originally regarded as a means of beholding the fairies, and that only by a later extension of the idea did it come to be employed for the purpose of looking into the future or foretelling death. It is clear from the account of it given by Robert Kirk in his *Secret Commonwealth*, written in 1691, that he regards it as chiefly designed for envisaging the fairies, as indeed the sub-

---

[1] L. Spence, *The Gods of Mexico*, pp. 317–18, 355–7.

title of his essay makes particularly clear. He fully describes the manner in which it could be acquired for this especial purpose. The English antiquary, John Aubrey, received several private letters from Scotland even before Kirk had written his pamphlet, which emphasized the same view, and numerous evidences of what is a very plain, but hitherto neglected, fact abound in Scottish folk-lore—instances which, unfortunately, I cannot elaborate in this place.

CHAPTER II

THE FAIRY SUPERSTITION (*continued*)

TABOO, as most people are aware, is a prohibition against infringing the sacred or forbidden. It has relationships with so many departments of folk-lore that it is scarcely surprising to find it intruding itself into the sphere of Faerie. The manner in which it does so is manifold. Its restrictions apply more particularly to the abuse of the fairy name and to the eating of fairy food. To the second instance, however, the term " taboo " scarcely applies as the elves, for reasons of their own, are invariably anxious that mortals should partake of their fare. Further, it is regarded as a distinct breach of elfin law or privilege to till fairy soil, or to remove stone, timber, or leaf from its precincts.

As regards the prohibition on the utterance of the fairy name by mortals, either that of the species as a whole, or of individuals, this undoubtedly issued from sources exceedingly ancient. It is implicit in animistic belief that the name of a man or spirit is a vital part of the individual. In some remoter areas of the world a person's name is still regarded as being equally vital or important with his spirit or soul, and to know it and pronounce it presumes power over the person or spirit to whom it belongs. Supernatural beings in general are indeed exceedingly touchy upon the subject of their names being freely bandied about, and to this rule fairies are no exception. It is for this reason that the fays have bestowed upon them such alternative titles or sobriquets as " the good neighbours," or " the wee folk." " We find," says Wentz, " that taboos of a religious and social character are as common in the living fairy-faith as exorcisms. The chief one is against naming the fairies."

> " Gin ye ca' me fairy,
> I'll wark ye muckle tarrie [trouble],"

says an old Scottish rhyme which popular belief put into the mouths of the elves. " The fairies," remarks Robert Chambers, " are said to have been exceedingly sensitive upon the subject of their popular appellations. They considered the term ' fairy ' disreputable." [1] There were times and seasons when it was

---

[1] R. Chambers, *Popular Rhymes of Scotland*, p. 324.

unlawful to mention the fairy name. If a dairymaid in the Outer Hebrides was asked to hurry in milking the cows, she would reply, " Hurry the woman of the town beyond," meaning Fairyland, thus averting the reproach from herself to those whom it was perilous to reproach.[1]

" As a rule, throughout Europe, the fairy is anonymous," says Alfred Nutt, " and is conceived by the peasant collectively rather than individually. It is the exception, outside Ireland, to find a definite name and personality assigned to members of the fairy world." [2] This is accounted for by the fact that those Irish fairies whose names are freely used by the peasantry are drawn from the ranks of the Tuatha Dé Danann (Folk of the Tribe of Danu) who were formerly gods, before they received fairy status, and whose names were matter of popular knowledge. Some fairy ladies even refused to acquaint their mortal husbands with their names, and the same applies to some fairy husbands. Even speech with fairies appears to have been regarded as actually dangerous in some British areas. In *The Merry Wives of Windsor*, Falstaff, beholding children dressed as elves, ejaculates: " They are fairies, he who speaks to them shall die." The Fairy Queen, in the ballad of *Thomas the Rhymer*, requests the hero to maintain silence in Elfland, whatever he may hear or see, and to speak no word there until he returns to the mortal sphere. In the romance of *Huon of Bordeaux* the hero is warned not to address Oberon on peril of his life.

Numerous tales are told of the anxious care with which fairy folk conceal their names. But should these be divulged by accident or inadvertence on the part of the elves themselves, they are bound to undertake any task which the lucky human eavesdropper may command, or free him from any vow he has made to them.[3] The knowledge of their names has magically placed them within his power.

One who does the fairies a service must never ask more than his just due in payment for the same. This idea certainly arose out of the belief that fairy spirits, in their ancient aspect of gods, personified the sense of justice and right-dealing—a doctrine I shall elaborate farther on.

To partake of fairy food placed a mortal entirely in the power of

[1] A. Goodrich Freer, *Folk-Lore*, X, p. 270.
[2] A. Nutt, *The Voyage of Bran*, II, p. 220.
[3] For taboo on fairy names, see E. S. Hartland, *The Science of Fairy Tales*, pp. 309 ff.

the elves.   After eating it he became to all intents and purposes a member of the fairy band.   In this we perceive the germ of the ancient idea of communion with supernatural beings.   Robert Kirk remarks upon the spiritual character of elfin fare, which he asserts is merely the essence of human food.[1]   In Scotland " the good neighbours " were said to subsist upon the root of the silver weed which is ploughed up in spring, and the tops of young heather, while they drank the milk of the red hind and extracted that of cows at a distance by means of drawing it magically through a hair rope or tether.   The fragments which fell to the floor after a meal were also believed in the Highlands to be perquisites of the fairies.[2]   In the old romance of *Thomas of Erceldoun* the Fairy Queen warns the minstrel that he must not eat the fruit of an orchard through which they pass, as if he does so he will remain in hell until doomsday.   The prohibition against fairy food is, of course, one and the same with that which places a taboo on the food of the dead or the pabulum of the gods.   The explanation is that, in barbarous opinion, to eat of food proffered binds one to the giver.   A mystic relationship is thus formed, in virtue of which the eater partakes of the nature of his host.   If there is any difference in relation to fairy food, it is that the prohibition is not recognized by the elves.   Concerning the taboo on fairy soil, it will be more convenient to deal with this question briefly in the chapter devoted to " Traces of Ritual in Fairy Belief."

Hunting and riding in procession were among the major amusements of the fairy court.   The elves would occasionally ride by moonlight through a district, with a great jingling of silver bells at their horses' bridles.   The fairy horses of the best strain are invariably described as milk-white in hue.   Horses which were found in the morning with their flanks in a lather of foam were considered to have been elf-ridden during the previous night.   In all likelihood we must look for the origin of this belief to the ancient European legend of " the Wild Hunt," which was probably inspired by the hurly-burly of the night-wind giving the impression of an aerial host sweeping past.   With this notion we must associate the idea that the gods, or supernaturals, the providers of food, were the masters or controllers of the game supply, and that they were regarded as themselves indulging in hunting it down,

---

[1] R. Kirk, *The Secret Commonwealth of Elves, Fauns, and Fairies*, pp. 67–8, 114.

[2] G. Henderson, *Survivals in Belief Among the Celts*, p. 252.

precisely as did early man. We know, too, that some bands of British fairies—the Sluagh of the West Highlands, for example—were actually thought of as hunting men with bows and arrows during their flight through the air, so that they might capture their souls. The Sluagh are sometimes regarded as fairies, at others as the dead, and the probability is that the fairies, in their form of the souls of the dead, were in this respect regarded as tracking down the souls of the living.

The association of the fairies with agriculture is important. That they retained the ownership of all waste land until it was cleft by the spade is generally accepted as genuine folk-belief. As we have seen, some of them, particularly the brownies, actually assisted in agricultural labour. In the West Highlands, if supplicated, they occasionally appeared in a swarm and speedily turned the soil until it was ready for planting.[1] In such cases, however, they not infrequently succeeded in escheating the ensuing crop by a trick, or through a bargain couched in obscure or garbled terms.

Fairies were, indeed, thought of as exercising control over the crops. In Savoy they are said to have taught the people the art of agriculture. In Brittany they are particularly partial to the agricultural class. Agriculture is the craft through which the primitive religious spirit most clearly manifests itself. " Its ritual," says Nutt, " must have been of a particularly rigid and inflexible nature." But with the advent of Christianity, he adds, it became disorganized and distorted. What would remain " would be a vague but ineradicable conviction that so-and-so must be done, or the powers would be displeased." [2] The ancient Irish Tuatha Dé Danann, the gods of Ireland were, he tells us, " chiefly concerned with the regulation of agriculture and the institution of festivals and ceremonies in connection with it." These godlike figures were the ancestors of the Irish fairies of to-day. And we find the same notion prevailing in England and Scotland. The Irish fairy was the guardian of the agricultural peasant, who must in his work exercise the same extraordinary degree of care as did the worshippers of the Tuatha Dé Danann, if he would not offend their successors, the Fairy Folk. To the fairies of the British Isles must be rendered the same tithe of corn, milk, and other agricultural produce as was exacted by the

[1] M. McPhail, " Folk-Lore from the Hebrides," *Folk-Lore*, XI, p. 441.
[2] A. Nutt, *op. cit.*, II, p. 222.

Tuatha Dé Danann of Ireland. In the Western Isles of Scotland it was until recently believed that the top grain of corn on every stalk belonged by right to the " good people." In that region, if a person had what was known as the *Ceaird Chomuinn*—that is, " the association craft," or a species of handicraft fellowship with the fairies—he could compel them to come to his assistance for planting or reaping whenever he chose.[1] This fact is eloquent of the existence of an ancient pagan cultus of which the fairies must have been the presiding gods or genii. It is facts such as this which make us realize the great importance of the fairy tradition for the study of primitive religion and ritual.

Vestiges of this framework of cult still linger in British tradition, more especially in those tales which speak of the quite extra-ordinary zeal of the fairies for neatness and decorum in all the circumstances of life. It is not only the brownies and the *glaistigs* who keep things ship-shape in houses, wash the dishes, and polish the furniture, and who pelt untidy cottagers with turfs and stones, as did a Highland brownie, or who " skelped " careless servants in the dark, as did another of his tribe. The fays of England, as we know from Shakespeare, were zealous guardians of order. If everything in house or dairy were not *point-device*, they severely pinched and otherwise tormented the sluttish maids responsible for disorder or untidiness. As Nutt remarks, the fairies, as " powers of life," " organized ordinary living and the ritual of life. Everyone will, in this connection, recall Bishop Corbet's poem *Farewell Rewards and Fairies*, which so strikingly displays the rigour of the English fairies in upholding cleanliness and domestic order. The ethical character of this régime extended even farther. In fairy tales vice and greed are invariably punished: the deserving poor take the places of the rich; the plain but virtuous become the beautiful. The fairy is a species of Providence for the worthy suffering from oppression. The elves appear as a moral force; they are invariably on the side of justice.[2]

Nutt concludes that part of his essay which deals with fairy decorum by remarking that from " a canon of rigid and exclusive practice " associated with the Irish Tuatha Dé Danann " there descended a body of folk-superstition concerning the necessity of recognizing the moral tenets they, or rather their ministers, had formerly compelled upon the folk, which the whole force of the

[1] J. G. Campbell, *Superstitions of the Scottish Highlands*, pp. 22–3.
[2] M. de Lescure, *Le Monde Enchanté*, p. xxxiv.

Church could not defeat, and probably did not wish to defeat, finding in it a ready-made code of simple moral behaviourism and orderly method." This, he thought, was "easily referrable to a time when all the operations of rural life formed part of a definite religious ritual, every jot and tittle of which must be carried out with minute precision." [1] Perhaps the most striking statement in our literature which bears this out is that of Lilly, who, in his *Life and Times*, says that fairies love neatness and cleanness of apparel, a strict diet and upright life, and " fervent prayers unto God." These, he adds, " conduce much to the assistance of those who are curious these ways "; that is, who wish to cultivate a knowledge of elfin manners and economy.

The association of the fairies with leechcraft or the healing art, reveals another link between them and those circumstances which invariably accompany primitive religious practice. The fairies of the old romances are famous for their skill in healing wounds and diseases. Most of " the folk " are knowledgeable in the lore of medicinal plants. At times they communicate their knowledge of these matters to human beings. It is, strangely enough, more in the Keltic areas of Scotland and Ireland that we find them acting as craftsmen—smiths, cobblers, and brewers. As spinners and dyers the elfin women were unrivalled, and in the former avocation they resemble the Fates of classical mythology.

Charms and spells against the fairies were exceedingly numerous in Great Britain, but only the several classes of these can be outlined here. Many charms were regarded as protections against the elves or as keeping them at a distance. Some were couched in general and inclusive terms; as, for instance, that Highland invocation quoted by Carmichael, which asks that:—

> " From every brownie and banshee,
> From every evil wish and sorrow,
> From every *glaistig* and *bean-nigh*,
> From every fairy-mouse and grass-mouse,
> Oh save me to the end of my day ! " [2]

Charms against fairies frequently consisted of some evil-smelling and pungent matter which would affect their olfactory sense and thus retard their entrance to a house. In the Highlands, stale urine [3] or a piece of smouldering sheep-skin was employed

---

[1] A. Nutt, *Folk-Lore*, XXXII, Presidential Address.
[2] A. Carmichael, *Carmina Gadelica*, I, p. 31.
[3] J. G. Campbell, *op. cit.*, p. 49.

to keep them away.[1]   To ensure that they would not steal milk from a cow, some of the mother's dung was smeared over the calf's mouth before it sucked the dam.[2]

There is division of opinion as to whether the crossing of a stream threw the fairies off the scent when they pursued human folk. In any case, many tales speak of them ferrying across streams and rivers. One way of getting rid of an unwanted fairy visitor was to tell him that disaster had occurred at his dwelling, threatening fire or injury to his kindred.

If a fairy woman struck a Highlander with her nine deadly cow-fetters—that is, the spancel or plait of horse-hair fastened round a cow's legs when milking her—the person so struck would be rendered " fey " and unlucky. To threaten anyone with a stroke from these fetters ensured that he must execute the speaker's will. In Ireland, spindle-whorls were tied to the horns of cows to prevent fairies from milking them.[3]   In Ulster, salt was sometimes placed on the heads of children to protect them from the elves.

English spells and charms against fairies are numerous from Anglo-Saxon times onward. One way of avoiding fairies in old England was to turn one's coat, or some other garment.

> " Turn your clokes.
> For fairy folkes
> Are in old oakes,"

says an old rhyme. Certain plants and flowers contained the power to repel the little people, especially greenish and yellow blooms, the fairy flax (known as *moan* in the Highlands), the St. John's wort, mug-wort, verbena, the cow-parsnip, and docken. Clippings from the rowan, or mountain-ash, of which crosses were made and worn in the lining of one's clothes, were a sure protection in all parts of Britain against being carried off by the elves.

The fairies had a decided aversion to iron in all its shapes and forms—a dislike shared by ghosts and other spirits in many parts of the world. A table-knife or a pair of scissors protected an infant against kidnapping by fairies in the Highlands.[4] If a man fixed his dirk, dagger, or knife in the door of a fairy mound it could not be closed, and thus allowed of his exit at a critical

[1] G. Henderson, *op. cit.*, pp. 263 ff.
[2] R. Kirk, *op. cit.*, p. 71.
[3] E. Andrews, *Ulster Folk-Lore*, p. 15.
[4] J. M. McPherson, *Primitive Beliefs in the North-east of Scotland*, pp. 110–11.

moment. This fear of iron on the part of the elves has been construed as the dislike of a Stone-Age folk for metal implements, which they regarded as magical.

In all parts of Britain and Ireland it was regarded as essential to keep on good terms with the fairies in a social sense. They were usually excellent neighbours, but relentless enemies. Occasionally they borrowed meal or kitchen utensils from human acquaintances, and never failed to repay the debt, usually with interest. If one resided in a house built above a fairy hill, it was only politic to attend to any complaints tendered by the inhabitants of " the flat below " respecting the droppings of water from above, or similar nuisances. Such kindnesses were generally repaid by fairy assistance at any time of emergency. It was also considered neighbourly to keep a supply of fresh water in the house overnight so that the fairies might bathe themselves or their children in the same. Failure to respect this custom not infrequently aroused elfin enmity. Kettles and such domestic implements were often borrowed, though they were not invariably returned.

But we arrive at a much more important section of fairy belief when we come to consider that associated with the even more intimately human connection between mortals and elves in the bonds of love and matrimony. The fairy mistress is a recognized type in folk-lore, and has been the subject of many essays and brochures. In the story of *Wild Edric* we have already encountered one of the very few English examples of this class of fairy tale. In the Highlands of Scotland and Ireland the fairy sweetheart was known as the *leannan sidhe*. Robert Kirk of Aberfoyle alludes to such an association as " the inconvenience of their Succubi, who tryst with men." [1] Such a union was invariably hedged round by taboos of the most rigid kind. The mortal lover might not, under heavy penalties, reveal his association with his supernatural mistress; he was forbidden to allude to her fairy nature, or to touch her with any articles made of iron. If any of these provisions was infringed, she at once and for ever deserted him, and if there were children of the union they were usually spirited away out of his ken. In general it was the fairy woman who made the first advances in such affairs. The superstition has, of course, a European and even a world-wide scope.

Sometimes the fairy lady appeared to her lover in the guise of a deer, hare, or other animal. She frequently tendered him some

---

[1] R Kirk, *op. cit.*, p. 80.

gift which had the property of protecting him. Fairy men were occasionally won by mortal women as husbands, but in such a case it usually happened that female curiosity got the better of discretion. The elfin lover's name was demanded; he disappeared, and was recovered only after a long and perilous search in which great hardships were undergone. In Scottish lore the male fairy-lover is not infrequently of homicidal tendency, as certain ballads reveal. In some cases the fairy bridegroom appears as a frog, and if his head be cut off he assumes mortal guise.

In Ireland a man could not be freed from such an alliance without finding a substitute to take his place. Misery and dejection usually followed upon connections of the sort. While the contract was not broken on the mortal side the fairy familiar remained the slave of the human partner. Beautiful young girls in Ireland were snatched away to be wedded to the Fairy King.[1] Fairy children, said one of Lady Gregory's informants, must be matched with mortal mates, their own species evidently being ineligible. It has sometimes occurred to the writer to suspect elements of totemic practice and belief in certain fairy associations. Thus the last-mentioned notion seems redolent of the totemic law that a person of one phratry, or totemic sub-tribe, must marry an individual from another, while the fairy kidnapping of women looks like marriage by capture, which has totemic antecedents.

The fairy records of Wales abound in legends of elfin sweethearts. In England the fourteenth-century romance of *The Green Knight* also deals with such a theme to some extent. The great French exemplar of the *genre* is the tale of Melusine, the fairy lady who wed with Guy, Count of Lusignan. Compelled to assume the shape of a serpent every Saturday, she begged him to refrain from seeing her on that day. But he broke the taboo, and she deserted him as a consequence.[2] In this connection the classical tale of Eros and Psyche will occur to most readers.

Professor G. L. Kittredge regards the fairy mistress as an immortal woman, resident in a land of perpetual youth, whose mortal lover is usually guided to her by a fairy damsel or an enchanted animal, frequently a deer. The hero may remain with the fay " for ever," but sometimes he returns to the mortal sphere. The antitype to this kind of story is that species of tale which tells how a fairy becomes for a time an inhabitant of earth and the wife

---

[1] Lady Wilde, *Ancient Legends of Ireland*, p. 34.
[2] J. d'Arras, *Melusine* (Eng. version), Early English Text Soc., XXII.

of a mortal lover.[1] These story-types have been worked out by Mr. H. Cross, particularly with reference to their classical origin.[2]

Andrew Lang, as I have already mentioned, suggested that the fairy mistress was " the representative of the Stone Age "; that is, she is associated with marital customs which appear to proceed from that period and which are surrounded with taboo. She must not be touched with iron; she must not be struck or maltreated; she must be permitted to withdraw from public gaze at certain periods. But these are taboos characteristic of savage existence to-day, although they may have descended from Stone Age times. It should be added that British tales of that class in which the mortal forsakes the world for an elfin lover are few, the outstanding example being that of Thomas the Rhymer, which is almost certainly drawn from a French model.

In folk-lore the tale has received a more modern setting. In Irish myth the fairy ladies of the Tuatha Dé Danann, the ancient gods of Ireland, became the mates of men of high descent. Later, in Scotland and Ireland, we find the *leannan sidhe*, or fairy sweetheart, consorting with men of lesser mould, cobblers and smiths. These, through the nature of their circumstances, might not follow the fairy damsel to her paradise, although a mortal woman might be borne off by a fairy man. " Other times, other manners " is often the rule in folk-lore, as in everyday life.

Dr. Von Sydow is of opinion that the fairy " was a creature of erotic dreams and hallucinations and ideas about trolls." He believes that the entire fairy-mistress legend is a monument of an early erotic attitude to supernatural beings. But that " erotic dreams " were the sole origin of the belief in fairy spirits, as he seems to maintain, cannot for a moment be accepted. No doubt man in his early stage dreamed dreams of spirit sweethearts, and thus initiated the long legend of the fairy mistress, and this early theme was later glorified by romance. But behind the earliest of these dreams there must have existed a definite belief in such beings. Man could not have considered himself in love with spirits concerning which credence had not been previously and soundly established, as Von Sydow himself appears to admit when he says that the notion originated in " ideas about trolls." [3]

In Scotland the fairy mistress is extraordinarily jealous of her

[1] C. L. Kittredge, *A Study of Gawain and the Green Knight*, pp. 231–2.
[2] H. Cross, *Modern Philology*, XII, pp, 585 f.; and *Revue Celtique*, XXXI, pp. 413 ff.
[3] C. W. von Sydow, *Folk-Lore*, XLV, pp. 291 f.

human mate. He is " under spells " to meet her every night, and should he break these, she administers to him such a trouncing that he never repeats the offence. ' She assists him in his trade or craft, tells him when he is to die, and when he will be married to a mortal woman. But the compensations of such a union are few. " Her voracity thins his herds," and when he leaves her, at last, the palace where she entertained him vanishes and misfortunes crowd upon him.[1]

The theme of " the loathly lady " is intimately associated with that of the fairy mistress. It is prominent in mediaeval romance and has its prototypes in Keltic story. It usually relates to a hero who meets with an ill-looking hag, who craves shelter, entertainment, and even affection from him. Out of his courtesy to all females he treats her gently, while others, his companions, jeer at and despise her. In the sequel she is transformed into a most beautiful woman, who weds with him, though the usual taboos relative to secrecy and good treatment are generally laid upon him.

In a Scottish Keltic tale, *The Daughter of King Underwaves*, Diarmid, a Fenian hero, and heir presumptive to the throne, meets with such a hag, who craves the shelter of his tent, but from whom his companions shrink. He accords her shelter and even a share of his couch, and she is transformed into a lady of surpassing beauty. But she assures him that if he should reproach her three times with the circumstances in which they met, she will be forced to abandon him. He does so thrice, and on the morrow of the third occasion he awakes to find himself, not in a magnificent castle, but weltering in a moss-hole. He goes in search of his wife, and finds her at the point of death. He secures a talisman which will cure her, a drink from a certain enchanted cup, but is advised by an elf to substitute for it a draught from a magic well, which has the effect of changing their love into aversion.[2]

In Irish stories of this class the hero usually obtains " the sovereignty of Ireland " through his gracious act. That is, the lady represents Erin, the land of Ireland, of which she is the genius or spiritual representative.[3] The mediaeval romancers, failing to comprehend the point of the Keltic story—which indicates that a candidate for the crown of Ireland must pass a test revealing his modesty and chivalry—give a wholly different turn to the incident.

[1] J. G. Campbell, *op. cit.*, pp. 8, 41, 127.
[2] J. F. Campbell, *Popular Tales of the West Highlands*, III, p. 421.
[3] W. Stokes, *The Academy*, April 23, 1892.

They make the loathly lady ask the hero, " What do women most desire? "; the answer to which is, " The Sovereignty "—that is, sovereignty over man, an obvious misreading of the original phrase. We find many analogies to these Scottish and Irish legends of the loathly lady in early English and Norman–French literature. Perhaps the best examples of it are to be encountered in Chaucer's " Wife of Bath's Tale," or in " The Marriage of Sir Gawain," in which the knight enables King Arthur to read a riddle put to him by such a hag by wedding the hideous crone himself and extracting this answer from her. She then assumes the shape of a beauteous lady and confides in her husband that what women most desire is " mastery over men." [1]

We also find this theme worked over in such later ballads as *King Henrie*. This type of tale appears to contain a memory of a ritual marriage between the High King of Ireland and a goddess of the soil. We encounter the remains of such ritual marriages not only in Irish tradition, but also in that of Rome, where King Numa Pompilius had a pact with such a goddess or genius, the nymph Egeria, who counselled him on occasions of difficulty. Frazer believes that a ceremonial marriage between the King of Rome and the nymph Egeria, a surrogate of Diana, was periodically performed. In such a manner, too, the Fairy Queen inspired Thomas the Rhymer, her lover, with prophetic prevision respecting the Scottish kingship and its problems.

The legend of the loathly lady is important as revealing the circumstances in which a goddess is later transformed by folk-lore into a fairy spirit. It is difficult to believe that the appearance in the mediaeval romances of hags who become beauteous damsels had their origin elsewhere than in the earlier Irish version of the theme that the spirit of Ireland, an ancient goddess of the soil, puts a mortal of royal race to the test not only with the object of discovering whether he be of the true hereditary line in which the kingship vests, but also whether he is of such a royal and generous nature as will fit him for the kingship.

We find in the myth of Conn, King of Ireland, that when he entered a mysterious rath or mound he beheld the sun-god Lugh, seated beside a woman of great beauty, who is described as " the Sovereignty of Erinn till the day of doom," and who typifies the Kingdom of Ireland. She was the bride of Lugh, and was married to him at the annual festival of the *Lugnassad*, the newly-

---

[1] Sir F. Madden, *Sir Gawaine*, p. 288.

risen sun. The earthly monarch of Ireland typified this god Lugh; he was his worldly representative, and that he was ritually married to this goddess-consort, or to a woman symbolizing her, at the time of his coronation is scarcely to be questioned, judging from what we know of Irish pagan procedure. In later story, however, the term " sovereignty " appears to have been construed in a totally different sense from that conceived in the ancient and original meaning. It becomes, in the hands of the romancers, merely part of a riddle in which the term degenerates into a vulgar and flippant assertion of female desire for mastery over mankind and nothing more, simply because the makers of romance failed to understand its original and ritualistic implications. The version given in the legend of Thomas the Rhymer, too, inverts the chief element of the old myth, making the fairy queen become hideous *after* being kissed, instead of before.

Another link between Faerie and humanity is that species of fay known to students of folk-lore as " the friendly fairy," or " the helpful fairy," regarding whom British tradition contains a number of examples. The usual formula is associated with a hero or heroine who, because of some small kindness to the fairy (who is generally disguised as an old man or woman, or an animal or bird), receives timeous aid at an opportune moment.

Perhaps the most suitable and the most popularly known example of the helpful or friendly fairy is to be found in the tale of *Cinderella*, which has at least four English versions and half a dozen Scottish ones. In it the friendly fairy is represented by the " fairy godmother " who equips Cinderella for the royal ball. Occasionally the fairies appear *en masse* to lend their aid, as in the tale of a woman in the island of Skye, who experienced difficulty in spinning a piece of cloth for her children. She was bemoaning the fact to herself when, on a sudden, the fairies appeared and finished the task as if by magic.[1] In Robert Chambers's story, *The Red Etin*, a Scottish variant of *Jack the Giant-Killer*, the hero is aided by a fairy disguised as an old woman, who gives him a magic wand which helps him to overcome the Etin, or giant with three heads.[2] In fact, the friendly fairy usually acts as the *dea ex machina* in fairy tale. Occasionally she manifests herself in animal form, as in the old French tale of *Puss in Boots*, or some of the

---

[1] M. J. MacCulloch, " Folk-Lore of the Isle of Skye," *Folk-Lore*, XXXVII, p. 206.

[2] R. Chambers, *op. cit.*, p. 89.

Scottish variants of *Cinderella*, in which she takes the form of a red calf or a grey sheep with magical powers.[1]   On the whole, however, the helpful fairy in animal form is not nearly so prominent in British and Irish folk-lore as in that of continental Europe.

As beseemed beings gifted with supernatural powers, the fairies, like the gods, were in the habit of endowing mortals with good qualities or presenting them with objects possessing magical virtues.   They could grant them treasures of gold or silver, rings, caps, and cloaks which rendered them invisible; clothes, baskets, and chests which held an inexhaustible supply of grain or meal— in short, there was scarcely any limit to the benefits they were capable of bestowing upon mankind.   A well-known Highland authority remarks, as a peculiarity of fairy gifts, that " the benefit of the gift goes ultimately to the fairies themselves," or, as it is expressed in the Keltic phrase, " the fruit of it goes into their own bodies."   " Their gifts have evil influences and, however inviting at first, are productive of bad luck in the end." [2]

It would, I think, be difficult to substantiate this statement, as the fairy lore of Keltic Scotland, and indeed of Europe, is replete with instances of elfin benefactions of lasting value to the recipient.   Sometimes the ugly, and even the loathsome, are loaded with benefactions and attributes of excellence to compensate for their personal drawbacks, and in tales dealing with incidents of this class we probably surprise the fairy sense of justice, of which I have spoken—such a sense of it, in short, as might emanate from a deity of established repute rather than from an inferior type of sprite.   A perfectly hideous smith, who was also an indifferent workman, fell asleep on a fairy mound in the Highlands one day, and three fairy women, who passed by, each bestowed a gift upon him, so that he became handsome, eloquent, and a good artificer.[3]   Mechanics frequently received from the good folk the endowment of peculiar excellence in their crafts. Other folk dreamt that somewhere in the hills, or by the sea-shore, strange medicaments were to be discovered which cured diseases such as jaundice or fever.   Sometimes fairy ladies bestow upon their lovers garments which endow them with titanic might in battle, or render them swift of foot.   Magic stones are presented to mortals which have the power of transporting them wherever

---

[1] *Folk-Lore Journal*, II, pp. 72–4; *Folk-Lore*, I, pp, 289–91; M. R. Cox, *Cinderella*, pp. 534–5.

[2] J. G. Campbell, *op. cit.*, p. 23.   [3] J. G. Campbell, *op. cit.*, pp. 153–4.

they may desire to go, or which confer unusual powers of milk-giving to their cattle.

An outstanding example of the fairy gift is that which tells how a MacLeod who was going to the Crusades was crossing a river by a ford, when a fairy lady rose out of the water and presented him with a box which contained several smaller boxes. In the inmost lay a magic banner which, if waved, would bring forth a host of armed men to succour his clan in the hour of need. But it must be employed for this purpose in an extremity only. If used within a year and a day from its last exhibition, no crops would grow on the MacLeod's land, nor would his flocks and herds bring forth young. On several occasions, says tradition, it has been produced for the purpose of bringing armed succour to the MacLeods, with results disastrous to their enemies. It still remains, a prized talisman, in the Castle of Dunvegan.[1]

A story common to all three British countries, and also familiar on the Continent and elsewhere, is that of the hunchback whose deformity was removed because he reminded the fairies of the name of a day in the week which they had missed out when chanting a rhyme on the week-names. Another hunchback, who was envious of his fellow's good fortune, imitated his example, but bungled the business, only to find, to his discomfiture, that the exasperated fairies had clapped his companion's discarded hump upon his own.[2]

Tales and traditions relating to fairy gold and treasure are more common in England than in Scotland or Ireland, but are certainly not so abundant in Britain as on the Continent. In England it was evidently unlucky to disclose the discovery of a fairy hoard, as Massinger remarks in his play of *The Fatal Dowry* (Act IV, Sc. I):

> "But not a word of it—'tis fairies' treasure,
> Which but revealed, brings on the babbler's ruin."

In a masque by Ben Jonson, Mab bestows a jewel on the Queen, saying:—

> "Utter not, we you implore,
> Who did give it, nor wherefore."

The spriggans, or diminutive elves, of Cornwall and Devonshire are notoriously guardians of treasure which formerly belonged to

---

[1] A. A. MacGregor, *The Peat-Fire Flame*, pp. 20 ff.
[2] For a long list of tales dealing with incidents of this kind, see M. R. Cox, *Cinderella*, p. 501, note 43.

the giants of these regions.[1]   Robberies of fairy treasure, especially of golden and silver cups and goblets, are also frequently noted in English fairy tale, and for a quite exhaustive collection of such incidents the reader is referred to the late E. Sidney Hartland's masterly treatise, *The Science of Fairy Tales*.

At a spot near Abernethy, in Fifeshire, the treasure of a Pictish king was said to be guarded by a " droughy," or pech, who fiercely assailed any prospector.   In Scotland few tales of buried treasure are associated with the fairies.   A laird of Craufurdland, who sought for a pot of gold said to be buried under a pool beneath Craufurdland Bridge, near Kilmarnock, was frustrated in his attempt to dig it up by a mischievous brownie.   He had just succeeded in damming up the stream when the tricksy elf called out from the shelter of a bush :—

> " Pow, pow,
> Craufurdland tower's a' in a low ! "

The laird, understanding from this that his residence had taken fire, hurried home, only to realize that he had been deceived, and when he returned to resume operations at the bridge, it was to find the water falling over the linn in full force, whereupon he desisted from his attempt to locate the treasure.[2]

Jacob Grimm tells us that fairy treasure, when buried, moves of itself, at the rate of a cock's stride every year, towards the surface. If not located within seven years, it sinks back to the original depths.   Near the surface it reveals itself by a glow of some sort. It must be removed by someone gifted with silence and innocence— qualities best found in a child.[3]   In Ireland the Tuatha Dé Danann and their fairy successors were, and are, credited with the possession of enormous wealth and treasure.   This they offer to mortals to gain their affections, or for other reasons.   It appears probable that the idea of fairy treasure had its inception in stories of gold and silver articles buried with the dead in mounds and tumuli. · Mr. L. Duncan remarks that at the end of last century the Irish peasantry believed that if they caught a white rabbit and ate it, such a repast gave them the power to see where fairy gold lay.   A very considerable proportion of fairy tales records that those who received fairy money from the elves found, upon

---

[1] R. Hunt, *Popular Romances of the West of England*, pp. 51, 90.
[2] R. Chambers, *op. cit.*, pp. 241 f.
[3] J. Grimm, *Teutonic Mythology* (Stallybrass's trans.), p. 970.

examining it later, that it consisted of withered leaves, beans, or other vegetable matter.[1]

The belief in changelings and in the abduction of adults by the fairies may ultimately cast more light upon the true nature of elfin spirits than any other of the numerous superstitions associated with them. The belief that fairies were wont to kidnap children of tender years, leaving in their places elfin substitutes, is vividly and copiously illustrated by the folk-lore of the several British regions. But from the first the ancient popular theory concerning changelings has revealed itself as among the vexed questions of traditional lore. The danger of a child's abstraction was greater while it was still unchristened, and every precaution was taken to ensure its safety from the fairy clutches.

A changeling, or fairy substitute for an abducted human child, might be known by its wan and wrinkled appearance, its long fingers, and slight bony development, as also by its fractious behaviour and voracious appetite. In Scotland its large teeth and fondness for music and dancing usually betrayed it. In all likelihood it exhibited the attributes of cretinous children. The fairies, we are told, preferred to exchange their own brats for the healthy and beautiful children of the peasantry. The whole question of *why*, precisely, they wish to kidnap children and adults is one which has agitated the schools of fairy lore for many years.

In Ireland and Scotland, and in Welsh lore, children were frequently said to be spirited away by a monstrous red hand which came through the roof whilst they were sleeping. But in general they were usually stolen by the fays when their mothers were engaged in domestic duties, or when working in the fields. The mother's unguarded moment is the fairy's opportunity. A changeling might be tricked into betraying himself under certain circumstances. In order to effect this, some unusual act was engaged in which would arouse the creature's surprise. Perhaps the most universal stratagem employed was to boil water in eggshells, which nearly always had the effect of extracting from the changeling the statement that, old as it might be, it had never before seen such a proceeding. The phrase usually employed by the changeling was that he had seen such and such a local forest grow and wane thrice, but that in all that extensive period he had never seen water boiled in eggshells. Putting a suspected change-

[1] See E. S. Hartland, *The Science of Fairy Tales*, pp. 48–50.

ling on a dunghill and leaving it there to cry is an old English method of discovering whether or not a child was actually a changeling. In Ireland the ceremony gone through was, as a rule, a long and complicated one, conducted by a " fairy doctor," or local wise man. Cases have occurred in Ireland within the last fifty years where suspected changelings have actually been placed on the fire in the hope that they would fly up the chimney and the genuine child be restored.

In some cases the fairies left behind them a puppet or " stock "— a rude likeness of the child abducted—instead of a fairy brat. This appears to have been a log of wood which had been given volition and the semblance of humanity by fairy magic. The stratagem was also frequently resorted to in the case of women whom the elves had decided to kidnap. A smith in Lowland Scotland overheard two fairy men fashioning one of these images, and discovered that it was intended to simulate his own wife. " Mak' it red-cheekit and red-lippit, like the smith o' Bonny-kelly's wife," said one of them, and because of this unwitting admission, the husband was able to circumvent the plot.[1]

As the thesis of this book is an endeavour to probe to the basic significance of the superstition concerning fairies, and as there is no intention to describe such beliefs as have little or no bearing upon that question, I cannot deal here with the very large number of spells and charms which were supposed either to protect children against the fays, or to restore them to their parents. More to the point is the belief that the folk of Faerie had a compact with the Father of Evil in respect of which they were compelled once in every seven years to render him a tribute of one of their own band. But it was possible for them to tender a substitute, and popular belief held that it was for this purpose that they spirited away human infants and occasionally grown-up folk.

The most frequent kind of adult abduction was that of the nursing mother. It was thought that fairy women were unable to suckle their own offspring, and that a human nurse was essential for the adequate nourishment of these. Men who were kidnapped were usually of those classes who could afford the elves amusement—pipers, minstrels, and so forth. If anyone chanced to sleep on a fairy mound, however, he or she was prone to be captured and borne off below. If he was sorely wounded, or had undertaken an unjust quarrel, he was particularly open to fairy appre-

[1] W. Gregor, *Folk-Lore of the North-east of Scotland*, p. 62.

hension, and if the hour was that of sunset he had little chance of escape. If discovered in an unlawful act, or if he gave way to some headlong and sinful passion, he was equally doomed, and once more, in respect of such a belief, we find the fairies regarded as ministers of justice and decorum. A kidnapped adult was permitted to revisit the haunts of men after seven years' confinement in Fairyland, but almost inevitably he found it impossible to adjust himself to mortal ways, and generally succumbed to the allurements of the fairy mound.

In some cases the fairies " took " the spirit of a person only, leaving his body behind, in which circumstances all the appearances of death usually manifested themselves. Such instances are extremely common in Ireland, where people old and young are still frequently regarded as having had their souls escheated by " the Gentry," many of them lying in bed for years in a condition of collapse or even semi-consciousness, brought about, of course, by some obscure nervous or other allied complaint.

The several theories which have been advanced to account for the kidnapping of mortals, young or old, by fairies can scarcely be regarded as satisfactory. In many lands, particularly those where a tradition of ancestor-worship prevails, a belief exists that ancestral spirits steal the souls of people of all ages, substituting one of themselves for the victim's spirit. It has been thought that this belief is a corrupted folk-memory of an ancient doctrine of reincarnation. A second theory associates fairy kidnapping with the notion that the elves steal people to increase their numbers, as do some savage communities. Professor A. C. Haddon pointed out that, in Ireland, " dwarf or misshapen children are held to be given to a mother by the fairies in place of a healthy child they have stolen from her *to renew* the stock of fairies." [1] The Leper Islanders believe that ghosts steal men, as fairies do, " to add to their company." [2] So long ago as 1914 I drew attention to the fact that certain American Indian tribes were in the habit of abducting white children to make up losses in the tribe.[3] Kirk believed the fairies to be the doubles or, as he called them, the " co-walkers " of men, which accompanied them through life, and thought that this co-walker returned to Faerie when the person died. This notion, as we shall see later on, is in accordance

[1] A. C. Haddon, " A Batch of Irish Folk-Lore," *Folk-Lore*, IV, p. 358.
[2] W. Y. E. Wentz, *The Fairy Faith in Celtic Countries*, p. 247.
[3] L. Spence, *Myths of the North American Indians*, p. 36.

with the belief of the Australian " Blackfellows," whose dead were regarded as continually awaiting reincarnation—evidence which helps to make it clear that the changeling idea was associated with the ancient doctrine of the reincarnation of spirits in human bodies.

Alfred Nutt thought that it was possible to explain the changeling belief only if we " recognize in the fairies representatives of the antique lords of life and increase," powers to whom primitive man " looked for the periodical outburst of new life, and whom he strengthened in their task by sacrifice." [1] Hartland remarks that " the same reasons which induce fairies to steal a child would probably render it an acceptable offering to a pagan divinity."

I have come to think that originally the belief was not associated with abduction, but rather with the notion that ancestral spirits awaiting re-birth ensouled the bodies of new-born infants of their own kindred. This, in time, and through a confusion of mental processes, was exchanged for a belief that the spirits of the ancestors actually purloined the infant's body, leaving a " changeling " behind. In certain instances the spirit only of the child appears to have been exchanged; in others the body; in still others both soul and body. Again we encounter the notion that an automatic but soulless image of the child might be left in its place. That this idea was not foreign to Britain is revealed by two passages in Robert Kirk's work on the fairies, one of which says that " women are yet alive (1691) who tell they were taken away when in child-bed to nurse Fairie Children, a lingering voracious Image of them being left in their place (like their Reflexion in a Mirrour)." The other mentions that the " Subterraneans " are in possession of " Pleasant Children, lyke inchanted Puppets." [2] This can hardly allude to anything else than the automatically magical stocks or images employed by the fairies to hoodwink mothers dispossessed of their offspring, and these extracts seem to point to a definite belief both in the existence of (1) a fairy soul left in the place of children and (2) a magically inspired image of the child. In my view, both these instances, as recorded by Kirk, descend from genuinely primitive sources.

A fair proportion of changelings, when surprised by some stratagem which tricks them into revealing their elfin character, are discovered as old men, who babble in a senile way of extensive territorial changes which have overtaken the district in

<hr>

[1] A. Nutt, *op. cit.*, II, pp. 229–30.   [2] R. Kirk, *op. cit.*, pp. 71, 72.

which the scene is enacted, thus showing their close acquaintance with it at a remote period. Such a changeling is obviously the ancestral spirit of a *distant* generation, which has taken lodgment in the body of an infant descendant. All this seems to me to point to a possible belief that human spirits were reincarnated again and again in the clan or tribe, the changeling usually remarking that he has witnessed recurring afforestations in the neighbourhood in which the story is located, or that he can recall the rising and sinking of river-beds in its area. That we find the doublet to this conception in Australian Blackfellow belief (the evidence for which will be given in the chapter on " Fairies as Ancestral Spirits ") makes it practically certain that the primitive theory underlying the changeling superstition had its origin in a crude dogma of human rebirth or reincarnation.

The idea that fairies could not function in certain ways without the assistance of mortals—particularly as regards their giving birth to children (at which time human midwives must assist them) and in nursing their offspring—seems to point to a belief that they were unable to do so without the aid of a mortal virtue or inherent quality which the fairies lacked. A fairy lady in Galloway insisted upon a countrywoman suckling her elfin infant.[1] In an Arabian tale a Queen of the Jinn appears to a woman and asks her to give suck to her child, which is " by fate obliged to taste the milk of a mortal, it being a command laid upon us by Allah." [2] These parallels, divided by half a world and centuries of time, appear to indicate the existence of a widespread and ancient belief that were supernaturals to partake of mortal milk they would acquire something of mortal vigour or kinship. May this not have been regarded as something in the nature of a ritual act, which consummated the fact of rebirth or reincarnation and rendered it complete and definite?

If the changeling superstition is capable of being explained by the theory of human reincarnation, it would seem to follow that the original belief must have been associated only with the idea that the soul, and not the body, was " taken " by fairy spirits. But the notion that soul and body were one and indivisible is a greatly more primitive belief. This phase of the superstition is more usually associated with the kidnapping of adults, and appears to indicate a difference in doctrine. Among primitive peoples it is

---

[1] R. H. Cromek, *Remains of Nithsdale and Galloway Song*, p. 242.
[2] Valentine, *Eastern Tales*, p. 363.

still thought that when an individual falls sick his soul has been carried off by an ancestral spirit.[1] But that these originally separate notions—if savage belief is capable of being described at any time as distinctive or highly specific—became merged into one, or confused in the primitive mind, little doubt can be entertained. That the doctrine of changelings has a very definite bearing upon fairy origins will be realized in respect of certain other evidence to be tendered in these pages in circumstances from which its implications will receive a greater degree of clarity.

In assessing the fairy nature and origins, facts of importance may be gleaned from a consideration of such data as we possess respecting the dwelling-place, or " background," of the fairy folk. In England this was generally believed to be a green knoll or mound, which was occasionally thought of as having widespread subterranean ramifications. At other times fairy spirits were considered as making their homes in barrows, or primitive tombs. In Scotland the Lowland elves were usually housed in similar hills, or in dwellings situated beneath ancient castles or duns. In the Highlands the name *brugh* is the word generally applied to dwellings of the elfin race, though more specifically this word denotes its interior, the term *sithein* (a green mound *pron.* shee'an) implying the residence as a whole. Occasionally the good folk dwelt in brochs, or ruined Pictish towers, sepulchral tumuli, or earth-houses, the abandoned homes of primitive man. In Ireland the names " fort," *dun*, *rath*, and *brugh*, are most generally encountered, as those of fairy dwellings.

If we examine the record of English fairy tale with the intention of gleaning from it a general impression of the English conception of Fairyland, we discover that idea as a fairly homogeneous one at all times and ages. The more ancient lore on the subject is, indeed, almost standardized. As I have already mentioned, William of Newbridge and Ralph of Coggeshall, two early writers, both allude to the finding of a couple of children in Sussex who had penetrated to the upper world from a subterranean land which they called St. Martin's Land. It was separated by a river from " a bright country," which could be seen from their own meadows. The first of these scribes also tells how a Yorkshireman beheld people carousing in a barrow, the door of which was open to the outer world. These tales date from about the close of the twelfth century. In the early English romance of

---

[1] J. G. Frazer, *Spirits of the Corn and the Wild*, II, pp. 97–8.

Orfeo and Heurodys, which is pre-Chaucerian, the hero, pursuing the band of fairies who have carried off his wife, enters a rock on their heels, and after following them along what appears to have been an extensive gallery three miles in length, he comes to " a fair country," in which it is bright as a summer's day. The landscape is flat and green, without hills and dales, and in the midst of it Orfeo perceives a castle with crystal battlements, adorned with gold and precious stones. Within its walls he beholds numerous folk in a recumbent position, whom those in the world regarded as dead. Some of these were headless and armless, others merely wounded, while still others had been strangled or drowned.

In the story of Herla, already alluded to, the King of that name is led by a fairy dwarf into a dismal mountain cavern, from which he at length emerges into a space brilliantly lit by torches. In the ancient romance of *Guy of Warwick* the fairy scene is almost the doublet of that in *Orfeo*, with its glittering castle and verdant swards.

More modern English stories provide some information regarding the general appearance of Fairyland. The Cornish tale of *Cherry of Zennor* tells how the youthful heroine found herself in a lane where apple-trees gave fragrance to the air. Thence she was conveyed across a crystal stream, and at length arrived at a beautiful garden, filled with flowers of every hue, and loud with the song of birds. In this demesne was set a noble house, which, however, contained a gruesome chamber. In the arcane apartment alluded to, Cherry found numerous people turned into stone. On quitting this decidedly dubious sphere it is significant that she had to climb upwards for miles in order to reach the outer world.[1] In a fairy tale from Osebury, in Worcestershire, the elves are described as dwelling in a cavern. Other fairies inhabited " a rather high hill " near Midridge, in the county of Durham. Another hill, near Taunton, was regarded as their residence. These modern instances I cull almost at random from scores of examples of the kind. I believe that it may be said with accuracy that the genuine Fairyland of England, as known to its more venerable folk-lore, was regarded as being situated in a subterranean sphere, and it is thus in alignment with similar ideas of Fairyland obtaining in Scotland and Ireland.

The general name for Fairyland in the Lowlands of Scotland

[1] R. Hunt, *op. cit.*, pp. 120 ff.

was Elfame, or Elfland. In more than one passage in old Scottish literature it is said to have been surrounded by a wilderness. But the notion also seems to have flourished that many fairy spirits dwelt in woods or forests, as more than one popular ballad makes clear. As in England, however, the most general view of the elfin region was that it was embowelled in the subterranean depths. The Fairyland alluded to both in the romance and ballad of Thomas the Rhymer is a land seemingly without sun or moon, where rivers of blood and water rush and swirl with resounding clamour and where the moaning of the sea is continually heard. But this region also contains orchards and a fair domain. We must be careful, however, in accepting this background as a genuinely Scottish description of Fairyland, as the romance in question has assuredly French or other alien associations, the aqueous portion of it being reminiscent of the old German " water-hell."

In Scottish fairy literature we frequently find references to Fairyland as " Mirry-land," " Maryland," or " May-land." This is probably a corruption of the Old English phrase " Mere-land," *mere* being an early English expression signifying " goblin " or " nymph." Some authorities, however, have seen in the name a corruption of " Middle-erd." The whole evidence contained in the famous essay of Robert Kirk, to which I have frequently referred, reveals that he believed the Fairyland of the people dwelling on the " Highland line " to exist in the subterranean sphere. In the Galloway tale of a young mother who nursed a fairy child, she is admitted by way of a door in a hillside into a beautiful land watered with twining rivulets and bright with golden corn.[1] Jamieson recounts a marvellous tale which he heard in his youth from an old man, which tells how a certain Childe Rowland sought to release his sister from Fairyland. This magical sphere was situated beneath a round hill surrounded with rings or terraces, and was reached by a door in the hillside. It led through a long passage encrusted with bright stones to a superb hall upheld by massy pillars and beautifully furnished with couches draped in silk and velvet.[2] In brief, I may add that a life-long acquaintance with Scottish fairy lore makes it impossible for me to credit that in the Lowlands the idea of Fairyland was associated with any other region than the subterranean.

---

[1] R. H. Cromek, *op. cit.*, p. 242.
[2] J. Jamieson, *Illustrations of Northern Antiquities*, p. 397.

As regards Highland belief on this subject, I think I am justified in summarizing here the testimony of the Rev. J. G. Campbell, an authority so experienced and trustworthy that it would appear merely absurd to discount his statements. The word *sithein*, he says, denotes a fairy hill of peculiarly green appearance and rounded form, sometimes almost conical. *Tolman*, he proceeds to say, " is a small green knoll or hummock of earth," while *cnoc*, another word used to denote a fairy dwelling, implies " a knowe," or knoll. But even lofty hills have been represented as tenanted by fairies, while rocks are sometimes alluded to as their dwellings, though caves are never so in the Highlands. " The dwellings of the race are below the outside or superficies of the earth, and tales representing the contrary may be looked upon with suspicion as modern." " These dwellings were occupied sometimes by a single family only, more frequently by a whole community." [1] But, as I have already said, certain fairies inhabited subterranean dwellings situated beneath ancient forts, *duns*, or castles. The exceptions to the above general statement respecting the homes of the Highland fairies are so few and unimportant as to be practically negligible.

When we come to examine the much more complex idea of Fairyland, as represented in the older and classically important myths and tales which describe it in the ancient literature of Ireland, we enter an environment where we must tread with circumspection. These accounts, which are derived from Irish manuscripts, many of which hail from the eleventh and twelfth centuries of our era, and which in some cases embrace material copied or otherwise drawn from writings or beliefs greatly more venerable, present us with a view of the fairy domain which can refer only to a land of the gods, a paradise of immortals, though some of these descriptions of it coincide with those of Fairyland in many later Irish, Welsh, and Scottish Highland tales of comparatively modern origin. This is not to say that the fairy hill does not appear in Ireland as the home of the elves from the viewpoint of the Irish peasant. It does, as also the " fort," *dun*, or *rath*. But in the more ancient view the country of Irish Faerie is as frequently an overseas paradise situated at some considerable distance from the Irish coast—a sort of Hesperides or " Summerland," where conditions frankly paradisical prevail. This sphere is known to Irish myth by numerous names, the more important of which are *Tire beo*, " the Land of the Living," *Tir n-Aill*, " the

---

[1] J. G. Campbell, *op. cit.*, pp. 11–14.

Otherworld," *Mag Mor*, or " The Great Plain," *Mag Mell*, " The Pleasant Plain "; while we also find such titles attributed to it as *Tir Tairngirre*, " The Plain of Happiness," *Tir-nan-Og*, " Land of the Young," and *Hy-Breasail*—that is, " Breasal's Island." Some of these may have been poetical denominations accorded to it by individual bards, but on the whole they appear to apply to one and the same region.

The accounts given of this overseas paradise make it very clear that it is by no means a world of the dead, but rather *a retreat of the gods*, in which they resided in the utmost bliss, and to which favoured mortals might be admitted while still alive in order that they might share the happiness of the Keltic divinities. Peace and plenty are its chief attributes. Viands and liquors of surpassing richness are constantly available within its island borders. The scenery is delectably beautiful, the people noble and amiable beyond all human standards. Old age is unknown, sickness vexes not its inhabitants, flowers blossom everywhere, streams of mead and fresh milk course through its meadows, while the chief tendency of its folk is towards amorous dalliance. The outstanding legends concerning this otherworld it would be impossible to summarize in any tolerable manner in the space at my disposal, and for the most satisfactory and critical account of these I would refer the reader to the admirable treatise of the late Alfred Nutt, *The Voyage of Bran*, where they will be found discussed with great fullness and erudition.

That the people of ancient Britain also believed in the existence of such an ocean-paradise is clear from the accounts of it which we possess in Welsh literature and folk-lore. The prime example of an island of the kind in British traditions is, of course, that associated with Avallon, " the Isle of Apples," to which King Arthur is said to have been transported after fighting his last battle.

But in both Irish and Welsh myth we encounter still other examples of elysiums, which appear to be of an even earlier character than that of the overseas island. One of these is known to both Irish and Scottish Keltic tradition as Lochlann, a submarine region which we cannot altogether dissociate from Fairyland because of the numerous resemblances its descriptions present to those of that sphere. Another is the country of Sorcha, which reveals many associations with Faerie and which is also situated beneath the sea. In Welsh myth we meet with a region known as Annwn,

" the Not-World," or Abyss, an underworld territory in which are stored many of the appurtenances of civilization, and which was occasionally raided by mortal heroes in order that they might reclaim these for the use and behoof of humanity. Certain of its characteristics recall those of Fairyland so closely that we must regard Annwn as at least one of the prototypes of British Fairyland.[1] Both Irish and Welsh lore contain numerous allusions to voyages and expeditions made to these mysterious insular and underworld territories, in which the courageous explorers experience the most marvellous adventures. To these beliefs I will return in the chapter which treats of " The Fairies as the Dead."

Now we find that when the Tuatha Dé Danann, the gods of ancient Ireland, were dispossessed of the land by the conquering Milesian Kelts, a number of them betook themselves to the overseas paradise, while others chose to remain in Erin and resolved to take up their abode in the *sidhes*, or hills, which were assigned to them by their king, the Dagda. These *sidhes* were barrows, or mounds, or natural hillocks, each opening upon an underground dwelling of extraordinary splendour. Here undoubtedly we observe a conflict of belief between the type of the overseas paradise and that of the hollow hill. The above story seems explanatory of the existence of the two kinds of Fairyland. The latter belief the Kelts in Britain possessed in common with the Teutonic peoples of the Continent, and this may point to its having been a pre-Aryan or earlier Aryan idea which the peoples of Europe had held in common for generations.

If we seek for contrasts between the types of Fairyland presented by the ideas of the hollow hill and the overseas paradise in modern folk-lore, we shall find that the former is peopled by spirits of a kind very different from those who inhabit the insular elysium. They are frequently of a goblinesque type, which does not at all correspond with the godlike and noble species which populates the overseas realm. Moreover, the habits of the two communities are different, the hill-spirits approximating in their crafts and general activities more to the human peasant. Even so, particularly in the older strata of belief, there is a decided resemblance between many of the tales recounted about both Fairylands. That the *sidhes* of the *earlier* Irish hill-abodes were one and the same with the deities of the island-paradise appears

---

[1] E. Anwyl, *Celtic Religion in Pre-Christian Times*, p. 60; L. Spence, *The Mysteries of Britain*, pp. 121 ff.; J. Rhys, *Hibbert Lectures*, p. 249

more than probable.   It is only later that they assume the character of rather unsightly and goblinesque spirits, and this may be accounted for by a reversion to aboriginal belief.

Moreover, the backgrounds of the two Fairylands, under-hill and over-seas, are frequently indistinguishable. We sometimes find the insular scenery, with its celestial beauty, duplicated in the subterranean sphere. It is apparent that at some time there must have been a definite fusion of the two ideas. Professor Zimmer (to summarize his view severely) thought that the earliest Goidelic Elysium in the western ocean was the dwelling-place of the older Goidelic gods. On the introduction of Christianity, these deities were, he believed, thought of as being dispossessed of their paradise and banished to the hollow hills, in which the Irish peasantry still speak of them as dwelling. Even the seventh-century Irish texts already confuse the earlier conception of the overseas island with that of the hollow hill, although the former idea persisted and is discovered in texts of the twelfth and thirteenth centuries.[1]

Alfred Nutt, on the other hand, thought that the hollow hill was quite as ancient a conception as that of the overseas paradise. He asks if we do not have here two strains of belief due to the conception of different races. Or did the pre-Christian inhabitants of the British Isles distinguish between the land of the supernatural beings they worshipped and that to which mankind went after death?[2] Elsewhere he indicated parallels between the Goidelic island-paradise and that known to the more ancient Greeks—an assumption which appears nowadays as rather a work of supererogation, as insular Elysiums are the common possession of many peoples.[3] It is more to the point, however, when he points out that the island-paradise idea in Ireland finds its earliest analogue in Greek religion, though if he had substituted " closest " for " earliest " he would probably have been nearer the mark.

Dr. Douglas Hyde noted that, in a collection of about sixty tales taken down from the lips of the Irish peasantry, about five contained allusions to an under-water paradise, four to an other-world within the hills, while the ocean-island idea was quite unrepresented.[4] Professor Kittredge points out that the island-

---

[1] H. Zimmer, quoted in A. Nutt's *Voyage of Bran*, Vol. I.
[2] A. Nutt, Intro. to A. MacDougall's *Folk and Hero-Tales from Argyll*, pp. 261 ff.
[3] A. Nutt, *The Voyage of Bran*, I, p. 203.
[4] D. Hyde, *A Literary History of Ireland*, p. 96.

paradise was inhabited by the Tuatha Dé Danann, whereas the Fairyland of the mounds was peopled by the *sidhe*, who, if not originally identical with the Tuatha Dé Danann, were confounded with them. But he adds that the Irish folk, after the introduction of Christianity, " found it no easier to carry two sets of fairies and two fairylands in the mind without confusion " than the Greeks did to distinguish between the Chthonian and Uranian gods. So they located the *sidhe* sometimes in the hills, sometimes overseas, which latter paradise had often " a fairy hill for its vestibule," or was perhaps dotted with such green mounds. In more than one tale such confusion is apparent, and indeed it seems to have become the general rule.[1]

Mr. Josef Baudiš gives it as his belief that the *sidhe* spirits of the mounds were identical with the chiefs of the Tuatha Dé Danann, whom he classes as the ancestral gods or spirits of the Irish folk. The name Tuatha Dé Danann, he thinks, probably belonged only to some of these *sidhe*, and by extension came to be used of all such godlike beings. " *Sidhe*," of course, means nothing more or less than " supernatural," so this might well be the case. But many fairies are of a highly unpleasant character, and the other-world of the Kelts came to have two aspects—one as a beautiful and blessed country, the other as a dangerous and unfriendly region. The Keltic conception of the other-world was a complex one, and when the insular Kelts arrived in the British Isles they had already absorbed many foreign elements and probably received others from the older inhabitants of these islands.[2] Dr. MacBain believed that the *sidhe* were the ghosts of the glorious dead dwelling in their barrows or tumuli, who received a species of ancestor-worship from the people, and that the Keltic gods, originally quite distinct from them, were afterwards confused with them. After the introduction of Christianity the *sidhe* were further confused with the elves, the earth and wood powers, so that the modern *sidhe*, or fairy, is " a mixture of tumulus-dweller and wood-nymph." [3] It may here be remarked that on the continent of Europe we find the hollow hill usually inhabited by spirits who appear to be the descendant forms of the gods of a former worship.

The above statements represent the outstanding theories con-

[1] C. L. Kittredge, " Sir Orfeo," *American Journal of Philology*, VII, pp. 195–7

[2] J. Baudis, " The Other-World in the Mabinogion," *Folk-Lore*, XXVII, pp. 31–6.

[3] A. MacBain, *Celtic Mythology and Religion*, pp. 148–9.

cerning the origins and character of British Fairyland.　The others, and less important, I have space to allude to only in a note containing the references where they can be found.[1]　But my purpose in this chapter is to detail their principles and not to discuss them, a fuller examination of them being possible only in association with other circumstances at a later stage.

It is necessary to add here that a marked difference in the sense of time distinguishes the person " taken " by the fairies, and doomed to sojourn in their sphere, from the ordinary mortal. Years in Fairyland sometimes appear as days; the distractions of the fairy realm destroy all sense of chronological proportion.　It is unnecessary to do more than indicate this phenomenon here, as it has been dealt with exhaustively and with admirable clarity and learning by the late E. Sidney Hartland in his *Science of Fairy Tales*.　Nor is there any need, I think, to make more than passing mention concerning the traditional means by which people " taken " by the fairies were released from their clutches by friends or enchanters, further reference to this point being essential only in such connections as bring it into association with the question of fairy origins.

Having furnished a précis of the fairy superstition as comprehensive, and I trust as lucid, as space and the highly complex nature of the subject permit of, I must now approach the main argument of this book—the endeavour to discover, if possible, the actual nature of the beings whose general economy we have been discussing.　In doing so, my first concern is naturally with the several theories which seek to explain this origin, a review or rather a description, of which will be found in the following chapter.

[1] J. A. MacCulloch, *Religion of the Ancient Celts*, p. 370; E. Hull, *Folk-Lore of the British Isles*, pp. 121 ff., E. S. Hartland, *op. cit.*, p. 365; W. Y. E. Wentz, *op. cit.*, pp. 291, 332 f.; W. J. Perry, " The Isles of the Blest," *Folk-Lore*, XXXII, pp. 150–80; D'Arbois de Jubainville, *The Irish Mythological Cycle*, pp. 195 f.

CHAPTER III

THEORIES CONCERNING FAIRY ORIGINS

THREE main theories have been advanced to explain the origin of the belief in fairy spirits: (1) that they are the spirits of the human dead; (2) that they are elementary spirits—that is, spirits of nature, the genii of mountain, flood, and forest; (3) that belief in them is due to reminiscences of former peoples or aboriginal races which have been thrust into the more distant and less hospitable parts of a country by the superior weight of an invading stock. The theory that they are ancestral forms is, of course, included in the first of these propositions. But it is also necessary to consider the possible derivation of the idea of fairy spirits from classical forms, such as pagan gods; from totemic forms; and, as we shall see, from still other, if less important, points of view. I will devote a chapter to the consideration of each theory where its importance seems to demand such a course, while less significant assumptions concerning the origin of the fairy race will receive more summary notice. In the present chapter my sole intention is to enumerate and briefly describe the several classes of theory respecting fairy origins in a prefatory manner, in order that my readers may receive a preliminary view of the general nature of these arguments before I proceed to their fuller discussion.

The conclusions of prime authorities on folk-lore regarding these several hypotheses are naturally of value in assisting us to arrive at a sound decision concerning fairy origins. Accordingly I shall summarize them in this chapter in such a manner that the reader may receive the general sense of expert opinion relative to the whole topic, before I proceed to discuss it from my own point of view in the chapters to follow.

Yet in this place I am not so much concerned with the proof associated with the several theories here set forth as with the theories themselves, the evidence being fully adduced in the chapters which deal with each hypothesis. As we shall see, the great majority of writers on the fairy problem do not adopt one or other of the theories outlined at the beginning of this chapter, but regard it, as did Andrew Lang, as " a complex matter," composed of a mingling of many beliefs. No outstanding authority,

53

for instance, has maintained exclusively the hypothesis that fairies were wholly spirits of the elementary class, and nothing more.

Professor A. H. Krappe, in discussing in brief the several theories about fairy origin, has given it as his opinion that many fairy-story types, probably the majority, are in accord with the theory that the fairies are the spirits of the dead. " They are almost universally believed to have their dwellings underground—like the dead—and they are fond of snatching the living down to their dark abode, in this resembling all chthonic powers. They are credited with superhuman wisdom, as are ancestors generally. They are attached to definite localities . . . which simply means that they are dead ancestors. More, like these very ancestors, they are the objects of a regular cult, for they expect to receive food, and if it is refused them they demand it and take their revenge. The Irish refer to them as ' the good people,' which strikes one as a literal translation of the Latin *manes*, designating, of course, the dead ancestors of the family." If the phrase *is* a translation of *manes*, it is inconceivably bad Latinity.

But Professor Krappe adds a warning as regards the necessity for caution in drawing a hard-and-fast line between such kinds of spirits as seem to us ancestral and elementary. " Such classificatory systems," he remarks, " though justified in modern scientific research, never existed in the minds of primitive populations. Nor do they exist there to-day." The dead are regarded as instrumental in the production of grain and fruit; they may enter trees, becoming indistinguishable from genuine vegetation spirits. " They naturally assume green, the colour of the fruit-bearing earth, which, for that very reason, becomes also the colour of death and of the nether powers." [1]

The late E. Sidney Hartland, in what is most evidently a designedly meagre and restrained summing-up of the question of fairy origins, advanced the view that " no theory will explain the nature and origin of the fairy superstitions which does not also explain the nature and origin of every other supernatural being worshipped or dreaded by uncivilized mankind throughout the world." [2] In short, he infers that the belief in fairies " arose out of the doctrine of spirits," and he practically leaves it at that.

---

[1] A. H. Krappe, *The Science of Folk-Lore*, pp. 87–9.
[2] E. S. Hartland, *The Science of Fairy Tales*, p. 351.

But this is not to say that a highly specialized body of belief such as that associated with Faerie is not capable of subsidiary explanations apart from this very general conclusion, especially in connection with those later and accretive ideas which must have grown up around it.   Admittedly there is a common basis for the origin of all beliefs associated with the origin of spirits, which is to be found alone in the doctrine of animism.   This notwithstanding, and with all due respect to the warnings of Krappe, Hartland, and others concerning the risks accruing to the scientific classification of spiritual forms, certain types of spirits with markedly separate characteristics have assuredly been conceived, and have been given diverse denominations and descriptions by those who believed in their existence.   Of this the fairy type is indeed a case in point; and however correct it may be to say that it cannot basically be separated from the ghost, the goblin, or the demon, it has, in the course of ages, assumed characteristics which in a secondary sense distinguish it sufficiently from all of these to permit the scientific observer, and to some extent the peasant or the savage, to rank it as a separate *variety* of spirit, if not as a distinct species.   From which it will be manifest that I regard the plea for the identity of all spiritual beings as slightly over-strained.

We have already seen that Alfred Nutt believed the fairies to be more closely associated with agricultural growth and ritual than with any other phase of superstition, which is of course to say that he regarded them as *primarily* elementary in character, though not perhaps exclusively so—spirits whose chief reason of being it was to ensure vegetable and cereal growth and the fertility of flocks and herds, as well as of mankind.   That this class of fairy came to be associated with moral and ethical ideas of social correctness was, of course, a secondary development, arising out of the proven necessity for care and caution in agricultural operations, which, by a later extension of the idea, came to be implied as influencing personal morals and habits.

Mr. R. U. Sayce is of opinion that any attempt to explain the fairy belief " must take into account ancestral and nature spirits." Fairies, he states, are usually regarded as spirits, though they are not thought of as being purely unsubstantial.   Both Arabian jinn and Icelandic elves, when killed, left bodies behind them. He thinks that illusions and defects of vision had much to do with the belief in fairies.   He quotes Ostyak belief as holding that life beyond the grave runs in reverse order to that on earth, departed spirits gradually growing younger and smaller. The distinction between ancestral spirits and those of plants and animals is, he remarks, far from clear. Mr. Sayce adduces many reasons for believing in the ancestral character of fairies, with which I shall deal in the chapter on that subject.[1]

The champions of the third theory hold that the belief in fairies is exclusively due to a memory of aboriginal or vanished peoples who have been compelled to betake themselves into the remote regions of a country because of racial pressure, and who have impressed their more civilized neighbours by exhibiting traits which are usually associated with elfin life—the kidnapping of women and children, sudden appearance and disappearance in jungle or bush, the shooting of poisoned darts—and by their general vindictiveness and *diablerie*, no less than by their dwarfish or stunted stature. The chief advocates of this hypothesis were by no means strained in their maintenance of a theory which has been strenuously opposed by the guardians of official folk-lore. Here I must content myself with a brief sketch of this theory on historical lines, leaving its fuller discussion for the chapter which deals exclusively with the subject.

The theory appears to have been introduced by Sir Walter Scott, who probably received it from Dr. Leyden, a Scottish Borderer who had made a profound study of the fairy problem. Scott identified the *duergar*, or dwarfish gnomes, of the North with " the diminutive natives of the Lappish, Lettish, and Finnish nations," who had retreated before the conquering Scandinavians. Through their knowledge of metal working and nature, thought Scott, they came to enjoy a reputation for sorcery, and the superstition of their larger neighbours invested them with the character of spirits.[2]   J. F. Campbell, the collector of the *Popular Tales of the West Highlands*, followed Scott in this hypothesis and drew a number of convincing parallels between Elfin and Lapponic traits.[3]

But the grand protagonist of the theory in more modern days was the late David MacRitchie of Edinburgh, who in successive works elaborated it very fully, imparting to it a setting of considerable literary charm. He believed that fairies were

---

[1] R. U. Sayce, " The Origin and Development of the Belief in Fairies," *Folk-Lore*, XXXV, pp. 99 ff.
[2] W. Scott, *Letters on Demonology and Witchcraft*, pp. 119–20.
[3] J. F. Campbell, *Popular Tales of the West Highlands*, I, pp. xcv–ciii.

nothing more than a confused memory of the dwarfish races of which I have spoken, stunted and hirsute folk, whose habits we see reflected in fairy folk-lore as those of a class of spirit.   According to his view they were mound-dwellers, and he held that traditions concerning them have attached themselves to mounds and earth-houses in Scotland and elsewhere which excavation has revealed as the former homes of a folk of dwarfish stature.   These people, so far as their North British associations are concerned, he identified with the Picts of Scottish history, being, like many another investigator, misled by the similarity between the term " Pict," which denotes a member of the Pictish race, and " Pech," a Lowland Scottish word meaning a dwarf or gnome of supernatural character, which is probably allied to the expressions " Puck " and " pixie."   But his investigations did not stop with the boundaries of this island, for he examined the legends and the ethnological notices of travellers referring to dwarf races in many parts of the world—Eskimos, Ainos, and Central African pigmies—from which he drew a large and plausibly convincing body of evidence to fortify his views.   Furthermore, he identified the fairies with the Feinne or Fenians of Gaelic romance and the Finns and Lapps of Scandinavia.   In the appropriate chapter I will summarize the arguments which other investigators have brought against the acceptance of this hypothesis.   But I may here remark that in very numerous conversations on the subjects which I enjoyed with my dear old friend—in which my expostulations respecting his general premises were naturally modified because of his seniority—I wholly failed to break down his amiable inflexibility.   At this distance of time I am glad to be able to state that although I still cannot agree either with his major propositions or with the method of proof by which he sought to substantiate them, I am convinced that the theory for which he laboured so long and so courageously cannot altogether be discarded, but must, if placed in its proper perspective, be regarded as one of the strands which go to make up the fairy superstition. I may add that I have also felt that the very severe criticism which his hypothesis received at the hands of certain opponents, although it seemed to be justified in the circumstances because of the damage which a whole-hearted acceptance of the " dwarf " theory was capable of inflicting upon more official and acceptable views respecting fairy origins, was still much too harsh and unsympathetic, especially in view of the fact that later responsible censors have accepted its content as explanatory of at least a part of the fairy problem.[1]

In her interesting volume *The God of the Witches*, Miss M. A. Murray, the well-known Egyptologist, has further elaborated the theory that fairies are the memory of a dwarfish race. She indicates that in many lands the fairy was regarded as a being of normal human stature, and lays the blame for the misunderstanding of the fairy problem at the door of " popular prejudice," which persists in regarding all elvish beings as diminutive. This notion, she thinks, was due entirely to the manner in which Shakespeare described the fairies. " Up to his time," she says, " English fairies were of the same type as in those countries where his influence has been least felt," but this influence reduced them in the popular view to mannikin proportions.[2] But, as we have already seen, the very diminutive fairy was well known upon English soil at least four centuries before Shakespeare's day. She adduces numerous examples of fairies who were of average human height, but a page or so farther on she lays it down that fairies, as a general rule, were slightly under the average human stature.[3] In a word, her method takes no account of the rather salient fact that differences in fairy stature are due to the existence of several fairly well-defined strata of belief in these beings which originated at periods relatively remote one from the other, all of which survived in folk-belief and literature to a later time. Her dwarfish folk, who came to be known as " fairies," dwelt, she thinks, in the wilder parts of the country, not because they were dispossessed, but because they were of pastoral habits and were not agriculturists. Indeed, they wholly differed from the agricultural population, existing on the produce of their cattle and inhabiting " bee-hive " huts. They were, in short, the remains of the Neolithic and Bronze Age populations, and their houses, constructed in groups, and covered with grass or brush, had collectively the appearance of mounds or small hills. In them she sees the upholders of the witch-cult, which, she is of opinion, represents the primeval faith of this island and of other primitive European communities.[4]

But before even MacRitchie had promulgated his theory that

---

[1] D. MacRitchie, *The Testimony of Tradition ; Fians, Fairies, and Picts* (*passim*).

[2] M. A. Murray, *The God of the Witches*, p. 41.

[3] M. A. Murray, *op. cit.*, p. 44.

[4] M. A. Murray, *op. cit.*, Chapter II, *passim*.

fairies were nothing but a memory of dwarfish races, Grant Allen had adumbrated a somewhat similar hypothesis which held that they were the ghosts of the Neolithic folk. These small and swarthy spirits haunted the primitive barrows and sepulchral mounds, and at length came to be thought of as a little people who dwelt underground.[1] The theory has much to recommend it, and may perhaps be regarded as a partial explanation of the fairy problem. Sir Harry Johnston, too, holds that most fairy myths originated in " the contemplation of the mysterious habits of dwarf troglodyte races lingering still in the crannies, caverns, forests, and mountains of Europe, after the invasion of Neolithic man," and he indicates certain traits of Central African pigmies as having a resemblance to those of European elves. At the same time, he is of opinion that this resemblance may be pressed too far.[2]

I must now summarize the views of that very considerable class of critic who has seen in the fairy superstition the evidences of a belief which contains a number of complex strands and which are by no means capable of being explained by reference to any single hypothesis. I may fittingly commence my review of this body of criticism with a précis of the opinions of Andrew Lang, which, because of his acuteness and long experience, have perhaps a prior right to our careful consideration.

Lang believed that fairies are " much older than their name; as old as the belief in spirits of woods, hills, lonely places, and the nether world." He regarded them as of the same class as the Slavonic *Wilis*, the *Apsaras* of India, the *Nereids* of ancient and modern Greece, and the Melanesian *Vuis*; that is, chiefly as elementary spirits. Just as the Scottish fairies were styled " the Good Folk," so Fauna, the daughter of Faunus, was known as " the Good Goddess," and her real name was tabooed. In Gaul, the *Fata*, the native spirits of woods and wells, survived the official heathen religion on the introduction of Christianity, and their rural or sylvan shrines remained unmolested. Indeed, Lang thought, with Maury and Walkenaer, that " the function of prophetic Gaulish maidens and druidesses " may have been confused with those of the fairies. To some extent, too, the fays resembled the Greek *Moirai* or the Egyptian *Hathors*, deities who presided over birth and who foretold the fate of children. But in

---

[1] Grant Allen, " Who were the Fairies? " in *Cornhill Magazine*, XLIII, pp. 338 ff.

[2] Sir Harry Johnston, *The Uganda Protectorate*, I, pp. 513 ff.

the popular mind they had many other attributes. They cannot be dissociated from the spirits of the dead. " They certainly inherited much from the pre-Christian idea of Hades." In such tales as that relating to Thomas of Erceldoun " the subterranean fairy world is the under-world of pagan belief." In such old romances as *Orfeo and Heurodys*, too, we encounter the pagan idea of the under-world, while in the same way Chaucer describes Pluto as " King of Fayrie," and in " The Merchant's Tale " speaks of " Prosperine and all her fayrie." In many a fairy tale, too, the dead are met with in Elfland.

But despite their associations with Hades, continues Lang, it does not follow that the fairies were originally ancestral ghosts, although such an origin has been claimed for them. " The stone arrow-heads of an earlier race are, when found by peasants, called ' elf-shots,' and are attributed to the fairies. Now the real owners and makers were certainly a dead race, as far as a race can die. But probably the ownership of the arrows by elves is only the first explanation that occurs to the rural fancy. . . . Some ancestral ghosts, however, such as the Zulu Amatongo, have much in common with Scottish and Irish fairies." [1]

Elsewhere, Lang laid some stress on the circumstance that Fairyland " was a kind of Hades, or home of the dead," in at least one of its aspects, while he was sufficiently complaisant to the theory of fairy development from the idea of a vanished prehistoric race to declare that " we cannot deny absolutely that some such memory of an earlier race, a shy and fugitive people who used weapons of stone, may conceivably play its part in the fairy legend." His conclusion respecting the fairy belief generally was that " we conceive it to be a complex matter, from which tradition, with its memory of earth-dwellers, is not wholly absent, while more is due to a survival of the pre-Christian Hades, and to the belief in local spirits—old imaginings of a world not yet ' dispeopled of its dreams.' " [2]

In his introduction to Tyson's *Philological Essay Concerning the Pygmies of the Ancients*, Dr. B. C. A. Windle had a great deal to say of the subject of fairy origins which, although it was written in 1894, is still very much to the point. He believed that one of the most effective ways of discovering the true nature of the

---

[1] A. Lang, Introduction to *Perrault's Popular Tales*, pp. xxxvi ff.
[2] A. Lang, Introduction to Kirk's *Secret Commonwealth of Elves, Fauns, and Fairies*, pp. 29, 31, 60.

fairies was by classifying them according to the nature of their habitations. They are found in mounds and in the interiors of hills, which may either be natural elevations or of a sepulchral character; or these fairy hills may have been the actual dwelling-places of prehistoric peoples. Or they might take up their abode in a castle or a house, the hill upon which such a building is erected, or a cave underneath it. Little people or fairies also occupy rude stone monuments or are connected with their building; or they may make their dwellings either in the interior of a stone or among stones. They may also inhabit forests, or single trees. Their association with water as a home is also well established. Regarding these several classes of fairy dwelling he provides copious examples. He treats of MacRitchie's theory respecting the origin of fairy belief at considerable length, and is of opinion that that writer " has gone far to show that one of the mythic elements, one strand in the twisted cord of fairy mythology, is the half-forgotten memory of skulking aborigines." In arriving at a general conclusion regarding fairy origins, he wrote: " One can scarcely fail to notice how much in common there is between the tales of the little people and the accounts of that underground world, which, with so many races, is the habitation of the souls of the departed. . . . It would appear that the underground world, whether looked upon as the habitation of the dead or the place of origination of nations, is connected with the conception of little races and people. That it is thus responsible for some portion of the conception of fairies seems to me more than probable." He adds: " That the souls of the departed, and the underground world which they inhabit, are largely responsible for it [the fairy superstition] is, I hope, rendered probable by the facts which I have brought forward." That animistic ideas have played an important part in the evolution of the idea of fairy spirits is, he thinks, not open to doubt. " That to these conceptions were superadded many features really derived from the actions of aboriginal races in hiding before the destroying might of their invaders—and this not merely in these islands—has been, I think, demonstrated by the labours of the gentleman to whose theory I have so often alluded [Mr. MacRitchie]. But the point upon which it is desired to lay stress is that the features derived from aboriginal races are only one amongst many sources." [1]

[1] B. C. A. Windle, Introduction to Tyson's *Essay Concerning the Pygmies of the Ancients*, pp. liii–civ.

If, like Windle, we consider the origin of the fairies with regard to their dwellings alone we should have little difficulty in concluding that they are in the nature of " genii," or animistic spirits which haunt hills, ruins, and so forth, or as the spirits of the dead haunting burial mounds.   But, unfortunately, they are capable of being classified in several other ways than by the nature of their haunts.   Moreover, ghosts, demons, vampires, and other supernaturals dwell in or frequent such places as well as fairies.   If the habitations of fairies, especially those situated underground, have a bearing upon the question of their origin—and it is admitted that to some extent they have—it is scarcely of such paramount importance as Windle appears to imply.

Professor Sir John Rhys was among those who believed that fairy origins were multiple.   He wrote: " I should hesitate to do anything so rash as to pronounce the fairies to be all of one and the same origin; they may well be of several.   For instance, there may be those that have grown out of traditions about an aboriginal pre-Celtic race, and some may be the representatives of the ghosts of departed men and women, regarded as one's ancestors; but there can hardly be any doubt that others, and those possibly not the least interesting, have originated in the demons and divinities— not all of ancestral origin—with which the weird fancy of our remote forefathers peopled lakes and streams, bays and creeks and estuaries." [1]

Canon MacCulloch, whose sound common-sense and scholarship mark him out for peculiar reliance in regard to the subject before us, in reviewing the evidence as a whole, also bears witness to the multiple origin of the fairy legend.   He concludes that " while some traits of dwarfs and fairies suggest an earlier race of men, others, when traced back, are found to be purely animistic in origin."   Many of these traits are non-human—the tiny size, the supernatural powers, the spirit aspect.   " Probably the belief in the manikin soul,[2] no less than general animism, and also human imagination and dreams had great influence in its formation.   Many traits of fairies are also those of supernatural beings with no human ancestry—a fact too often forgotten—Greek Nereids, Slavic Vily, spirit foxes in Japan, spirits of all kinds. . . . Primitive animistic, or even pre-animistic, ideas are the basis of

[1] J. Rhys, *Celtic Folklore, Welsh and Manx*, p. 455.
[2] As will be seen later, one view respecting the size of fairies is thought to have been developed from the idea among primitive races that the soul is diminutive.

the fairy creed, attached now to groups of imaginary beings, now to all kinds of supernaturals, now to traditions of actual men. On the other hand, these traditional memories doubtless gave definiteness to the fairy creed, or to certain parts of it. Yet it must be remembered that man always tends to regard the beings of his creed in his own likeness." Canon MacCulloch agrees with Andrew Lang that we cannot deny that the memory of an earlier and ruder race may conceivably play its part in fairy belief, but he concludes that " there has been interaction between animistic belief in groups of imaginary beings and folk-memory of earlier races regarded always more and more from an animistic and mythical point of view." [1]

In a lecture given at Cardiff on " The Legendary Character of the Fairies " so long ago as 1894, the late Professor A. C. Haddon of Cambridge summarized his attitude to the question of fairy origins as follows: " It is evident from fairy literature that there is a mixture of the possible and impossible, of fact and fancy. Part of fairydom refers to (1) spirits that never were embodied: other fairies are (2) spirits of environment, nature or local spirits, and household or domestic spirits: (3) spirits of the organic world, spirits of plants, and spirits of animals: (4) spirits of men or ghosts; and (5) witches and wizards, or men possessed with other spirits. All these and possibly other elements enter into the fanciful aspect of fairyland, but there is a large residuum of real occurrences; these point to a clash of races, and we may regard many of these fairy sagas as stories told by men of the Iron Age of events which happened to men of the Bronze Age in their conflicts with men of the Neolithic Age, and possibly these, too, handed on traditions of the Palæolithic Age." [2]   This classification, by one of the most prudent and well-equipped of our anthropologists, stresses the value of the theory that fairy belief was developed at more than one period in the past, and that it consisted of various strata, all of which seem to have survived and commingled.

Moses Gaster, a celebrated authority upon Oriental and East European Folk-lore, found " no direct indication . . . as to the antiquity of the fairy in Irish popular tales."   " The fairy, such as it appears in our tales, is, in any case, something quite different

---

[1] J. A. MacCulloch, *Folk-Lore*, XLIII, pp. 362–75. See also his *Mediaeval Faith and Fable*, pp. 28–44.
[2] A. C. Haddon, quoted by J. Rhys, in *Celtic Folklore*, pp. 683–4.

from the Norns of northern mythology, or the fata of the Latin popular belief, or the moirai of the Greeks, or the parcae, more or less sinister figures, differing entirely from the real fairy or fay. It would thus be difficult to say where the origin of the European fairy is to be sought." He did not think such a figure made its appearance before the time of the French romances of chivalry and the Arab influences from Spain. " The more one studies the connection between these romances and some of the tales found in Arabic—and let me add in Jewish writings of an earlier period—the more clear does the connection appear." [1] Gaster was certainly influenced by his Oriental studies. There can be no question whatsoever of the existence of a belief in fairies in Europe at a time long antecedent to the romances of chivalry, which themselves contain numerous reminiscences of the purely European fairy and of European fairy traits.

Having briefly summarized the outstanding theories entertained by British writers on the subject of fairy origins, I will proceed to examine the several classes of belief from which the fairy superstition as a whole has emerged, and of which these theories treat. Occasionally I shall find it necessary to draw upon examples other than British in illustrating them, and at times shall have to examine hypotheses of foreign provenance, as the nature of the subject demands. Before closing this chapter I should like to add that I have not thought it necessary here to draw any conclusions from such evidence as it contains, as that will be greatly added to in later chapters; and in any case that which draws to a close is, as I have already indicated, more or less intended as an introduction to theoretical ideas concerning fairy origins—a brief conspectus of the several hypotheses which seek to explain these origins, rather than a review of the evidence which might justify them.

[1] M. Gaster, " Collectanea," *Folk-Lore*, XLII, p. 157.

CHAPTER IV

FAIRIES AS SPIRITS OF THE DEAD

IT is wellnigh impossible to pursue the study of tales and legends associated with the fairies for any length of time without being most forcibly impressed with the community which exists between their background and general economy and the vulgar conception of that other-world which the souls of the dead are thought of as inhabiting. Fairies, indeed, have many things in common with ghosts. In some cases they have even taken over the burial tumuli formerly supposed to be haunted by the spirits of the dead. Many a legend of Fairyland tells how human explorers came face to face with persons dwelling there whom the mortal adventurer recognized as deceased friends or dead celebrities of human origin. Some European peasants, says Jacob Grimm, believe that the dead " belong to the fairies, and they therefore celebrate the death of a person like a festival, with music and dancing." [1] At the festival of Hallowe'en, ghosts and fairies were thought of as mingling together in unholy revels, the world on that occasion being given over to their sway. In modern Highland and Irish legend the dead and the fairies are at times scarcely to be distinguished. Persons who succeed in escaping from Fairyland often reveal the marks of incipient mortality, and in some instances, if they set a foot on upper earth, they crumble to dust, as might a corpse. To eat the food of fairies has the same results as when one partakes of the food of the dead. Indeed, a greater number of resemblances seem to exist between the dead and the fairies than differences divide them.

Many barrows and other sepulchral spots in Britain and elsewhere are pointed out as fairy dwellings. The famous Brugh of the Boyne, in Ireland, was at once a fairy hill and an ancient burying-ground. The hill of Tomnahuriach (" Hill of the Fairies ") at Inverness is another case in point, as is the sepulchral barrow of Willey How, in Yorkshire, popularly believed to be a fairy dwelling. These are merely concrete illustrations culled from hundreds of instances. In Cornwall the " spriggans," or elves, haunt only those standing stones which are associated with sepulture. As we shall see when we come to examine the connection of

[1] J. Grimm, *Teutonic Mythology* (trans. by Stallybrass), III, p. 122.

fairies with circles and standing stones which have been used as burial sites, these are so numerous as to constitute a powerful body of evidence that in many parts of this country fairies were connected in the popular mind with the last resting-place of the dead.

Alesoun Pearson, a Scottish witch who was brought to trial in the sixteenth century for trafficking with the fairies, bore witness that in the course of her sojourn in Fairyland she met with the spirits of young Maitland of Lethington and the old laird of Buccleuch, Scottish notables both of whom had been dead for some considerable time.[1] The fairy man who introduced one, Bessie Dunlop, an Ayrshire witch-wife, into the sphere of sorcery, was a certain Thome Reid, slain at the battle of Pinkie, a good many years before.[2] A " black man " who waylaid a peasant in Lochaber described himself as " a fairy man," but was found to be " John Stewart, who was slain at the down-going of the sun, and therefore neither dead nor living." [3] Another Scottish witch, Elspeth Reoch, entered into a relationship with " a fairy man," known to be one of the dead.[4] In one of J. F. Campbell's West Highland Tales we are told that a man saw a number of fairies spinning wool in a shieling where he was lodging at the time. Among them was Miss Emma MacPherson of Cluny, who had been dead about a hundred years.[5]

Tales of this kind simply abound in Irish folk-lore. One Jimmy Doyle, who penetrated to a fairy palace at Scollagh Gap, beheld there several people known to him to be dead.[6] Sometimes fishermen in Ireland encounter a strange boat filled with people " whom they recognize as the dead who have been carried off by the fairies to dwell in fairy palaces." [7]

Writing on the subject of Celtic fairy belief in Ireland and Scotland, Mr. Wentz gave it as his opinion that " when analysed, our evidence shows that in the majority of cases witnesses have regarded fairies either as non-human nature-spirits or else as spirits of the dead." [8] " The old people in County Armagh," he remarks, " seriously believe that the fairies were the spirits

[1] W. Scott, *Border Minstrelsy*, II, p. 340.
[2] W. Scott, *Letters on Demonology and Witchcraft*, p. 145.
[3] J. G. Dalyell, *The Darker Superstitions of Scotland*, p. 536.
[4] J. A. MacCulloch, *Folk-Lore*, XXXII, p. 236.
[5] J. F. Campbell, *Popular Tales of the West of Scotland*, II, p. 76.
[6] P. Kennedy, *Legendary Fictions of the Irish Celts*, p. 104.
[7] Lady Wilde, *Ancient Legends of Ireland*, p. 75.
[8] W. Y. E. Wentz, *The Fairy Faith in Celtic Countries*, p. 53.

of the dead; and they say that if you have many friends deceased you have many friendly fairies." [1] Elsewhere he says: " As I have found to be the case in all Celtic countries equally, fairy stories nearly always, in accordance with the law of psychology known as ' the association of ideas,' give place to or are blended with legends of the dead." [2] He cites the case of one Steven Ruan, a piper of Galway, who told him that the fairies are " nobody else than the spirits of men and women who once lived on earth." [3] He adds to this evidence, farther on: " The striking likenesses constantly appearing in our evidence between the ordinary apparitional fairies and the ghosts of the dead show that there is often no essential and sometimes no distinguishable difference between these two orders of beings, nor between the world of the dead and fairyland." [4]

In his *Popular Tales of the West Highlands* (Vol. II, p. 76) J. F. Campbell includes eight stories " which show that according to popular belief fairies commonly carried off men, women, and children who seemed to die, but really lived underground. In short, that mortals were separated from fairies by a very narrow line."

In Wales some fairies are closely associated with the dead. " The fairies of Wales are indeed frequently to be found on the best of terms with the ghosts," says Mr. Wirt Sikes. " These races have much in common, and so many of their practices are alike that one is not always absolutely sure whether he is dealing with a fairy or a spectre, until some test-point crops up." Elsewhere in his most entertaining book, *British Goblins*, Mr. Sikes mentions that " the popular theory of the origin of the fairies in Wales is that the Tylwyth Teg ("The Fair Family," i.e., the elves) are the souls of dead mortals, not bad enough for hell nor good enough for heaven." In modern Welsh folk-lore, Gwynn ap Nudd, the king of the Fairies, is also the ruler of the dead.

As Mr. J. G. Campbell once indicated, the foxglove in the Highlands is known in Gaelic as *Miaran nan cailleacha,* " the thimble of the old fairy woman," though more commonly as *Miaran nan cailleacha marbh,* " the thimble of the dead old woman."

The Sluagh, or flying fairies of Scotland, who are supposed to wander through the air at nights, shooting arrows at men and

---

[1] Wentz, *op. cit.*, pp. 74–5.

[2] Wentz, *op. cit.*, p. 95.

[3] Wentz, *op. cit.*, p. 39.

[4] Wentz, *op. cit.*, p. 109.

animals, are very frequently identified as the host of the dead by the peasantry of the West and of the islands. I have already indicated that persons carried off by sudden death were usually suspected of having been spirited away by the fairies, and unless redeemed from their power were doomed to spend the rest of their lives with them. Thome Reid, the fairy man above mentioned, appears to have been " taken " by the elves when wounded or slain at the battle of Pinkie, and Scott alludes to a similar case in his ballad of " Alice Brand," an interlude in *The Lady of the Lake* (Canto IV). People who indulged in " wild or unholy passions," or who were surprised in the commission of crimes, were likewise prone to be borne off by the fairies, probably because they infringed the elfin code of morality. To be caught by the fairies at sunset or sunrise was also fatal. Such cases seem to recall tales where malevolent ancestors, lying in wait for the souls of men, spirit them away when wounded, off their guard, or when defenceless through moral weakness, either to punish them, or to make them minister to their wants in the realm of the dead.

" We are confronted," says Mr. Wimberley, " with striking resemblances between the ballad ghost and the ballad fairy." [1] Quoting Hans Neumann's *Primitif Gemeinsschaftskultur* on this head, he agrees with that writer that " in substance, the conception of the living corpse did not in the primitive mind necessarily carry with it the conception of a soul or spirit." [2] He adds that " in British folksong the colour green is occasionally associated with the dead, or with death," and as the fairies favour this colour " it is possible that here again we encounter a significant resemblance between the dead and the fairies." [3] He is on sure ground, too, when he draws the conclusion that " the helpful ghosts of the savage stories and the kindly fairies of the ballads instance, of course, the significant mingling, or paralleling of ghost and fairy beliefs, or, perhaps we should say, the identicalness of such beliefs." [4] Mr. Wimberley also suggests that the dead give and are the guardians of treasure, as are the fairies. " The riches housed in ancestral graves suggest an origin for the belief that underground fairies are wealthy."

The diminutive size of certain fairies appears to have a bearing upon their relationship with the spirits of the dead. A Manx

[1] L. C. Wimberley, *Folk-Lore in the English and Scottish Ballads*, p. 165.
[2] L. C. Wimberley, *op. cit.*, p. 225.
[3] L. C. Wimberley, *op. cit.*, pp. 240–1.
[4] L. C. Wimberley, *op. cit.*, p. 280.

tale relates how a farmer who had lost his way in returning home from Peel heard a sound of music and merriment, which led him into a great hall, where there were a number of little people feasting. He seemed to recall some of their faces, and when one of them offered him something to drink, another forbade him to partake of the cup unless " he wished to be as they were and return no more to his family." [1] I cite this story more particularly as it actually links up the " little folk " either with the dead or with persons who have for some reason grown diminutive and who are in no respect different from fairies, but who are dwelling in a state similar to that in which primitive man believed the departed to survive. I may here recall the circumstances of the Cornish tale of *Cherry of Zennor*, already alluded to, in which we find a community of diminutive folk dwelling in an underground situation side by side with a " chamber of horrors " in which the maimed bodies of ossified dead people are stored. Here we seem to have both body and soul separately preserved in one " hades."

In Dr. Douglas Hyde's tale of *The King of Ireland's Son* we encounter " a short green man," who is revealed at the close of the story as a dead man. [2] Such references to the dead as diminutive are fairly numerous in folk-lore and old literature. In the Scottish poem known as *The Laying of Lord Fergus's Ghaist* the spirit is more than once alluded to as " a little ghaist," not much bigger than a midge. [3] This links up with Balkan stories of vampires, the souls of the wrathful dead, who take the shape of flies or other insects.

The spirits of the dead seem to assume the proportions of fairies. The night before the Rout of Moy, an attempt to surprise and capture " bonnie Prince Charlie," a certain Patrick McCaskill, a man gifted with the second sight, met a famous piper of the MacCrimmon family at Inverness and saw him contract to the size of a boy of five or six (the average height of the fairies in Scotland) and once more expand into his usual proportions. The man was slain in the morrow's skirmish. [4] Henderson recounts a story of an innkeeper in the Highlands whose wife made him drunk with brandy, cut off his head with an axe, and buried

[1] G. Waldron, *A Description of the Isle of Man*, p. 28.
[2] D. Hyde, *Beside the Fire*, pp. 18 ff.
[3] D. Laing, *The Early Popular Poetry of Scotland*, I, p. 284.
[4] A. Lang, Introduction to R. Kirk's *Secret Commonwealth of Elves, Fauns, and Fairies*, p. 59.

his body in the bracken. When the crime came to light, the woman admitted that she had been haunted by the spirit of her slaughtered spouse. One day, as she was out herding, she saw a number of small men playing around her, her husband among them. He came up to her and gave her a blow, which left a blue mark, from the effects of which she died later.[1] A daughter of Sir Charles Lee (says Beaumont, in his *Treatise of Spirits*) beheld the apparition of her mother in the shape of " a little woman," who prophesied her death.

A. E. Crawley, in his *Idea of the Soul*, has made it clear, by a substantial array of evidence gathered from ancient and modern sources, that among primitive folk " first among the attributes of the soul in its primary form may be placed its size," and that " in the majority of cases it is a miniature replica of the person, described often as a manikin, or homunculus, of a few inches in height." [2] Sir James Frazer has also made it clear that primitive people think that " if a man lives and moves, it can only be because he has a little man or animal inside who moves him. The animal inside the animal, the man inside the man, is the soul." This is, of course, a part of the familiar doctrine of animism, which so substantially governs primitive thought.[3] Writing of the size of fairies, Canon MacCulloch pays tribute to this idea. He remarks that it is not impossible " that the small size attributed to them [the fairies] in many regions may have been suggested by the common belief in the soul as a manikin," not only among savages, but in ancient Greece. On some Greek vases the soul is seen issuing from the body as a pygmy. In Egypt, the *ka*, or double of the dead man, is frequently represented, sometimes on bas-reliefs, as a dwarf.[4]

" The Hindus," says Carey, " believe that the soul of a person deceased exists but in ethereal or unsubstantial form, until certain necessary funeral ceremonies have been performed. It then passes into a more substantial form, described as about the height and length of a man's thumb." [5] There is, indeed, little need to stress the truth of this theory farther, as through the researches of Crawley, Frazer, and other writers, it has passed

[1] G. Henderson, *Survivals in Belief Among the Celts*, pp. 30–41.
[2] A. E. Crawley, *Idea of the Soul*, pp. 200–1, 206.
[3] J. G. Frazer, *Taboo and Perils of the Soul*, p. 26.
[4] J. A. MacCulloch in Hastings' *Encyclopedia of Religion and Ethics*, V, p. 683.
[5] Carey, *Ramayana*, III, p. 72.

into the more strictly accepted assertions of the science of Folk-lore.[1]

More than a century ago Jacob Grimm raised the question that elves and dwarfs were possibly the souls of the dead, and he quoted several passages from Teutonic folk-lore to fortify his theory.[2] Sir John Rhys also remarks upon it as a factor in fairy belief which must not be neglected.[3]

We now approach another and important question which has affiliations with the subject of the fairies when considered as the spirits of the dead. I allude to the belief which formerly prevailed in this island, and which actually does prevail in the remoter parts of Ireland, that when people were " taken " or lured away by the fairies, their souls took on a different quality from that which they possessed when in the strictly mortal state. A change which can only be described as " magical " appears to have come over them, for which it is difficult to account, but which must be recognized as important to the revelation of the origin and nature of elfin existence.

In the Irish *Book of Leinster* we read of an incident which well illustrates this belief. When Loegaire, son of the King of Connaught, returned from Mag Mell, or " The Pleasant Plain "— that is, the Irish home of the gods—he was advised by Fiachna, one of the dwellers in that place, that he and his fifty comrades should not dismount from their horses when they returned to Connaught. When they arrived on their native soil, the folk of Connaught sprang up to give them greeting, but were implored by Loegaire not to touch him or his companions, as they had merely come to bid them farewell. In the end Loegaire returned to Mag Mell.[4] In criticizing this tale, Wentz remarks that when he recounted it to an Irish peasant, the man said that " the spirit and body [of a mortal] are somehow mystically combined by fairy enchantment, for the fairies had a mighty power of enchanting natural people, and could transform the physical body in some way." This peasant, who appears, by the way, to have been gifted with powers of intellectual conversation, unconsciously

---

[1] For the origin of the idea of a soul, see E. Clodd, *Myths and Dreams*, pp. 182 ff.; E. B. Tylor, *Primitive Culture, passim*; A. E. Crawley, *op. cit., passim.*

[2] J. Grimm, *op. cit.*, p. 1414.

[3] J. Rhys, *Celtic Mythology, Welsh and Manx*, p. 459.

[4] D'Arbois de Jubainville, *The Irish Mythological Cycle* (Eng. trans. R. I. Best), pp. 201 ff.

F

alluded to a doctrine which is fast gaining ground among students of folk-lore—that in primitive belief, body and soul are not discriminated between, but are regarded as one. Mr. Wentz writes: " Some unknown bodily transmutation seems to have come about from the sojourn of people among the Tuatha Dé Danann—a transmutation apparently quite the same as that which the ' gentry ' are said to bring about now when one of our race is taken to live with them." In another place he ventures the opinion that " the old fairy faith and the new combine to prove the People of the God whose mother was Danu (that is, the Tuatha Dé Danann, or fairies) to have been and to be a race of beings who are like mortals, but not mortals, who to the objective world are as though dead, yet to the subjective world are fully living and conscious." [1]

In Walter Map's English tale of the British King Herla, who accompanied the dwarf king into Fairyland, we read of a similar injunction on the part of the elfin monarch. He warned Herla and his courtiers that they must not alight from their horses once they had returned to the mortal sphere, but some of them neglected his advice, and at once crumbled into dust.[2] The alteration of the body or spirit in Faerie is also mentioned in connection with King Arthur, of whom Sir Thomas Malory tells us that some men say that he is not dead, and that he would appear again in days of peril. " I will not say that it shall bee so," adds Sir Thomas, " but rather I will say that heere in this world *hee changed his life.*" [3] Here we have allusion to an ancient doctrine which the relatively modern writer could not definitely explain, and of which his day had lost the secret.

When Ossian returned from the enchanted country of Tir-nan-Og, he was warned by his sweetheart, Niamh of the Golden Hair, that he must not let his feet touch earthly soil. But when he reached Ireland he discovered that his Fenian comrades were merely names in the mouths of the people, generations having passed since he quitted the Green Isle. The men of the new time appeared puny to the brawny hero, and when he beheld three hundred of them trying in vain to raise a marble slab, he leaned from his horse and lifted it with one hand. But his saddle-girths broke with the strain, he slipped and touched the earth

---

[1] W. Y. E. Wentz, *op. cit.,* pp. 113, 296, 289.
[2] W. Map, *op. cit.,* Dist. I, c. 11.
[3] Sir Thomas Malory, *Morte d'Arthur,* III, p. 339.

with his feet, his fairy steed disappeared in a twinkling, and he rose from the ground a blind and decrepit old man.[1] But fatal was the end of Crimthann, High King of Ireland, who espoused the goddess Nair, and was wafted to the Oceanic Otherworld. Some six weeks of that enchanted sphere seems to have sufficed him, and he returned to Erin with a vast treasure of precious goods. Another six weeks passed in his native patrimony, but at the end of that time he sustained a fall from his horse—and perished as a result.[2] Nechtan, son of Collbran, returning to Ireland with Bran and other companions from a long voyage among the islands of the gods, leapt from his coracle in his haste to feel his native soil under his feet, but immediately on touching the earth he was transformed into a heap of ashes.

It is not unusual to find human beings suddenly transformed into fairies in certain circumstances. Bobd, King of the *Sidhe*, or fairies of Munster, and Ochall Ochne, King of the *Sidhe* of Connaught, had each a swineherd who had undergone several transformations in the course of their quarrels with one another, and they were at length born in the shape of the two famous bulls, the Brown of Ulster and the White of Connaught, so celebrated in connection with the great Irish saga of *The Cattle Raid of Cualgne*. In one passage of this saga, while in the form of Irish chieftains, they encourage two of their followers, Rinn and Faebar, both human warriors, to undertake a duel. These men fight for three days, and so sorely wound each other that at last their very lungs are visible, after which they become *siabur*, or fairies, " hideous to behold." [3] This is, of course, a mere euphemism, implying that death had overtaken them. Thomas Stephens, in his *Gododin of Aneurin*, tells us that when Gwenddolau and his allies were defeated and slain by the hostile chief Rhydderch at the battle of Arderydd, near Carlisle, in the year 573, when the rival Cumbrian princes unhappily waged war upon one another, a score of Gwenddolau's men, including Merlin the bard, took refuge in the Caledonian forest, " until they became sprites and were compelled to submit by starvation." [4]

Before attempting to find a solution for the belief in this state of enchantment I should like briefly to direct the reader's attention

---

[1] B. O'Looney " The Lay of Oisin in the Land of Youth," *Trans. Ossianic Soc.*, IV; A. Nutt, *The Voyage of Bran*, I, p. 15.

[2] D'Arbois de Jubainville, *op. cit.*, p. 206.

[3] See " Irische Texte," 2nd series, p. 254.

[4] T. Stephens, *The Gododin of Aneurin*, p. 71.

to a group of statements made by Irish peasants to Lady Gregory, when her researches into the subject of the fairy superstition took her into some of the more remote parts of Ireland. Most of these statements were made about persons who were obviously suffering from the effects of cretinism or from an obscure nervous complaint of some kind, but their relatives one and all appear to have believed that the soul of the sufferer had been hypothecated by the fairies, and that the body, or simulacrum, which remained was inhabited by a fairy spirit. In other cases death had occurred, and strange conclusions were drawn concerning its advent and character.

One man, whose son was supposed to have been " taken," said to Lady Gregory: " I don't know what's wrong with my son unless he's a real regular pagan [that is, " a fairy "]. He lies in the bed the most of the day and he won't go out till evening and he won't go to Mass. And he has a memory for everything he ever read or heard. I never knew the like." A girl called Katie Morgan, who suffered from a wasting disease, was known locally as " a fairy." From being a well-built colleen, she wasted away, her teeth grew very long and at last dropped out. She went out only at night, and ate what she could find in the fields. Another girl went out to gather nuts for three nights in succession, heard music in a wood on each occasion, and died. When her body was prepared for burial the neighbours beheld the corpse of an old woman with very long teeth and a wrinkled face. A young woman who, after her bridal, was being escorted home on a relative's horse, shivered as she passed a churchyard. Her uncle, who sat in front of her, put back his hand to steady her, but all he could feel was something like " a piece of tow." A year later, when her baby was born, she died, but people said she had been " taken " on her wedding-night. This sort of thing, said a shepherd in explanation to Lady Gregory, " was not death; it was being taken away." An old man assured her that the kind of people usually " taken " were those " that are good for singing or dancing, or for any good thing at all. And young women are often taken in that way." [1]

Must we distinguish between the changes consequent upon kidnapping or abduction by the fairies—that is, an obvious superstition that the afflicted person is possessed by a fairy spirit—and those passages in Irish myth which tell of persons returning from

[1] Lady Gregory, *Visions and Beliefs*, pp. 148, 176, 193, 233.

the oceanic other-world? In both cases the signs apparent are, or are thought to be, those of extreme old age, an access of unusual wisdom, and a generally " pagan " and anti-social disposition on the part of the sufferer. I conclude, therefore, that the modern belief is in some measure a reminiscence of the much more ancient notion. In the case of changelings it would appear that the mortal body of the possessed person has also been spirited away and that only a simulacrum of it has been left behind, which, at the moment of apparent death, reveals itself as the body of the old fairy who has actually taken the place of the kidnapped person. So far as the senile appearance of the returned adventurer into the sphere of the gods is concerned, he assumes this because of the length of time he has spent in that region. But that both ideas spring from a common source relative to a definite belief that a change of body overcame the visitor to a supernatural sphere, is, I think, clear enough.

What was the nature of the species of enchantment undergone by human beings who had either sojourned in the fairy sphere or who had suffered undue stress and strain in warfare? For these statements and tales I can discern no more probable origin than a euphemistic or aetiological, (i.e., explanatory) mythus which itself has drawn upon and elaborated the very primitive notion that death is an unnatural thing, a calamity brought about by the malevolent magic of supernatural beings, spirits, ghosts, or wizards. Early man could not account for death; it seems to have puzzled him exceedingly. Illness, in his purblind view, was due to the interference of an ancestral spirit or to the great malignant host of the dead, who desired his presence in the other-world, either for the mere sake of his company, or because one of their number wished to be reincarnated and to take his place in the land of the living. Or, if he infringed any of their taboos, they might punish him with death. Once he has sojourned in the land of Faerie, or Deadland, he assumes the cardinal nature of its inhabitants; he is transformed into something non-human; his spirit and substance alike become alien to the mortal sphere, which is unfriendly to his novel condition and which rejects him should he seek to return to it. So much is clear. He is like a fish out of water, a creature belonging to another element; or rather, one who has, in nearly all essentials, become so acclimatized to another environment that he is unable to exist in his original surroundings.

Such a change cannot be explained except through the existence of supposititious taboos, which appear to have automatically affected a man once he entered the fairy sphere or the land of the dead. But it will not do to omit record of the fact that the " Fairyland " of Keltic story in which the majority of the doomed heroes undergo this alteration is the Land of the Gods, and not the Elfland of later folk-lore or fairy tale. From the more modern Faerie one might return, although he was seldom able to adapt himself again to human ways, and in the end usually drifted back to the country of Elfland. And it falls to be added that the Land of the Gods, at least as we know it from Irish myth, was by no means a sphere of the departed, although certain passages in the myths of the ancient Britons make it seem probable that the underground paradise of our remote forefathers, as apart from that of the Kelts of Ireland, was in some sense a country of the dead. Keeping this in mind, I feel that it is not improbable that the later view of the lethal possibilities accruing to a return from Fairyland may have been a reminiscence of fatalities consequent upon a return from the Land of the Gods, such as occurred in the cases of Ossian, Crimthan, and Nechtan. But it is to be remarked that a return from such a sphere in any mythology other than that of the Kelts, so far from being perilous, is usually associated with an enhanced virility and a bestowal of all the gifts and graces of the culture-hero upon the adventurer when once again he reaches the earth-sphere. Here, I think, we are in the presence of a body of legend which, originating in a very primitive perplexity regarding the nature of death, attracted to itself notions associated with lowly and aboriginal views concerning changes in spirit and body which might be wrought through a sojourn in the country of the ancestors, the most primeval of all the abodes of the dead. There is, at least, a general consensus on the part of students of tradition that certain esteemed humans were, on occasion, invited or borne off to the ancestral paradise, the home of the great dead of the tribe, so that in regarding the Land of the Gods as a sphere in which sojourn might bring about radical changes in the body and spirit of a man whilst still alive, and in applying this doctrine to the Fairyland of a later tradition, the Kelts of Britain and Ireland were possibly harking back to the notions of their earlier forefathers, or of aboriginal predecessors on the soil which they had conquered. To employ a cant phrase of the older anthropology, the belief in the disastrous results of a voyage to the Land of the Gods is " non-Aryan " rather than " Aryan."

This naturally leads to a consideration of the resemblances between Fairyland and the place of the dead in British myth and legend. I have already summarized the evidence relative to the several types of fairyland conceived by British tradition. It now remains to describe such associations connected with fairy lore as may insinuate that, at some period or periods, what we know as the fairy sphere was regarded as a place of departed souls. Of course, post-Christian sentiment saw a Hell in Faerie, but we are at present dealing with conceptions possibly current at a period anterior to the Christian era. Andrew Lang believed that the idea of Faerie was " due to a survival of the pre-Christian Hades."

The early English poets habitually confuse Fairyland with the classical Hades. Thus Chaucer describes Pluto, the King of Hades, as " Kyng of Fayrie," and alludes to Prosperine, his queen, as associated with " fayrie," though in this sense the word may well apply to sorcery. In the romance of *Orfeo and Heurodys* the character of the elfin land is subterranean, and the idea of it must have been adapted from the Greek myth concerning Orpheus and Eurydice, the scene of which is laid in Hades. In an old Scottish play, *Philotus*, one of the characters adjures another: " Gang hence to Hell or to the Farie," which seems to imply that in the author's mind these spheres must have borne a close resemblance one to the other.

It must not be thought, however, that in pagan Ireland Fairyland was altogether conceived as a Hades or place of the dead. We have already seen that in some of its types and aspects it was inherently nothing of the sort; as when, for example, it came to be confused with the Land of the Gods. In all likelihood these separate paradises and deadlands of a nature so various were the result of the stratified beliefs of successive races dwelling in the same region. A conquering race would scarcely credit that its heroes would, after death, betake themselves to the deadland of the beaten and enslaved aborigines. The gods of vanquished races might be conceived as presiding over spheres of the dead for which their victors would have nothing but contempt, and which, because of that very contempt, might come to be conceived as hells or places of a debased and grovelling kind, pestiferous regions which only the spirits of despised " natives " or the undesirable might inhabit.

Thus, to the Kelts, the Fomorian deadland, the resort of

departed Fomorian spirits, the dead men of a race expelled by the conquering and superior Tuatha Dé Danann, came to be looked upon as a species of hell, exactly as, when the Tuatha Dé Danann themselves retired to the hollow hills of Ireland before the conquering Milesians, their own underground dwellings assumed a more or less unsavoury reputation in the eyes of their victors. This reveals the manner in which, out of a kind of deadland or Hades of vanished gods, the idea of a Fairyland may have arisen—a Fairyland which, in the sight of the pagan conquerors and their Christian successors alike, might readily assume an infernal reputation as the resort of discredited and banished deities unfriendly to a new population. The godlands of the conquerors became heavens, homes of the gods; those of the conquered, uncanny spheres resembling Fairyland, which in post-Christian times assumed nearly all the arrtibutes of a hell.

Nearly all the more unpleasant passages in ancient British myth which describe the gloom of the British or Welsh Annwn and its region of Caer Sidi; or the horrid Underworld caverns peopled by "giants" and monsters, with which we meet in Scottish Gaelic story, appear to be the abodes of a titanic race of "aboriginal" gods overthrown. It is the story of the Titans defeated and banished by the Gods of Olympus over again. The sagas of King Arthur and his Round Table, their conflicts with giants and monsters, are nothing else than memories of forgotten sagas of warfare between the gods of a conquering and more highly civilized race and those of a less developed folk. Some of these gloomy spots are even localized in legend; as, for example, Glastonbury, where an underworld ruler had his seat at Avalon, to which he spirited away Queen Guinevere.[1] Nutt has concluded that the ancient Kelts had no precise country of the dead. However that may be, they certainly believed in a land of dead or discredited gods, and their predecessors nourished an equally decided belief that the dead carried on a dead-alive existence in the burial mounds or beneath the burial cairns.

As has been indicated by Miss Rosa Burstein, at a higher level of culture such myths are told of gods; at a lower, of human beings.[2] That is, the dead come to take the place of the gods in later and debased story. The sites in which the gods took refuge

---

[1] J. L. Weston, *Sir Lancelot*, pp. 59 f.; F. Lot, "Nouvelles études sur la provenance du Cycle Arthurien," in *Romania*, pp. xxvii and xxviii; E. Hull, "The Development of Hades in Celtic Literature," *Folk-Lore*, 1907.

[2] Rosa Burstein, "The Harrowing of Hell," *Folk-Lore*, XXXIX, pp. 122-5.

probably came to be thought of as the burial-places of the defeated races, and the old tales once recounted of the vanished deities are now told about the folk entombed there. We cannot altogether dissociate the idea of Fairyland from a place of the dead in one or other of its phases. Indeed it stands to reason that if the fairies are capable of being identified with the dead, wholly or partially, their abode must naturally possess some of the attributes of a place of the departed.

Summarizing these conclusions concerning Fairyland as a place of the dead, we find that Early English literature confuses Fairyland with the classical Hades. This conception of it was not, however, universal in ancient and mediaeval times, and was probably not entertained by the conquered races, whose deadland it probably was. Many of the more unpleasant and gloomy resorts of the older pre-Keltic gods appear to resemble the abode of the Greek giants or Titans, whom Uranus imprisoned in the bowels of the earth. Such myths about these gigantic and unpleasant gods who resided underground came later to be told of the dead folk of the aboriginal races who were interred in sites to which such gods were said to have been banished, and which would seem sacred to the folk. In a great measure this would account for the infernal reputation of Fairyland, though post-Christian hostility probably heightened its unprepossessing character. At the same time, it is well to bear in mind the warning of Keltic authorities of standing that much of the evidence respecting the Land of the Gods and the fairy sphere in general which proceeds from Irish sources must be accepted with caution because of its occasionally conflicting nature and its general obscurity.

Between the taboo which forbids a mortal to partake of the food of the elves and that which prohibits him from eating food proffered him in the land of the dead, no actual difference exists. But it would be rash to infer from this alone, as do some authorities, that the fairies and the dead are one and the same. In some parts of the world the food of kings or priests is taboo, and kings or priests are neither the dead, nor are they elves. We are, in fact, faced with that ancient belief that if one ate the food of a person or spirit they would magically partake of his nature. Such an act was strictly to be avoided, as it presumed fellowship with the spirit race and the renunciation of that with mortals. In other words, to eat fairy food at once gave one a fairy nature, and scores of tales utter warnings as to the danger of such a proceeding. In the romance of *Thomas of Erçeldoun* the Queen of Elfin warns him against eating of the fruit of a fairy orchard. Ogier the Dane is actually prostrated by partaking of an apple from the garden of Morgan la Fay, and in many British fairy tales a kindly elf, not infrequently a dead friend or neighbour, admonishes the wanderer in Fairyland against the consumption of fairy viands.[1]

As Krappe indicates, it is a more than suspicious circumstance that numerous stories exist of fairies and troll-folk ferrying over streams in such a manner as recalls the passage of dead souls across the Styx. In a random note on the subject, in *Folk-Lore*, Sir James Frazer mentions that Isabella Ross, an old servant in his father's family, told him that " the fairies of the Highlands are all supposed to be drowned in a place called the Ferry." They wished to cross the ferry, and " they asked an old woman if the water was deep; she replied, in Gaelic, ' Although it's black, it is not deep.' "[2] In North Jutland a strange man came to the ferry of Sund and engaged the ferry-boats there to ply all night long. The ferryman could see nothing, but observed that in course of time the boats sank deeper and deeper as though under a heavy freight. But one ferryman put some clay from under his right foot beneath his cap, and, being thus temporarily gifted with clairvoyance, beheld the banks of the stream swarming with trolls.[3] That the custom of ferrying the dead across water to the place of sepulture has sanctions in Breton tradition we know, and this practice still exists at Tréguier in that region.[4] Procopius, a Greek annalist of the sixth century, alludes to a story that Breton or Frankish fishermen were compelled to ferry the shades of the dead to the coasts of Britain at the darkest hour of night.[5]

In the Highlands of Scotland a burial tumulus was frequently to be found in close proximity to the local churchyard. Such mounds, says Robert Kirk, were known to the people as " fairy hills," from which it was impious or dangerous " to remove earth or wood, as it was believed that ' the souls of their predecessors ' dwelt there." " And for that End," adds the minister of Aberfoyle, " a Mote or Mount was dedicate beside every Church-yard, to receive the souls until their adjacent bodies arise and so become

---

[1] W. Y. E. Wentz, *op. cit.*, p. 275; A. Lang, *Myth, Ritual, and Religion*, pp. 11, 26; and in his *Custom and Myth*, p. 171.

[2] J. G. Frazer, *Folk-Lore*, I.

[3] T. Keightley, *The Fairy Mythology*, pp. 128, 225. See also J. Grimm, *op. cit.*, p. 1417.

[4] L. Spence, *Legends and Romances of Brittany*, p. 383.

[5] Procopius, *De Bello Gothica*, Bk. IV, cap. 20.

as a Fairie-hill; they useing Bodies of Air when called Abroad." [1]
This, remarks Lang, is " putting the cart before the horse," as the
tumuli are much older than the churches.   Obviously the statement
has reference to a tradition that the souls of the dead inhabited
fairy hills, or tumuli, a belief which was later construed as signifying that the bodies only of the departed rested in the adjacent
churchyard, their souls dwelling in the fairy hills.   I think, too,
that the statement reveals a change-over from the primitive belief
that body and soul were one to that which conceived them as
being separate.   Kirk's reference, however, provides the best
evidence that the Highlanders actually believed the souls of their
dead ancestors to inhabit fairy hills, and it follows that they either
believed the dead to be fairies, or inextricably confused them with
fairy spirits.   In some parts of the Highlands, when a person died,
the mattress on which he had breathed his last was carried to the
nearest fairy hill and burnt there.

In Orkney, Katherine Jonesdochter, a witch, gave evidence at
her trial that she had seen " the trows (trolls, or fairies) rise out
of the kirkyard of Hildiswick and Holiecross Kirk of Eschenes, and
on the hill called Greinfall."   They came, she added, to any house
where there was feasting or great merriness, especially at Yule. [2]
This provides further evidence of the superstition that the fairies
were identified with the souls of the dead.   On the eve of Hallowe'en, the old Keltic festival of Samhain, the dead and the
fairies were thought of as mingling in their revels.   The original
Keltic story may be referred to an earlier belief that the dead
and the fairies were one and the same, for the Irish tale of Nera,
which tells how Ailyill, King of Connaught, offered a reward to
any man bold enough to venture abroad that night on a certain
errand, makes it clear that the inhabitants of the fairy mound
were the spirits of the dead.   Miss E. Hull, writing on this particular passage, says : "" In the minds of our pagan ancestors there
was very little distinction between the dead and the fairies, who
were, perhaps, only the spirits of an earlier race. . . .   All the
demons at the fairy raths are dead human folk who are out for
their Hallowe'en revels, after which they must go back to their
graves for another year."   She adds that in the story of Nera " we
have the connexion between the two emphasized." [3]

In considering the fairies as derived from the idea of the dead

[1] R. Kirk, *op. cit.*, p. 79.   [2] J. G. Dalyell, *op. cit.*, p. 532-3.
[3] E. Hull, *Folk-Lore of the British Isles*, pp. 245-7.

it seems important to stress the fact that they possess many human traits. Their temperament is, indeed, frequently revealed as only too human, as are their avocations, and their dress, as Kirk remarks, is usually that of the area which they inhabit. In passing I should like to make a point which I feel has been unduly neglected—if, indeed, it has ever been touched upon. I refer to the appearance which the goblin tribe, and indeed male fairies in general, present. Whence comes the inspiration which depicts the masculine fairy in art and illustration with enormous eye-sockets, in which roll large and " goggling " eyes? From what model is drawn the emaciated face, prominently revealing the bony structure, the skinny frame, the wasted hands? To anyone whose avocation has at any time brought him into touch with the wards of great hospitals, the origin of the goblin face and form is only too clear. It represents humanity sick unto death, on the verge of mortality. The goblin or male fairy is, outwardly, artistically, a reminiscence of the dying man; he is a replica of the manner in which generations of artists have sought to depict either the dead soul, or the dead body returned from the grave. As regards the female fairy, romance has dictated a different representation in art. Yet in folk-lore many stories describe her as wan, haggard, and unlovely. And if she is kissed by a mortal, she is all too likely in some cases to reveal the appearance of a dead woman.

Canon MacCulloch has summarized his conclusions on the subject of the relationship between the fairies and the dead with neatness and lucidity. " The similarity of beliefs regarding fairies and ghosts, while yet the two classes of beings are regarded as different," he writes, " rather points to their *not* having a common origin, but reminds us that similar traits are ascribed to all kinds of supernaturals, and that through the mingling of traditions the traits of one class easily pass over to another. If fairies began as ghosts of an earlier race, they became in time more or less mythical spirits, *not* now envisaged as ghosts, but transformed into fairies; while more or less recent ghosts retained their ghostly aspect. Probably, however, the ghost origin is only one of several. Popular tradition does actually regard certain fairies as souls of the dead, or rather of certain classes of dead persons; but perhaps we need not lay too much stress on this any more than on folk-etymologies, interesting but erroneous. If some fairies took their origin from ghosts, this probably occurred in extremely remote times and the

Nereids of Greece—a kind of fairies, the fées of mediaeval romance, and the stately fairies of early Irish story, are certainly not derived from ghosts." [1]

I find myself in agreement only with part of this summing-up. Especially would I lay stress on the statement that " if some fairies took their origin from ghosts, this probably occurred in extremely remote times." Canon MacCulloch's conclusion seems in no sense unfriendly to the theory that fairies were primarily the dead. Those fairies who exhibit the closest resemblance to the dead are naturally of that type who haunt, or are supposed to reside in, the burial mound, the tumulus, the stone circle, or the isolated standing-stone, and of these I shall have a good deal to say in a later chapter. It is precisely such elves as have associations with the burial-places of the dead who most resemble the dead, or the idea of the disembodied souls—a fact which, so far, has been lost sight of in the great welter of the fairy debate. The goblinesque appearance of the British mound-fairy reveals his likeness to the dead man. The Irish fairies (the Tuatha Dé Danann), were " dead " gods who became fairies, precisely as dead men became fairies. The same applies to the Nereids of Greece, and the fays of French Romance.

Here I must pause, for anything more I have to say in connection with this part of the subject of fairy origins must be said when comparing the value of the evidence I have adduced for it with that which supports other theories respecting fairy descent. But I feel that I have at least produced enough proof to show that it is not possible to regard fairy spirits in general as otherwise than spirits of the dead in their remote origin, although I freely admit that a few diverse and dissimilar forms and types must be included as factors in the fairy genealogy. I think it is clear, too, that Canon MacCulloch's argument that fairies and ghosts did not have a common origin is scarcely borne out by his later tacit admission that they were ghosts " transformed into fairies." The mere fact that more modern predilection has come to regard fairies as a separate class of mythical spirits, not now envisaged as ghosts, has nothing to do with their origins and is, after all, quite an artificial conception of them, encouraged chiefly by literary tendencies.

[1] J. A. MacCulloch, " Were Fairies an Earlier Race of Men ? " *Folk-Lore*, XLIII, p. 365.

CHAPTER V

THE ANCESTRAL CHARACTER OF FAIRY SPIRITS

As I have already indicated, the theory of the derivation of fairies from ancestral spirits is to some extent a part of the larger hypothesis that fairies are the spirits of the dead. But I have thought it best to separate the material which treats of their ancestral character from the proof which reveals them as deceased mortals; for if that evidence is sufficiently telling, it will not only make plain to us that fairies, in one of their aspects, were regarded as the spirits of dead people, but of a certain type of dead folk, thus disclosing their nature more particularly and classifying them with greater clarity and precision.

Here it is necessary briefly to consider the question of the cult of ancestors before venturing farther. The spirits of the departed are believed to be possessed of supernatural powers which they did not enjoy in the flesh. They may also be dissatisfied or malignant in consequence of being suddenly deprived of life, and if they are neglected by the living, are apt to be revengeful. Therefore they must be cajoled and propitiated. Fear of beings belonging to a mysterious state or sphere of which he knew nothing continually haunted and terrified primitive man and induced in him what is known as " the dread of the sacred." It was every man's personal duty to attend to the demands or requirements of his deceased ancestors. At first he would succour his own immediate forebears with food and gifts; but it must have been borne in upon him that when his parents joined the great majority, the care of the spirits of *their* parents likewise devolved upon him . . . and, by degrees, he might even come to regard himself as responsible for the well-being of a line of spirit ancestors of quite formidable genealogy.

These, through his neglect, might starve in their tombs; or, alternatively, they might crave his company. Because of vengeance or loneliness they might send disease upon him, for the savage almost invariably believes illness to be brought about by the action of jealous or neglected ancestors. The loneliness of the spirit-world is the dead man's greatest excuse for desiring the company of his descendants.

Again, the ancestors may reappear in children. Among many primitive folk the child is regarded as an ancestor reborn. This appears to me to indicate that the ancestral cult can have come into being only after the institution of the family, and not during any phase of promiscuity. Among the peoples of the African Gold Coast and Slave Coast, for instance, a distinction is drawn between the ghostly self which continues the dead man's existence in the spirit world after death and his *kra*, which is separate and capable of being born again in a new human body. Much the same idea prevails among the Blackfellow tribes of Australia. But in the African areas alluded to these spirits never animate a newly-born child in a strange family. This tacit recognition of the family state perhaps provides us with a horizon for the beginnings of the ancestral cultus, and therefore for a belief in the type of spirits known as fairies. It is also clear that the spirits of the dead ancestors frequently behave very much as do the fairies, who are wont to be irritable and exacting, who expect tributes of food and drink, who remain invisible, and who exercise a close and sometimes almost " governessy " oversight of human affairs.

If we can discover parallels between beliefs associated with ancestor-worship and those connected with the fairies, the theory of their ancestral origin will be considerably fortified. Any attempt to explain the fairies, says Mr. R. U. Sayce, " must take into account ancestral and nature spirits." He adds the warning, however, that " the distinction between ancestral spirits and those of plants and animals is far from clear " in the primitive mind.[1] Many tribes, as we shall see later, believe that spirits haunting rocks, trees, and so forth were once those of men. It is a fact in folk-lore that most ancestral spirits are regarded as the conservators of tribal virtue and decency, and this would go far to explain the fairy insistence on decorum and neatness. The ancestral spirits of the African Bantu, for instance, are, says Willoughby, " vigilant defenders of clan morality and decorum, sure to vent their wrath upon those who waste the patrimony which they conserved, or fail to honour the law and customs which they held as a sacred trust from their earliest forefathers." [2]

Mr. Sayce finds resemblance between ancestral and fairy belief in the following circumstances: the belief in rebirth, which reveals itself in both connections; the frequent associations with the idea of an ancestral cult to be found in Keltic fairy stories. Other resemblances are to be discovered in the constant and intimate

---

[1] R. U. Sayce, *Folk-Lore*, XXXV, pp. 99, 114.
[2] Willoughby, *The Soul of the Bantu*, p. 87.

association of fairies and mortals, fairy intervention in human affairs, fairy warnings of misfortunes, fairy associations with the hearth and with ancient dwelling-places; in human concern for the welfare of the fairies, such as the provision of drinking-water and baths in farm-houses, the lending of cooking utensils, offerings of food and blood to the elves, and of teinds or tenths. The case would certainly have been strengthened by adding that the folk in general have a much more intimate association with the fairies than with any other class of spirit. If, adds Sayce, fairies are not more generally regarded as ancestral spirits by those who believe in them, it is probably because of the great antiquity of the belief in them, which has come to be regarded as relating to a distinctive and separate class of spirit. This idea in particular chimes with Canon MacCulloch's view concerning the later belief that fairies are a distinct spiritual type. Sayce is of opinion that later immigrants into the British Isles brought with them their own ideas of the nature of departed spirits (the English ghost, for example, is never a dwarf, while the fairies, he thinks, possess a " Mediterranean " spirit and vivacity) and that the conquerors considered it wise to placate the native ghosts.[1]

It is chiefly in Scotland and Ireland, among British communities, that the ancestral qualities of the fairy are more particularly evident, as these areas are certainly peopled by races of older provenance than is the case with England. The *banshee* is notoriously an ancestral form, haunting families of distinction. The name simply denotes " fairy woman " or " supernatural women," and has no other special significance. In Scotland, however, she assumes more than one form, the *glaistig*, the *cointeach*, or " keener," and the *bean-nighe*, or " washer," which latter appearance she also takes in Ireland. Most great families in the Highlands of Scotland " possessed a tutelary spirit of the kind," remarks Sir Walter Scott. Sometimes the *cointeach* is alluded to as " a little white thing, soft as wool," and without flesh, blood, or bones—clearly a popular rendering of a very ancient idea of the rather amorphous appearance and condition in which the soul was supposed to exist in its separate state. The *cointeach* howled outside the doors of those about to die. In the Highlands of Aberdeenshire, says Wentz, two hills were pointed out where travellers were wont to propitiate the *banshee* with cakes of barley-meal, and if such an offering were neglected, death or misfortune

---

[1] R. U. Sayce, *op. cit.*, pp. 135. f.

was sure to ensue. This reveals very clearly the incidence of a belief in that species of offering usually devoted to ancestral spirits.[1]

The name *glaistig* means " grey woman," and the spirit thus described has been classed as a female of human race who has been put under enchantments and to whom a fairy nature has been given. " She is said to have been at first a woman of honourable position, a former mistress of the house, who had been put under enchantments." [2] The clan MacLean enjoyed the dubious ministrations of such a tutelary spirit at Breachacha Castle, as did the MacDougalls of Dunollie in their own stronghold.

In Ireland nearly every distinguished family had a *banshee* of its own. Such hags sat on rocks or fences, moaning horribly in premonition of a death in the family. The *banshee's* skeleton face and generally grisly appearance are eloquent of mortality. The *banshee*, the *glaistig*, and the Welsh *cyhiriaeth*, are, indeed, creatures of the most repellent kind. As their descriptions have come down to us, they represent the more ancient and horrible idea of the family spectre, with long and tangled locks, ghastly faces, green or grey in hue, talon-like nails, and raucous voices. They are symbols of death, corpse-like shapes haunting the spots where they dwelt in life, closely resembling the old English type of ghost popularly known as " Raw-head-and-bloody-bones." In a word, they represent the dead ancestress, jealously anxious concerning the welfare of the family whence she sprang.

I have already indicated how closely the brownie resembles the Roman *lar*, or ancestral genius. Like the *lar*, brownie frequently rises from the hearth, with which he is closely associated; he basks in front of it, he is " placated " with offerings of milk or cream, he refuses to quit the family, with whose fortunes he is identified. He departs only if he is offered clothing, and I have formed the impression that he may have done so out of chagrin because he was not offered the body of the person to whom the clothing belonged—the substitution of clothing, or a part thereof, being notoriously a late subterfuge on the part of humans who desired to escape their indebtedness to deities or ancestral spirits of a more or less discredited and jealous kind. " He continues in a family," says Jacob Grimm, " so long as a member of it survives,

---

[1] P. C. Maclagan, "The Keener in the Scottish Highlands and Islands," "*Folk-Lore*", XXV, pp. 84f.
[2] J. G. Campbell, *op. cit.*, p. 155.

G

and hence he is the heirloom of an ancient and respected house. Besides unparalleled fidelity, he is unremitting in promoting his master's interest, and his services are still further enhanced by the gift of foretelling future events." " In the Orkneys," adds the great German folk-lorist, " the brownie is a family spirit requiring sacrifice "—a statement which, however, I cannot substantiate.

Brownie, remarks Canon MacCulloch, " is almost certainly a transformed ancestral spirit, helpful and kindly, yet apt to take offence on slight provocation. A study of his traits and habits with those of ancestral spirits, will show that he is more nearly allied to spirits of the dead than are fairies in general." [1]   Indeed, in one outstanding instance, a certain English brownie, " the Cauld Lad of Hilton," was said to be " the ghost of a servant-boy, slain by an old baron of Hilton in a moment of passion." [2]   A mischievous " fairy boy " who haunted a house in the Shiant Islands was described as " one of the family." [3]

Rogers remarks that the *lares familiares* of the Scottish Highlanders were the ghosts of departed ancestors.[4] The " Billie Blin," a Scottish domestic sprite of the brownie species, gives the impression of being the spirit of a dead ancestor. He appears as the tutelar of the family, arranges matrimonial alliances, and presides over births. The name is also employed to describe a Scottish form of the game of blind man's buff which suggests some kind of bogey.[5] The domestic association of fairies with the hearth—the altar of the *lar*—is indicated by Milton in at least two passages which should be familiar to everybody (unless British people have ceased to draw upon the richest vein of poetry in their heritage); and indeed it scarcely seems necessary to say that Jonson alludes to the fairy " that doth haunt the hearth and dairy," and that frequent indications of this predilection of the fairies for the hearth abound in English poetry of the older sort. The *lar* of the Romans was originally of Etruscan provenance, and is known to-day among the people of Tuscany as the *lasio*, who appears in a house when one of the family dies. " They are the ghosts of the ancestors of the family, who come at such a time," said a Tuscan peasant to Leland.[6]

J. A. MacCulloch, *Folk-Lore*, XLIII, pp. 365–6.
W. Henderson, *Folk-Lore of the Northern Counties*, p. 266.
J. H. Dixon, *Gairloch*, pp. 159–60.
C. Rogers, *Scotland Social and Domestic*, III, pp. 340–1.
A. B. Gomme, *Traditional Games*, I, pp. 39–40.
C. G. Leland, *Etruscan-Roman Remains*, pp. 82 ff.

Many of the circumstances associated with British fairies identify them with ancestral spirit-forms. As we have already seen, " teinds," or portions of barley and milk, are allotted to them, especially in the case of the *brownie, glaistig*, and *gruagach*. As lately as the seventies of last century an old woman at Alnwick, in Northumberland, used to set aside for the fairies " a loake of meal and a pat of butter." [1] In Ireland you must " never drain your wine-glass at a feast, nor the poteen flask nor the milk-pail " if you wish to " keep in with " the fairies.[2] " When the people drop crumbs," says Carmichael, of the West Highlanders, " they leave them for the Frids," or elves. Such persons are invariably fortunate.[3] All this is traceable to a folk-recollection of an almost world-wide religious attitude to the dead which appears to have had its beginnings in ancient Babylon and Egypt. Egyptian and Babylonian ghosts grew wroth unless food and drink were left at their tombs by their relatives, and visited them with disease and misfortune or haunted them as vampires and sucked their blood. Of the ghosts of savage races the same may be said. I have already alluded to Kirk's statement that the Highlanders refused to remove soil or timber from a fairy hill because they believed their dead ancestors reposed there.

A schoolmaster in the Ben Bulbin country in Ireland assured Mr. Wentz of the implicit belief of the local folk that the fairies were the spirits of their departed relatives.[4] The Irish Tuatha Dé Danann, or fairies, were regarded as " royal or famous ancestral spirits " identified with the god-race of that name, " who being reborn as mortals, ruled Ireland." Pilgrimages were made to their tumuli and offerings rendered there.[5] Bishop Calloway has pointed out that what the Highlanders say of the fairies, the Zulus say of the ancestors. George Henderson indicates the existence of the survival of ancestral ideas among the Highlanders—how it is " a matter of extreme importance to call a child by the name of a deceased ancestor; death is but a minor affair so long as the name is kept up." The physiological fact that many children closely resemble their grandparents rather than their immediate parents appears to have been recognized by primitive man, and to have caused him to believe that the souls of his own immediate

---

[1] *Denholm Tracts*, II, p. 143.
[2] Lady Wilde, *Ancient Legenas of Ireland*, p. 143.
[3] A. Carmichael, *Carmina Gadelica*, II, p. 280.
[4] W. Y. E. Wentz, *The Fairy Faith in Celtic Countries*, p. 35.
[5] W. Y. E. Wentz, *op. cit.*, p. 413.

predecessors had taken up their abode in the bodies of his children. The hereditary use of Christian names is still most common among the humbler folk of Scotland, both Highland and Lowland. " Every birth," says Henderson elsewhere, " revealed a return. . . . Nature is believed to be full of spirits. . . . The mother forms her own inferences wherever she may chance to experience the feeling of quickening, and readily forms a sympathetic association with some object or other at the place and time. A spirit part of some ancestor, she believes, has entered her, a soul has become incarnate."[1] That this belief forms a part of Australian Blackfellow doctrine will be made clear on a later page. For a woman to sleep on a fairy hill or burial-mound in the Highlands was to tempt conception from elfin sources.[2]

" Many of the deities of the Irish," says Wood-Martin, " appear to have been *sidhes*; that is to say, deified mortals, for they dwelt in the *sidhes* or places where the dead had been deposited (that is in the fairy hills). These receptacles were scattered all over the land and in or around them assembled for worship the family or clan of the deified person; hence it might be termed really a species of ancestral worship."[3] " They are still on earth," said an Irish peasant woman to Mr. Wentz, referring to the fairies. " Among them are the spirits of our ancestors."[4] This latter statement seems to be indicative of the fact that some idea of a distinction between fairies and the dead was entertained by the speaker, or that such a belief was beginning to be accepted.

The great feast of the dead among the Kelts, as I have already mentioned, was that of *Samhain*, when offerings or sacrifices of various kinds were made to ancestral spirits and to the Tuatha Dé Danann in common, while *Bealltainn*, or the first of May, was another day anciently dedicated to festivals in honour both of the dead and the fairies.[5]

Many fairy tales, in which a friendly or guardian fairy appears, so describe her that she seems to partake of the nature of an ancestor, if indeed she does not represent some folk-memory of a time in which personal totem-spirits were thought of as presiding over the fortunes of men. In the tale of *Cinderella* we find a guardian fairy of this kind smoothing over difficulties and guiding the heroine to a brilliant future. Incidents of this nature are more

[1] G. Henderson, *op. cit.*, p. 58.
[2] W. Scott, *Lady of the Lake*, II, note E.
[3] W. G. Wood-Martin, *Pagan Ireland*, p. 85.
[4] W. Y. E. Wentz, *op. cit.*, p. 76. [5] W. Y. E. Wentz, *op. cit.*, p. 439.

commonly to be met with in continental than in British fairy tale, from which circumstance we may perhaps divine either that this rather antique type of belief had never any great acceptance in our island, or that it had died out here at a comparatively early period. At the same time numerous vestiges of totemic belief exist in British tradition. In my view such incidents as deal with the friendly fairy represent an idea which may have had its inception in the Near East. That the *lar* expressed an idea borrowed by the Romans from the Etruscans is undoubted, and we know that the Etruscans were in turn indebted to Greek, Egyptian, and Keltic sources for many of their beliefs. In English folk-lore I can find only vestiges of the friendly fairy, whereas in Scottish tradition she (for this form is nearly always feminine) is more commonly met with, as the tales of *The Red Etin, The King of the Glens, Bens, and Passes*, and the several recensions of *Ashiepattle* (the Scottish *Cinderella*) reveal. On occasion the guardian fairy assumes animal form, as in the tales of *Puss in Boots* and the Inverness-shire version of *Ashiepattle*, known as *The Sharp Grey Sheep*, in which the Scottish Cinderella's mother takes the form of a sheep. It may be that such examples as this indicate the existence of some totemic recollection. We certainly find totemic-seeming guardian beasts aiding their human charges in many instances in savage folk-lore. In their amours with men, too, fairy ladies are prone to assume the form of deer, or to dispatch messengers who disguise themselves in this form when leading a mortal hero to the abodes of their mistresses. In these circumstances one finds it difficult to define where the totemic influence (if any) actually ends and ordinary magical shape-shifting begins. In its due place I will return to the subject of the possible totemic association of fairies.

It is well known to students of folk-lore that one of the most unpleasant attributes of the ancestral spirit is its tendency to attack its relatives should they have failed to minister to its alimentary wants by leaving a sufficiency of food beside its tomb. In such circumstances it satisfies its hunger by drinking their blood. This barbarous superstition, which appears to have had its more official inception in ancient Babylonia, came to be recognized at a later period in many parts of the Near East, propagating the horrible belief in ghouls and vampires. But we certainly discover marked traces of it among the peasantry of the Balkans and Russia and even in the folk-lore of Germany, France, and Britain. That it found its way into fairy lore seems to add to the proof substantiating the theory that fairies possessed an ancestral significance. Sir Walter Scott remarks that in some parts of Scotland consumption was regarded as due to fairy malignity, which is only another way of saying that the fairies drained the blood of mortals. He adds that in Moray consumptive persons were passed through wreaths of oak and ivy cut in the increase of the March moon as a remedy for decline.[1] Miss Gordon Cumming remarks, in her book *In the Hebrides* (p. 267), that people attacked by consumption are said to be the victims of the fairies. The reason for bringing water into the house at night, says J. G. Campbell, was that the fairies would suck the sleeper's blood if they found no water to quench their thirst.[2] In one part of Ireland, says Wentz, " it is a common opinion that when consumptives died they are there [in the hill of Knock Ma] with the fairies, in good health." [3] Hugh Millar, in his *Scenes and Legends*, refers to " the Lady in Green," who carries her child from cottage to cottage, and " bathes it in the blood of the youngest inmate of the household, who would be found dead next morning." [4] The late Mr. J. G. McKay described as " vampires " certain " green fairy women with bone beaks, or with cloven hoofs, who in some tales crack men's bones and drink their blood." [5] A story from the Central Highlands tells how some girls tending cattle were begged by an old woman to give her shelter for the night. One of them could not sleep, and beheld the crone sucking the blood of the slumbering maidens. She was a water-kelpie in disguise.[6]

Four young hunters mistook as many *glaistigs* for their sweethearts on the Braes of Lochaber. One of the lads, however, entertained suspicions of them and kept the maiden who seemed to be his inamorata at bay with his dirk. When daylight appeared he found his comrades lying dead, " with every drop of blood sucked out of their veins." [7] Lady Wilde assures us that some sixty years ago the Irish peasantry had a strong objection to being bled, as they feared that " the good people " would be angry.[8] This surely indicates a belief that the elves must have regarded " cupping " as a waste of good sustenance. The fairies themselves

W. Scott, *Minstrelsy of the Scottish Border*, II, p. 317.
J. G. Campbell, *op. cit.*, p. 20.
W. Y. E. Wentz, *op. cit.*, p. 37.
H. Millar, *Scenes and Legends*, pp. 361 f.
J. G. McKay, " Gaelic Folk-Lore," *Folk-Lore*, XXXVI, p. 169.
R. C. Macleod, *The Island Clans*, pp. 174–5.
MacDougall and Calder, *Folk-Tales and Fairy Lore*, p. 259.
Lady Wilde, *op. cit.*, p. 209.

were regarded as bloodless. In County Tyrone a man who was annoyed by them asked if among them all they could show one drop of blood. But they could not respond to the challenge.[1] We must be careful, however, to take into consideration the equally ancient belief that wherever blood was spilt, spirits immediately swarmed at the spot, to lap it up. Whether this is a proof of vampirism or is associated with the idea of sacrifice is by no means clear. In either case it reveals that the hungry dead regarded human blood as in the nature of pabulum. It is also to be kept in mind that burial mounds or barrows may have originated the notion of the hungry dead in European lands, and that where the ghosts of the departed came to be classified as " fairies " the notion of their blood-sucking propensities would persist—a view which, if well founded, makes it only more clear that the fairies were formerly regarded as the spirits of dead ancestors.

Let us now examine certain passages in tradition which appear to make it probable that the fairies are in some measure associated with the doctrine of reincarnation—a belief which is to a great extent associated with the idea that ancestral spirits reappear in the bodies of their descendants. Among the Kelts of Ireland a belief existed that the souls of heroes of the race of the Tuatha Dé Danann, who later came to be regarded as " fairies " and who dwelt in the fairy mounds, were subject to reincarnation.[2] If, indeed, we more particularly examine the Cuchulain, or " Red Branch " cycle of Irish saga, we find that practically all its principal figures were regarded as reincarnations of the earlier gods or heroes of that race, and that the tales which narrate their births indicate this more or less clearly. Concerning this belief, Alfred Nutt remarks that all these instances, which are fairly numerous, are of one and the same character, and that the spirit of the person to be reincarnated usually entered the maternal body in the form of an insect or some other material shape, and was reborn from it as a child. In any case " personality may be assumed to continue." The same thing occurs in the case of Welsh myth. So far as Ireland is concerned, therefore, it was only the favoured few born of the race of these gods who afterwards degenerated into fairies who underwent reincarnation. The belief does not apply to all living beings, as in the case of Indian reincarnation. But Alfred Nutt finds nothing to identify the Tuatha Dé Danann with ancestral

---

[1] E. Andrews, *Ulster Folk-Lore*, p. 99.
[2] W. Y. E. Wentz, *op. cit.*, p. 368.

worship;[1] an opinion which is in direct opposition to that of most authorities on Keltic faith.

But, as I have already indicated, the most express evidence that the fairies were regarded by the folk at large as the spirits of their ancestors is to be gleaned not only from peasant statement, but from the belief in " changelings," which prevailed among them. That the changeling was frequently regarded as a soul the owner of which had lived before in the locality where it appeared, and which had seemingly enjoyed more than one reincarnation, appears evident from the terms of quite a number of tales.

Later we shall encounter ideas among primitive Australian and other tribes which reveal strong resemblances between savage beliefs and those of our British forebears concerning the ancestral nature of spirits which have all the characteristics of fairies, but which, on examination, are found to be no other than the souls of dead ancestors awaiting reincarnation. For the present, however, I must pause to summarize the contents of this chapter and draw such conclusions from it as seem to be justified.

It must be clear from what appears above that a close resemblance exists between the dead ancestors and the fairy, who equally demands a portion of human sustenance as his right and who reveals a close interest in human affairs which he seeks to control by a code of decorum, as do the ancestral spirits. Many great families in Scotland and Ireland were and are in possession of fairy tutelars who present all the qualities of ancestral spirits. The brownie in particular reveals all the insignia of the Roman *lar*, or ancestral ghost of the hearth, and receives the same stipend of food and drink. In some cases he actually dictates the policy affecting matrimonial alliances. This " teind," or offering of pabulum, resembles that granted to the dead in ancient Egypt and Babylonia. The peasantry of some parts of Scotland and Ireland asseverate that the fairies are the spirits of their ancestors. The friendly or guardian fairy is rather obviously an ancestral spirit. Fairies occasionally act like vampires—a haunting and hungry shape unquestionably developed from the notion of the neglected ancestral ghost. Irish saga makes it abundantly plain that the spirits of the Tuatha Dé Danann, or ancient deities of Ireland, were regarded as undergoing reincarnation into human form from age to age, and that the modern fairies of Ireland are descended from the Tuatha Dé is beyond question.

[1] A. Nutt, *The Voyage of Bran*, pp. 71, 96, 235.

I think, therefore, that we are justified in believing that the fairies of these islands were at least in part spiritual forms which were regarded by the folk at large as the spirits of their ancestors, although one must qualify this statement by remarking that in course of time they came to be looked upon as a somewhat separate and specialized class of spirits. We cannot dismiss the ancestral soul as one of the factors which went to make up the general idea of the British fairy.

CHAPTER VI

FAIRIES AS ELEMENTARY SPIRITS

ELEMENTARY spirits may be defined as those which are believed to animate nature, inhabiting or ensouling trees, rocks, rivers, waters and clouds, plants, grain—or any natural object. Indeed, they are seldom, if ever, recognized as apart from a specific object; that is, as spiritual entities free of all bodily associations. They may appropriately be described as nature-spirits, and belief in them is the direct outcome of those doctrines of Animatism and Animism which play so great a part in the religious experience of primitive man. In an early stage of thought man regarded everything in the objective world as a living and sentient being in the same sense as he himself is. At a later stage in his development this idea was replaced by the notion that every object possesses an indwelling soul or spirit. These superstitions were the direct sources out of which arose the " doctrine of spirits," as it has come to be called.

Many circumstances in the fairy tradition seem to permit us to conclude that certain fairies must be regarded as nature-spirits. Some of these at first appear to have attributes seemingly so different from those of the familiar fairy of the mound or hillside as to make them appear as more or less distinct from the elfin species. But I find it necessary to repeat in this particular place that the division into classes, which is so salient a part of modern demonology, had, and has, little significance for primitive man or for the peasant in a comparatively low state of mental development. To such people, spirits of all kinds—fairies, the ghosts of the dead, and even witches and water-kelpies—are all creatures of the supernatural class between which he scarcely differentiates. The local incidence of some forms, too, is marked. In Wales, for example, we find many " true " fairies inhabiting lakes, whereas in England such forms are rare. In Scotland water-fairies are fairly numerous, water-spirits such as the kelpie scarcely being regarded as of the fairy class. In Slavonic lands, again, water-fairies abound.

The Gaelic Kelts describe all supernaturals as *sidhe*, which is by no means a designation of the fairies alone, but appears to embrace giants, *gruagach*-wizards, fairies proper, *cailleachs*, *banshees*, and the ghosts of the human dead. All are the creatures of a sphere which stands in opposition to the terrestrial, but which has yet certain undoubted associations with it. Still some differentiation there is. I have frequently, when pondering this tangled question, been tempted to believe that fairy spirits not only became differentiated from ghosts and other supernatural types because of the long distance of time which must have elapsed between the several " realizations " of such types in the popular imagination. It might seem that the fairies were the ghosts of, say, late Stone-age man, while what we call " ghosts " are the shades of the dead of more modern times. Again, elfin spirits may represent the shades of the dead who are as yet in a state of contact with the living and not finally translated to a more distant bourne. Indeed, I find such spirits in the folk-lore of Provence, where they are known as *armettes*. These are the dead who have not yet wholly severed associations with the living and who visit the earth on the eve of All Souls' Day. They must closely resemble fairies, for they reveal that highly moral, not to say " governessy," attitude to human weaknesses which is so marked a characteristic of the fairy species. Children in Provence are told that if they are good the *armettes* will kiss them on All Souls' Night; while if they are fractious or ill-behaved the spirits will scratch their feet—which recalls the rewards granted by the elves to industrious dairymaids and the pinching bestowed upon the idle and uncleanly.[1] These reflections might lead to the reasonable deduction that the difference between fairies and the dead is chiefly one of time and epochal realization, though the direct evidence for such a theory is certainly far to seek at present.

In some countries the fairy as nature-spirit is more apparent than in others. In Russia we find the *Rusalka*, or water-fairy, who inhabits lakes and rivers. She has green hair and teeth, and appears symbolic of the element in which she disports herself. In Yugoslavia we encounter the *Vilé*, the *Povodni Moz*, or Water Man, the *Hostnik*, or Forest Man, and other fairies with whom the popular imagination has peopled the air, the water, the forests, and mountains. In Germany we discern an immense variety of fairy forms—*Gnomes*, *Nixes*, *Kobolds*, *Elle-wives*, associated with one or other form of nature, and an ancient Anglo-Saxon manuscript divides early English fairies into *dun-elfen*, *berg-elfen*, *munt-elfen*, or spirits of downs, hills, and mountains, as well as

---

[1] Countess Martinengo-Cesaresco, *The Study of Folk-Songs*, p. 185.

feld-elfen, wudu-elfen, see-elfen, and *waeter-elfen,* or those of the fields, woods, the sea, and the meres; though one may suspect, with Grimm, that these names are arbitrary translations of those of fairy types alien to our islands.

In Italy, too, we learn of the *Folletti,* so well described by Domenico Comparetti and Charles Godfrey Leland. These tiny spirits ensouled plants, trees, and rocks, and seem to have been strictly aboriginal sprites, familiar to the peninsula for countless centuries. The list could be extended from the folk-lore records of every European country and from those of many Asiatic lands as well, the *Jinn* of Arabia showing a marked resemblance to European fairyhood, as do the *Phi* of Siam and the *Patupiarehe* of New Zealand.

It is known that in some parts of the world the belief is entertained that the spirits of dead men ensoul trees, stones, and other natural objects. A mass of tradition, for which there is overwhelming evidence, makes it clear that for ages primitive men in Britain, France, and elsewhere thought that, if a standing stone were raised over the burial-place of a deceased person, it served not only as a memorial for him, but that it actually represented him in the body and became the receptacle of his spirit, which took up its abode in the monolith. The considerable literature which has grown up in France explanatory of this belief is reflected in this country by only a handful of significant books and essays, but our native folk-lore makes it self-evident that the idea was as fully entertained by our ancestors as by the folk of primitive France. In Ireland and the Orkney Islands, and in some parts of Northern Scotland, such stone monuments were popularly known as " false men," the phrase indicating that they were formerly regarded as the " statues " or representations of the dead; while the circumstance that fairy spirits were believed to reside in them is part of the lore of the country folk, which seems to make it plain that these standing stones were also thought of as the receptacles of the souls of the dead. I mention this in passing, but when I come to consider the significance of these monuments more fully, in dealing with the fairy cultus, I shall have occasion to enlarge upon the subject.

Among races still in a primitive condition the association of the dead with trees is also a prominent feature of their superstitions, and is worthy of some examination as it appears to throw considerable light upon the theory that certain types of nature-spirits may be nothing else than the ghosts of the dead. As Professor Krappe remarks: " The souls of the dead may go into trees, becoming indistinguishable from genuine vegetation spirits. They naturally assume green, the colour of the fruit-bearing earth, which for that very reason becomes also the colour of death and of the nether powers." [1] " Ghosts and apparitions," says Wentz, " are commonly said to live in isolated thorn-bushes, or thorn-trees." [2] Frazer has made it " abundantly," and thus character-istically, clear that among savage peoples trees are regarded as sheltering the spirits of the dead. " The Dieyerie tribe of South Australia regard as very sacred certain trees, which are supposed to be their fathers transformed," he quotes, " hence they will not cut the trees down, and protest against the settlers doing so. Some of the Philippine Islanders believe that the souls of their fore-fathers are in certain trees, which they therefore spare. . . . The story of Polydorus will occur to readers of Vergil." [3] Among the Balla folk of Northern Rhodesia the ghost frequently goes to dwell in a tree until it is reincarnated. In Ecuador the Indians believe the spirits of plants to be their ancestors. Among the Ignorrotes every village has a sacred tree in which the ancestors are thought to dwell. In Luzon trees in clearings are left standing to serve as the abodes of the spirits of the dead. The mountaineers of New Guinea believe that the spirits of their ancestors dwell in the branches of trees, and the Indians of British Columbia are convinced that trees are transformed men. The sacred Chili tree of Gilgit, on the North-West frontier of India, is supposed to bless women with offspring, to make the herds to multiply, and to fertilize the corn. Frazer points out that in some lands the tree-spirit " is often conceived and represented as detached from the tree and clothed in human form, and even as embodied in living men and women." Moreover, it is frequently represented " simultaneously in vegetable form and in human form, which are set side by side as if for the express purpose of explaining each other." The long list of references to such beliefs in Miss Cox's *Cinderella* may also be consulted (note 7, p. 477), as may the seventh chapter of Grant Allen's *The Evolution of the Idea of God*. I have already quoted, more than once, Kirk's statement that the Highlanders at the end of the seventeenth century would

---

[1] A. H. Krappe, *The Science of Folk-Lore*, p. 90.
[2] W. Y. E. Wentz, *The Fairy Faith in Celtic Countries*, p. 70.
[3] J. G. Frazer, *The Golden Bough*, I, p. 62.

not remove timber from a fairy mound because they believed that the spirits of their ancestors dwelt in such places. " The soul of the dead," says George Henderson, speaking of Scottish Celtic tradition, " was believed to pass into the tree." [1]   To cut down a " skiough " or thorn bush in Northern Ireland was regarded as most hazardous to the woodman.[2]   " A superstition was current among the Celtic races," says Mr. John Cameron, " that for every tree cut down in any district one of the inhabitants in that district would die that year." [3]

In Scotland and Wales, as we shall see when we come to consider the circumstances of the fairy cult, numerous groves formerly existed which were looked upon as sacred and which might not be levelled or even clipped.   In Scotland these are still generally known as " Bell trees," and the assumption is that they were regarded as harbouring the spirits of the dead.   Such a grove is to be found at the Chapel of St. Ninian in the parish of Belly, and another the branches of which must not be cut, was formerly to be seen in the Isle of Skye; while still another stood near Ellery, at Loch Caolisport, Knapdale.   Certain kinds of trees in Morocco are haunted by Jinn, and among the Bathonga of South Africa the woods where the ancestral spirits live must not be disturbed.

Now we find that in certain parts of Britain fairies were believed to have their abodes in trees.

> " Fairy folks
> Are in old oaks,"

says an old English folk-rhyme.   A writer in *Folk-Lore* mentions that a certain lady dwelling in the island of Barra, in the Hebrides, " very often saw the Highland ' Tree ' or Forest spirits, all green coloured, or dressed in green, disporting themselves amongst the trees."   These green elves or spirits, it is added, " are well known in the Highlands." [4]   The Scandinavian elves not only frequent trees, but make an interchange of form with them.   In the church-yard of Store Heddinge, in Zealand, there are the remains of an oak wood.   Its trees, says local tradition, are the Elle-king's (elf-king's) soldiers.   By day they are trees; by night warriors. In the wood of Rugaard, in the same island, is a tree which by night becomes a whole Elle-people.   To damage this tree is

---

[1] G. Henderson, *Survivals in Belief among the Celts*, p. 179.
[2] E. Andrews, *Ulster Folk-Lore*, p. 57.
[3] J. Cameron, *The Gaelic Names of Plants*, p. 24.
[4] E. J. Begg, *Folk-Lore*, I, pp. 80–1.

regarded as sacrilegious. Those who gash, or otherwise deface, such trees usually die mysteriously.[1] In the Outer Hebrides a fairy maiden inhabits a tree standing on a knoll, and on a certain day she comes forth to give the " milk of wisdom " to the women of the island.[2]

The ancient Scandinavians, says Thoilacius, an old Swedish writer, thought that the trolls, or fays, dwelt in sombre woods. " Their lives are attached, like that of the Hamadryads, to the trees, and if anyone causes by friction the inner bark to loosen, a wood-woman dies." [3]

But nature-spirits also dwelt among the crops—wheat, barley, and so forth—as Sir James Frazer and his fore-runner Mannhardt have so painstakingly proved. I need scarcely go very profoundly into a phase of the subject which must now be fairly familiar to most people. It is sufficient for my purpose here to mention that the " corn-spirit " makes itself visible to the peasant at harvest-time in the form of a hare, quail, or other animal presence. For us the question is, how far such corn-spirits may be identified with fairies. Although the corn-spirit cannot be differentiated from the fairy in the animistic sense, it seems to be possible to distinguish the twain in the folk-lore sense. It has even been stated that in Scotland the " barley-maiden," the last handful of oats cut on a farm, " was meant as a symbol that the harvest had been secured, and to ward off the fairies, representatives of the ethereal and unsubstantial, till the time came for a new crop." [4] Of course, the last phrase is " poetic," or imaginative; still the reference helps to reveal that a difference was recognized between corn and fairy spirits. But how reconcile this with the idea that the fairies were in one sense agricultural spirits, as Alfred Nutt so positively asserts? It is obviously a case of the local and chronological overlapping of superstitions, disclosing that beautiful if tantalizing uncertainty of primitive belief which is so frequently the despair of the student of folk-lore.

In connection with this particular theme I may once more allude to the opinion of Dr. von Sydow, the Swedish folk-lorist, that Frazer and Mannhardt bungled sadly respecting the origins of European vegetation-spirits. Dr. von Sydow claims that neither Mannhardt nor Frazer " knew anything at first hand

[1] T. Keightley, *The Fairy Mythology*, pp. 92–3.
[2] D. A. Mackenzie, in *Book of the Highlands*, p. 99.
[3] Thorlacius, quoted by Keightley, p. 62.
[4] A. Nicolson, *A Collection of Gaelic Proverbs*, pp. 415 f.

about European peasant life," and that what they took for animism in connection with beliefs concerning the spirits of vegetation was really more of the nature of *orenda* or " vivism," as folk-lorists call it; that is, vital indwelling magical power of a more or less vague kind.   This would mean that those objects— maypoles, sheaves of corn, and so forth—which were supposed by Mannhardt to embody vegetation-spirits were merely vitalized by vague magic forces of some sort, conceived in the primitive age before the idea of spirit proper had taken form, and that they were not ensouled by definite supernatural entities.   The arguments of Mannhardt and Frazer are certainly open to the strictest criticism, but I feel that Dr. von Sydow has not given sufficient consideration to the fairly obvious and numerous evidences of cult and worship with which such spirits were certainly associated, and which serve to denote their actual nature.   Moreover, it is possible to compare and rank them along with well-known deities of growth in Egypt, Greece, Mexico, and other areas.   Indeed, he has treated the subject rather as a psychologist than as a student of folk-lore.

Whatever Frazer's deficiencies in respect of circumlocution and the occasional evasion of conclusions, he at least made it clear that he believed the corn-spirits of early Europe to have been primitive in their conception and that they belonged to a definite and recognized class.   He further indicated that they were usually called by impersonal names, such as " the old woman," " the maiden," and so forth, applicable respectively to the corn of the harvest past and that about to be reaped.[1]

But the point at issue refers to the precise nature of Frazer's corn-spirits and their mythological " position," particularly with regard to Nutt's statement that the Tuatha Dé Danann of Ireland were the givers of harvests, and thus " the lords of life " in that land.   In what, then, do the Tuatha Dé, who degenerated into fairy spirits and who stimulated growth, differ from the spirits of the grain, as recognized both by ancient and modern peasant agriculturists? The Tuatha Dé assuredly presided over the breeding of cattle and flocks, and even the progeniture of mankind, as well as over the growth of the crops; whereas the spirits of grain, whose rites are and were celebrated at harvest time, were regarded as controlling the crops alone.   For further comparisons we must confine our inquiry to Ireland, for though the tradition of the Tuatha

---

[1] J. G. Frazer, *Spirits of the Corn and the Wild, passim.*

Dé appears to have reached and interpenetrated English fairy lore, by way of British (" Welsh ") myth, the vestiges of its tradition there are somewhat too delicate for practical handling; while in Scotland, though visible, they bear all the marks of comparatively late introduction and arbitrary influence. Let us examine the Irish evidence first, before we draw further analogies.

Nutt's argument, stated in brief, is that the Tuatha Dé Danann, or " People of the Goddess Danu," were a mythological folk whose " history " has been known to us for a thousand years, as revealed in ancient Irish literature. These powers are discovered by that literature as purely agricultural spirits " concerned with the origin and regulation of agriculture and the institution of festivals and ceremonies in connection with it." The Tuatha Dé Danann spirits, Nutt believed, were " gradually developed out of primitive spirits of vegetation." [1]

As will shortly appear, I have the best of reasons for accepting this statement. Let us apply it to modern agricultural peasant belief in Ireland. In that country in modern times, or at least in some parts of it, much the same harvest rites were celebrated by the peasantry as in Scotland, as Miss Eleanor Hull assures us.[2] But if we go much farther back we find that in an ancient Irish document known as the " Tain Bo Cualnge " (" The Cattle-Raid of Cooley ") a distinction is made betwixt two classes of spirit, the *dee* or " gods " and the *an-dee* or " non-gods," the former being explained as " the people of (magic) power " and the latter as " husbandmen." This last designation is, of course, an obvious metaphor for spirits controlling the crops, and cannot signify mortal farmers. In any case, properly translated, *an-dee* means " the people of ploughing." " It looks," remarks Miss Hull, " like a division into an aristocracy of the fighting class and Druids and the plebeians or agricultural class." [3] This, of course, is to euhemerize, or humanize, entities obviously spiritual in character, for in my view the two classes represent respectively a higher and a lower stratum of belief, the first probably referring to the Tuatha Dé Danann, the agricultural deities or spirits of a later conquering race, and the other to the more grossly fetishistic spirits of an aboriginal folk, the forerunners of the " kirn-baby," the " old woman," and the " maiden " of a general and earlier

---

[1] A. Nutt, *Presidential Address to the Folk-Lore Society, passim.*
[2] E. Hull, *Folk-Lore of the British Isles*, pp. 233–4.
[3] E. Hull, *op. cit.*, p. 31.

H

European agricultural ritual of which we still retain the vestiges, and which appears to have survived side by side with the more advanced belief in departmental deities.

My reasons for so believing are founded upon an extensive study of the agricultural ritual of ancient Mexico, in which I have specialized for nearly half a century. It is necessary to remark that, although Frazer and others have examined the literature of Mexican rite with care, their treatment of it is naturally scarcely so precise as a specialist acquaintance with the subject would have dictated; and they almost invariably appeal to standard authorities, neglecting those of lesser note who frequently cast a more particularly illuminating ray upon Mexican agricultural ritual. As so much of value to their hypothesis hinges upon their recognition of the value and importance of Mexican agricultural rite, and as they lay so much stress upon the same, I am surprised that the poverty of their literary handling of the theme has not received more critical attention.

Now, if we tread those bypaths, which I have no space to particularize, but which I have fully examined elsewhere,[1] it will be seen that the position was almost precisely the same as that which obtained in ancient Ireland, a circumstance indicated by me to Alfred Nutt so long ago as the year 1907, and which he appreciated at the time although he made no use of a parallel which I still believe would have fortified his theory concerning the agricultural status of the Tuatha Dé Danann.

In ancient Mexico we discover a pantheon of maize spirits or " gods," obviously the creation of a more advanced race, who, like the Tuatha Dé, were regarded as powers conferring fruit-fulness upon the soil, and who, like their Keltic congeners, demanded blood-sacrifice as a part of the bargain by virtue of which they yielded a full harvest to mankind. The pact also included the observance of a strict and inflexible moral code, such as we find emerging in ancient Ireland, and which is apparent in the fairy creed, its degenerate descendant. But, side by side with this there existed numerous fetishistic powers of he soil, almost precisely similar to the " kirn-baby," " corn-mother," and " corn-maiden " of folk-lore. Statuettes, carved in stone, of these lower powers, evidently the spirits of a more aboriginal folk, were erected in the maize-fields, and those which have been retrieved reveal most clearly by their appearance and symbolism a close

[1] L. Spence, *The Gods of Mexico*, pp. 153–267.

resemblance to the figures which, within the memory of man, were manufactured out of corn, barley, or oat sheaves by the peasantry of the British Isles to represent the presiding or animating spirits of the grain at harvest time. These Mexican spirits were worshipped side by side, at the seasons of planting and harvest, with the greater gods, some of whom themselves bore a close resemblance to the lesser images of which I speak, and indeed may have developed from them in certain localities. Just as we find in Scotland that the " maiden " or " clyack " sheaf, the grain newly reaped, was regarded as the spirit of this year's grain and dressed in woman's clothing, and if reaped later was known as a " carlin," " *cailleach*," or " auld wife," so in ancient Mexico we find a mother and daughter goddess of the maize-plant. " The goddess Chicomecoatl, spirit of the corn, was apparently believed to lurk in those ears which had been hanging in the house since their blessing," and these were used as seed at the time of planting.[1] From all this it seems reasonable to infer that, while the great agricultural gods of the Irish Kelts " degenerated " into fairies, the more primitive aboriginal fetishes of the soil retained their original character as " old women," " maidens," and " kirn-babies."

To turn to the fairy association with water as revealing an elfin connection with elementary spiritism, many British fairies are thought of as dwelling in wells and lakes, more particularly in Wales and Scotland. Isle Maree, in the loch of that name and the adjoining island of Eilean Suthain, are reputed to be their haunts. The name of Loch Shiant, in Skye, has reference to the fairies, and coins and scraps of clothing were offered to them at this loch.[2] They are also associated with St. Mungo's Well at Huntly.[3] Those who drank the water of the well at Tobar Bhile na Beinne, in Argyll, left some equivalent to the fairy who was supposed to guard it.[4] Sometimes fairies inhabiting such wells took the form of a fish or worm. At Brayton, Harpham, Holderness, and Atwick, in Yorkshire, and at Wooler in Northumberland, such wells were under the protection of fairies or sprites.[5] At the Cheese Well on Minchmoor, in Peebleshire, " the country

---

[1] J. E. Thompson, *Mexico before Cortez*, p. 63.
[2] M. A. Martin, *A Description of the Western Isles of Scotland*, p. 140; *Old Statistical Account of Scotland*, II. p. 556.
[3] C. F. Gordon Cumming, *In the Hebrides*, p. 212.
[4] G. Henderson, *op. cit.*, p. 185.
[5] G. L. Gomme, *Ethnology in Folk-Lore*, p. 85.

girls imagine that the well is in charge of a fairy or spirit who must be propitiated with some offering." [1]   The famous fountain at Baranton, in the haunted forest of Broceliande, in Brittany, is associated with the fairy Vivian, who bewitched the enchanter Merlin.   The Breton fairy known as the *Korrigan* is regarded as a well-spirit.   It was at the Fount of the Fées that the fairy Melusine first appeared to her future husband, Raymond of Toulouse.   Graelent encountered his fairy sweetheart at a fountain.   At Domremy, the home of the heroic Joan of Arc, a similar fount existed at the foot of a tree; there the French patriot maiden was accused by her captors of having communed with the fays which repaired to it.   Nine fairy sorceresses guarded the thermal waters of the city of Gloucester. [2]

Scandinavia has a wealth of tradition respecting the *necks*, or fairies, who haunted its meres and water-courses, and the *rusalkas* of Russia are among the best representatives in folk-lore of fairies who are also nature-spirits.   They dwell principally in the rivers and streams of Russia, and resemble the *necks*.   In Wales we find such water-fairies as the Lady of the Van Pool, in Carmarthenshire, who became the bride of a local swain.   The *Tylwyth Teg*, or " Fair Family," also haunt a lake in the mountains near Brecknock, where a door in the rock leads to an enchanting garden. One must also recall in this connection the very considerable number of Keltic Irish, Scottish, and Welsh tales which allude to a fairy kingdom beneath the sea, usually known as Lochlann, Lychlyn, or Sorcha, which I have already mentioned in connection with the Keltic other-world.

Some notice must also be taken, when dealing with fairies as nature-spirits, of those vestiges of tradition which appear to associate the elves with creatures of the wild, for a certain type of fairy assuredly reveals in general appearance and characteristics the traits of animals, more particularly those dwelling in wooded places.   To these I have already referred as " rough " fairies of a primitive kind.   Puck is generally depicted as having animal ears, and is described as rough and hirsute, as is the brownie, the rugged creature who refuses to wear clothes.   The Highland *ourisk* and the Irish *phooka* both resemble the satyr, as did the elfin king who led King Herla of Britain into his subterranean palace.   The *bean-nighe*, the fairy of the Western Isles,

---

[1] W. Henderson, *Folk-Lore of the Northern Counties*, p. 230.
[2] A. Maury, *Les Fées du Moyen Age*, pp. 27–8.

who washes the clothes of those about to die, has webbed feet and
waddles like a duck.   Even the classic naiads of Greece and Rome
take animal shape when pursued.   Tam Lin, who was rescued
from Fairyland by his lady love, went through a series of animal
shapes before he finally emerged from the fairy condition to man-
hood again.

I shall deal later on with the possible totemic origin of such
fairies as reveal these animal traits.   Here, I only wish to make
it plain that they were regarded as akin to the spirits of nature—
those who inhabited trees, stones, or who dwelt in streams or
lakes.   But though these latter might well be conceived as spirits
of the dead awaiting rebirth in natural objects, may we regard
those who show animal characteristics in the same light?

We must consider a certain type of animal-seeming fairy familiar
to the people of ancient Gaul, and known to post-classical writers
as *pilosi* ("hairy ones") and *dusii*, which I will translate as
"devilkins."   The name is probably derived from the Latin
deus, "a god," and has come down to us as "deuce," although
it may have been derived from the Keltic *diù*, "a god."   Cassianus,
a Christian priest of Marseilles, who "flourished" in the fifth
century of our era, describes certain little beings "which the
people call forest spirits," who delight in gambols and entice men.
They have no desire to harm anyone, he says, but merely to tease
them and laugh at them.[1]   Isidore of Seville, writing of the
pilosi at the beginning of the seventh century, says of them that
the Greeks call them "Pans" and the Latins *incubi*, while the
Gauls describe them as *dusios*.   "They are those *incubi* whom
the Romans called Fauns."[2]   Grimm, in dealing with this text,
states that they are "the hairy terrestrial elves," and he compares
them with the brownie and the German *rauche Els* or rough elf.
St. Augustine speaks of the *dusii* as engaging in amours with human
women,[3] as does Hincmar, Archbishop of Rheims, who wrote in
the ninth century.[4]   Du Cange does not believe the name *dusius*
to be the same as *deus*, but says that it is found in almost all the
Slavonic, Celtic, and Teutonic tongues of Europe as *dus*, as
descriptive of a kind of devilkin who cherishes aspirations to love-
affairs with human folk.   Thomas of Canterbury speaks of them

[1] Cassianus, *Collectiones Patrum*, VII, c. 32.
[2] Isidore of Seville, *Etymology*, Bk. VII, 11, 103–4; Bk. VIII, last chapter,
and Bk. XI, 22.
[3] Augustine, *The City of God*, C. 23.
[4] Hincmar, in Migne's *Patrologia Latina*, CXXV, pp. 716, 725.

as forest or sylvan gods in Prussia, and adds that the people there dare not cut down the woods consecrated to them. The *dus* also turns up in modern Tuscany as " a mischievous little *folletto*, or goblin, who inspires love-dreams." There he is also known as *Dusio*, and *Diosio*; that is, a being who *may* rank as a god. I have also traced him to Britanny in the shape of Teuz, a demon of much greater bulk.[1] In Tuscany he continually annoys the female servants of the house, as does brownie on occasion.

Such forms appear to be descended from wood or forest spirits, and I cannot escape the impression that in them we discover a tradition which held that the souls of dead men betook themselves to the forest—as many savage races still believe. It follows that their sylvan environment bestowed upon them something of its wild and rugged spirit, both as regards their outward form and their habits. Just as spirits who dwell in seas and rivers are mainly human in appearance, yet possess decidedly aqueous, and even " fishy " characteristics, their kindred of the woods exhibit the marks of the forest animal—the hirsute hide, the slant eye, the prick ear.

Mr. Wentz draws a striking parallel between European and Siamese folk-belief as illustrating the theory that fairies are associated with the spirits of nature, which I feel I must quote *in extenso* to do it justice. " According to the Siamese folk-belief all the stars and various planets, as well as the ethereal spaces, are the dwelling-places of the *Thevadas*, gods and goddesses of the old pre-Buddhist mythology, who correspond pretty closely to the Tuatha Dé Danann of Irish mythology; and this world itself is peopled by legions of minor deities called *Phi*, who include all the various orders of good and bad spirits continually influencing mankind. Some of these *Phi* live in forests, in trees, in open spaces; and watercourses are full of them. Others inhabit mountains and high places. A particular order who haunt the sacred trees surrounding the Buddhist temples are known as *Phi nang mai*; and since *nang* is the word for female, and *mai* for tree, they are comparable to tree-dwelling fairies, or Greek wood-nymphs. Still another order called *Chao phum phi* (gods of the earth) are like house-frequenting brownies, fairies, and pixies, or like certain orders of *corrigans* who haunt barns, stables, and dwellings." [2]

[1] L. Spence, *Legends and Romances of Brittany*, p. 100.
[2] W. Y. E. Wentz, *op. cit.*, p. 229.

We must not neglect the possibly important association of nature-spirits with the earth itself in connection with the theory that such spirits were, or came to be, regarded as fairies. Andrew Lang, in his introduction to Robert Kirk's *Secret Commonwealth*, lays stress on this phase of the subject. He says : " The *Subterranean Inhabitants* of Mr. Kirk's book are not so much a traditional recollection of a real dwarfish race living underground (a hypothesis of Sir Walter Scott's) as a lingering memory of the Chthonian beings ' the Ancestors.' " [1] This word is derived from the Greek *chthon*, meaning " the ground," and its derivative has reference to beings of Greek myth regarded primarily as presiding over the crops, as well as exerting a species of " infernal " or subterranean influence, more particularly the goddess Kore, or Ceres, to whom sacrificial rites were offered as a deity of corn and harvests. The Chthonian powers were therefore not only " the Ancestors," but, like the Tuatha Dé Danann, deities of agriculture. That some fairies, such as the Tuatha Dé, were developed from Chthonian powers cannot be denied, as the tribute of milk and grain offered to them makes plain. The dead were certainly thought of as in some way assisting in the growth of grain. In their mysterious underworld they contrived its fructification by magic, and that they also furnished certain domestic animals to man, especially the pig, is revealed by the Welsh myth of Pwyll, Prince of Dyved, as by many another pagan story gleaned from more than one part of the world. That the fairies took over this tradition from them we cannot doubt, having regard to numerous tales of their agricultural associations, as of their equally close concern in domestic cattle and the folk-lore of the byre and stable.

I think, too, that it is not unimportant in this place to say a few words concerning the more or less intimate association of fairies with that class of spirit known to Germanic folk-lore as the *poltergeist*, which has of late years come to be regarded as a sprite to be piously considered by our Spiritualists, who claim for him a reality of existence by no means extended to him by students of folk-lore. The name implies " rattle-spirit," and is derived from the habit of this creature of knocking or rattling upon walls or furniture, throwing stones at windows, and juggling with domestic crockery. In Friesland we find him identified with the

---

[1] A. Lang, Intro. to R. Kirk's *Secret Commonwealth of Elves, Faun s, and Fairies*, p. 29.

local *Puk*, and the house-spirits.[1]   In old Scotland poltergeists were well known.   Kirk alludes to such spirits as throwing " great stones, pieces of earth and wood " at people,[2] and John Major testifies that they entreated the folk of his native place in a similar manner, though in that neighbourhood they took the form of brownies.[3]   A well-known case of such haunting is afforded by the " devil of Glenluce," described in Sinclair's *Satan's Invisible World Discovered*, and that of " The Drummer of Tedworth " is familiar to most.   Some *nisses*, or *necks*, seem to have acted as poltergeists in Denmark, casting old shoes about and generally making a nuisance of themselves.[4]   Giraldus Cambrensis alludes to such spirits as tormenting people in Pembroke in his time.[5] " Brownie Clod," in Scots folk-lore, was so known because he cast " divots " at passers-by.   The Spanish *duende*, or fairy, likewise pelts people with stones and clay, as we learn from Torquemada's *Spanish Mandeville*.   There is thus no question that the belief in these spirits as fairies is a widespread one, and, judging from the general evidence, they appear to be invariably associated with " witch-doctors," or local wizards, who employ them in revenging themselves upon those who have slighted or injured them.   Such, at least, was the case in three well-known examples of poltergeist haunting—the devil of Glenluce, the Drummer of Tedworth, and an instance in the department of Seine Inferieure, in France.   But I prefer to leave our Spiritualistic sages to draw their own conclusions from such data.

To sum up: all nature-spirits are not the same as fairies; nor are all fairies nature-spirits.   The same applies to the relationship of nature-spirits and the dead.   But we may safely say that a large proportion of nature-spirits became fairies, while quite a number of the dead in some areas seem to take on the character of nature-spirits.   We cannot expect any fixity of rule in dealing with barbaric thought.   We must take it as it comes.   It bears the same relationship to " civilized " or folk-lore theory as does the growth of the jungle to a carefully designed and meticulously labelled botanical garden.   As Victor Hugo once exclaimed when writing of the barbaric confusion which underlies the creative function in poetry: " What do you expect?   You are among savages! "

[1] T. Keightley, *op. cit.*, pp. 233, 240 ff.   [2] R. Kirk, *op. cit.*, pp. 79, 104.
[3] John Major, *Exposition of St. Matthew*, folio xlviii.
[4] W. A. Craigie, *Scandinavian Folk-Lore*, pp. 193–4.
[5] Giraldus Cambrensis, *Itinerary of Wales*, Bk. I, C. 12.

If we look for anything approaching precision in the emanations of the primitive mind, we are pretty sure to be disappointed. It knows neither rule nor law, and the man who seeks for anything approaching uniformity or definite pathway in its vast deserts is wasting his time. Specialists in folk-lore persist in the manufacture of classifications many of which are of little or no avail to the science they profess. And probably no one would be more astonished than the savage, from the consideration of whose habit and custom their classifications are compiled, were he capable of comprehending the processes by which they had been arrived at. True, there exists a surprisingly uniform appearance in the manner in which the savage in all parts of the world does envisage certain among the major conditions of existence; as, for example, in respect of the origins of that world, the presence of supernatural powers, and the fortuitous nature of death. But when anything in the nature of absolute or minute classification confronts him he is almost immediately at a loss. And if we seek to ransack the records of the greater religions, in the hope that their more advanced beliefs may reflect some gleams of light on the darkness which surrounds their earlier forms, we shall certainly discover but little to encourage us to proceed in the quest. We shall probably find that, as in the case of Christianity, or any of the Oriental faiths, their later eschatology is merely an elaboration of primitive notions disguised in the terms of a mock mysticism and set forth in those of a more sophisticated mythology.

It may be possible, however, to explain in part the train of thought by which the idea of nature-spirits originated in the primitive mind. I certainly do not desire to father such a theory— if it deserve the name—on any other worker in the vineyard of tradition, as it is solely the result of my own experience as a groper in the sphere of mythology, and I would lay stress upon the necessity of taking it for what it is worth. It is founded upon certain savage myths which seem to describe the origins of mankind, animals, and plants as emanating from one and the same generalized type of creature. Let us briefly examine some of these myths. I may add that in this place I shall not take into account their possible totemic implications, which I hope to deal with at a later stage.

The Urabunna tribe of " Blackfellows," in Australia, believe that in the remote and mythical ages there existed at first a comparatively small number of individuals, who were half-human and half-animal, or half-plant. These creatures were endowed with greater powers than mortals now possess. They could walk on the earth or beneath it, or fly through the air. Wandering over the face of the land, they deposited at some striking natural feature a number of spirit individuals, which after a time became changed into men and women, and since that period, they aver, these spirit-beings have been continually undergoing reincarnation as Urabunna folk.[1] The Dieri of South-eastern Australia similarly believed that mankind were perfected out of shapeless and generalized creatures, who entered into rocks or trees.[2] In the central, northern, and north-eastern areas of Australia the same idea is indulged in.[3] The Central Australian Warramunga hold that their totem clans originated each from a single ancestor, half-beast or half-plant, from whose body emanated a number of spirit children.[4]

Among the Banks Islanders the spirit which animates a child about to be born is invariably that of an animal or plant.[5] It may be remarked in passing that in ballad and folk-tale the soul is frequently transformed into a plant, an animal, a bird, a fish, or even into an inanimate object.[6] Among the American Indians of Puget Sound myths are told about a time " before the world was changed," when the animals were human beings, who, when occasion demanded, readily assumed any animal characteristics that were necessary to the situation.[7] Another American Indian story recounts that the world of the first men was a harmonious one, but that the minds of the people altered and a season of conflict and disturbance supervened. This resulted in the transformation of the folk into beasts, birds, reptiles, fish, and insects, as well as into trees, plants, grasses, rocks, and mountains.[8]

If these myths do not explain entirely the savage doctrine of spirits, they throw a good deal of light, I think, on the primitive

---

[1] J. G. Frazer, *Totemism and Exogamy*, I, p. 181.

[2] M. C. B. Howitt, " Some Nature Legends from Central Australia," *Folk-Lore*, 1902, p. 403.

[3] E. S. Hartland, *Primitive Paternity*, pp. 236 f., quoting Spencer and Gillen.

[4] E. S. Hartland, in Hastings' *Encyclopedia of Religion and Ethics*, XII, p. 400.

[5] J. G. Frazer, *op. cit.*, II, 93.

[6] L. C. Wimberley, *Folk-Lore in the English and Scottish Ballads*, pp. 33, 52.

[7] S. Gunther, " Accretion in the Folk-Tales of the American Indians," *Folk-Lore*, XXXVIII, p. 40.

[8] J. Curtin, *Creation Myths of Primitive America*, p. 490.

belief in the unity of spirit life.   And I am of opinion that even if they were subsequently manufactured to explain this belief, such invention and explanation is in line and sequence with earlier notions regarding the nature and origins of spirit.   In my view, too, they go far to account for the belief in nature-spirits and, consequently, of fairies.   To the primitive mind there is no line of demarcation between the spirits of men, animals, plants, and natural objects, any more than there is between the bodies of men and animals or birds, which are described by savage man as composed of clans or tribes similarly to his own, gifted with speech, and capable of union in marriage with him.   When he thinks of a bear or a wolf, he thinks of a creature which differs scarcely at all from himself, which has the same instincts and which reasons in much the same way.   And he naturally regards the spirits of these creatures as being similar to his own.   It is to the dim border-land of human thought which nurtured such ideas that we must seek to return, if we can, should we desire to cast light upon the origins of nature-spirits, and consequently of the fairies, with which they have so much in common.

Now it is a notable thing that in Great Britain and Ireland the nature-spirit remains to us in a vestigial form only.   To make a list of British nature-spirits as known to our islands to-day is very nearly as difficult as, say, to find people of Chinese extraction in Glasgow, or Hottentots in London.   I can think of no genuinely English earth- or tree-spirits, while English water-spirits appear to be confined to " Jenny Greenteeth " and a few " white ladies," or " green ladies " who inhabited wells.   In Scotland the kelpie remains the solitary water-sprite, excepting the water-horse and water-bull, if these may be so termed.   The *urisk*, obviously at first a water-spirit, is now regarded as a member of the fairy tribe. There are no tree-spirits anywhere in Britain to-day.   If this latter sentence sounds a trifle naïve, I cannot help it.   I am merely stating a professional fact, as might a grocer who had to confess that he was " out " of sugar.   In Ireland the *phooka* may be the " remains " of a tree-spirit.   He sometimes takes the form of a goat, and may represent an earlier Keltic Faunus.   The Welsh water-sprites have all gone over to the fairies.   Indeed, it is manifest that almost every species of nature-spirit which formerly inhabited this enchanted island of ours has long become absorbed in the fairy multitude.   The process has not gone so far in France, particularly in Brittany; while the Balkans are still rich in degrees of elfin difference. Of the British fairies we know, it would be difficult to discover which had been born of earth, wood, or water. Only, perhaps, by virtue of a prick ear or an incipient webbing of the feet may we guess whether an elf was formerly a denizen of forest or flood. Many German and Scandinavian elves, and notably the great host of Slavonic fairies, retain the insignia of difference; but in the British " Commonwealth of Elves, Fauns, and Fairies," as old Kirk called it, things are more standardized, and only in Cornwall and the Highlands of Scotland, in an island whose demonology was once the most various in Europe, do types divergent at all from the common hill fairy, the standard elf of folk-lore, still remain. And even these are in danger of being banished into the limbo of forgetfulness by the quite artificial fairy of juvenile literary commerce, with gauzy wing and skirts reminiscent of the ballet. It has always seemed to me extra-ordinary that literature has been able to create wings where none were before, for our native fairies are as wingless as ourselves. But for such an innovation the Elizabethan poets and playwrights were probably responsible—a topic which we must consider in another chapter.   In a word, practically the whole range of British goblin forms and nature-spirits have become merged in Faerie; they are associated with the standardized elf, who, generally speaking, represents the deceased ancestor; but not without reason, because the deceased ancestor so frequently sought their demesnes and was identified with them in appearance and habit.

CHAPTER VII

WERE FAIRIES A REMINISCENCE OF ABORIGINAL RACES?

In an earlier chapter the ground has already been prepared for the discussion of the much-vexed question at present under consideration. As I have said, the outstanding protagonist of the theory that fairy spirits were a reminiscence of aboriginal races of dwarfish stature was the late David MacRitchie, and here I must discuss the terms of his hypothesis a little more fully. Although he was of opinion that the belief in fairies had originated in many parts of the world through the medium of tales concerning dwarfish races who possessed fairy-like traits, his researches were more particularly confined to the material presented by the fairy legend in Scotland.

It was mainly the writings of J. F. Campbell, of Islay, and of Professor Nillson (in his *Primitive Inhabitants of Scandinavia*), which inspired in MacRitchie the belief that the notion of fairy spirits had originated in traditions concerning small or stunted races in Scotland and some other countries. At first he identified these hypothetical dwarfish races with the Feinne, or Fenians, the ancient heroes of Irish legend, whose leader was the celebrated Fionn, or Fin, known also as Fin MacCoul, the father of the bard Ossian, with whom the Fenian saga is so intimately connected that it has come to be known as " Ossianic." This appeared all the more strange as the Feinne are said to have been of almost gigantic height. The Feinne, again, he sought to equate with the Finns of Finland. These " Finns," or Fenians, had for him a further relationship with the Picts or pechs of Scottish tradition and history, whom he also regarded as a stunted race, although archaeology can discover no traces of Pictish dwarfishness. He further saw in the mounds, barrows, and tumuli of Scotland the dwellings of the aforesaid Feinne, Finns, or Picts. These mounds, he averred, had not been burial-places, but the actual dwellings of dwarfish races, though it is only fair to say that in some cases, particularly in those of earth-houses, he correctly described certain subterranean structures as the abodes of primitive men.

In advancing his theory MacRitchie drew very fully upon the

fairly numerous legends respecting " dwarfish " folk to be found in Scottish folk-lore, the Gaelic tales concerning *urisks* and *avusks*, and similar goblins, which he regarded as savage aborigines, the stories of dwarfs who dwelt beneath castles or houses, and who, because of their proximity to the inhabitants of these places, struck up a neighbourly association with them.   He also collected those incidents in tradition which allude to the building of castles, cathedrals, and churches by the pechs in many parts of Scotland. In doing so he gathered such a mass of evidence as certainly enriched Scottish folk-lore.   In one sense his works may safely be regarded as repositories of much that is curious and not easily found elsewhere, if care be taken to disentangle the traditions he garnered from the terms of his theory.   This evidence he certainly employed to the full in its illustration, on occasion extending the analogies thus provided much farther than was warranted by reasonable caution.   But it must be added that the result was such as to impress almost as many students of folk-lore as it estranged or exasperated.   Frankly, MacRitchie succeeded in setting the whole world of fairy speculation by the ears, with results not altogether unfavourable to its general enlightenment because of the debate occasioned.   Despite his frequent exaggerations and not a little juggling with philological derivations (as, for example, the resemblance of " Finn " to " Feinne "), he did much to prove that a memory of aboriginal peoples was at least one of the strands which go to compose the fairy belief.

At a still later stage in his researches he added to the catalogue of those pigmy peoples who had been regarded by the larger races as fairies, or who had given colour to that idea by their traits and habits, the Lapps of Lapland and Norway, the Ainu of Japan, and other tribes who are certainly not pigmies in any sense of the term. From the habits and general appearance of these various stunted tribes, he believed, by their custom of dwelling in mounds and hills, their rapid appearance and evanishments, and their withdrawn mode of life, the general notion of fairy spirits was fostered among the taller races.[1]   But here I may say, at once, that neither he nor any of the other protagonists of the " aboriginal " theory have sought to explain the widespread belief in fairies as supernatural or spiritual beings, except as a confused or degenerate phase of the idea that they were originally a dwarfish and aboriginal race.

[1] D. MacRitchie, *The Testimony of Tradition ; Fians, Fairies, and Picts, passim.*

This—in itself—is, I feel, perhaps the weakest link in the none-too-powerful chain of evidence forged by this school of thought, and, oddly enough, one which has been least commented upon by its antagonists. I consider the above to be a fair, if succinct, account of MacRitchie's hypothesis. In a work dealing with the whole range of surmise concerning fairy origins it is naturally impossible to give its due weight to every minor argument adduced by any one writer, and if I have here omitted any of the more vital considerations advanced by my old and valued friend, these will surely make their appearance in such criticisms of his general theory as I shall have occasion to quote.

Some other contemporary writers shared MacRitchie's views, in part, or in their entirety. Professor Sir John Rhys believed that the historical Picts of Scotland had " made slaves and drudges of the mound-haunting race," that they had possibly amalgamated with that race, and that the traditions of them as fairies or small folks arose to some extent from such amalgamation. He thought that in Ireland such races might have " retreated before the Celts and concealed themselves after the manner of the little people—in underground dwellings in the less accessible parts of the country." But he took care to add that " true fairies " were the creatures of imagination, while the aboriginal folk of small stature formed " only a sort of substratum, a kind of background to the fairy picture." This view of the fairy scene, he believed, was " the result of our ancestors projecting on an imaginary world a primitive civilization through which tradition represented their own race as having passed, or, more probably, a civilization in which they saw, or thought they saw, another race actually living." [1]

Sir Lawrence Gomme, commenting generally on the theory that fairies are the traditional representatives of an ancient pigmy race, remarked that " it is important to note that these beliefs must have originated not with the aboriginal pigmy race themselves, but with the conquering race who overpowered them and drove them to the hills and out-parts of the land." The influence of the conquered race must have remained, however, and have produced in the minds of their conquerors mythic conceptions which, with the lapse of time, " became stereotyped into certain well-defined lines of fairy lore." He further compared the origin of witchcraft and fairy-craft in an endeavour to elucidate the problem of fairy origins. The former, he thought, was the survival of beliefs about the

[1] J. Rhys, *Celtic Folk-Lore*, pp. 660, 669, 683–85.

aborigines from aboriginal sources, while fairycraft was the survival of beliefs about the aborigines from Aryan sources.[1] Personally, I cannot extend absolute credence to a classification so definite. It is, I feel, precisely this kind of clean-cut definition which finds little or no support from actual folk-lore record and content. It is, I admit, possible in certain cases to distinguish between aboriginal and " Aryan " tradition, so called, but the criteria which enable us to do so are severely limited in their scope.

Jacob Grimm appears to have entertained some such theory, if only in passing, for he gave it as his belief that " the dwarfs retiring before the advance of man, produce, like the Thurses, Jotunns, and Hunes, the impression of a conquered race." In Devon and Cornwall, he adds, " the Pixies are regarded as the old inhabitants. In Germany they are like Wends, in Scandinavia like Lapps." [2] Elsewhere in his great work he states that elves and dwarfs became confused in the popular imagination.[3] But I would point out that in Teutonic lands dwarfs were invariably regarded as non-human and supernatural beings.

In his valuable treatise on *Folk-Memory* Mr. Walter Johnson has discussed the problem of the origin of fairy belief from aboriginal sources, and he is of opinion that it is " in a large measure, an obvious retention in folk-memory of a small, mysterious, magic-loving folk, who were, in the mind of the Celtic peoples, the aborigines of the island." " The little folk of the Neolithic period lived often in underground chambers " or in circular pits roofed with branches or turfs. " Hence the Iron Age folk peopled every mound with fairies." [4] In a later passage he faces a difficulty. The fairies live in mounds, or barrows, but these are known to contain remains of the dead. The fairies are little people; those who recount tales concerning them, big folk. But the mounds to which superstitions are attached are generally those of the " Round " or Bronze Age type. In other words, the barrows which should, according to the theory, entomb small Neolithic folk, actually contain the skeletons of a larger race.[5]

Sir Harry Johnston, the well-known explorer, has in more than one place expressed the opinion that certain dwarfish races

<hr>

[1] G. L. Gomme, *Ethnology in Folk-Lore*, pp. 63–4.
[2] J. Grimm, *Teutonic Mythology* (trans. by Stallybrass), p. 1417.
[3] J. Grimm, *op. cit.*, p. 449.
[4] W. Johnson, *Folk-Memory*, p. 59.
[5] W. Johnson, *op. cit.*, pp. 151–2.

may have given rise to the idea of fairies.   To do justice to his view
I must quote it at some length.   He writes :—

" Other dwarf races of humanity belonging to the white or
the Mongolian species may have inhabited Northern Europe
in ancient times, or it is just possible that this type of Pygmy
Negro which survives to-day in the recesses of Inner Africa,
may even have overspread Europe in remote times.   If it did,
then the conclusion is irresistible that it gave rise to most of the
myths and beliefs connected with gnomes, kobolds, and
fairies.   The demeanour and actions of the little Congo
dwarfs at the present day remind one over and over again of
the traits attributed to the brownies and goblins of our fairy
stories.   Their remarkable power of becoming invisible by
adroit hiding in herbage and behind rocks, their probable
habits in sterile and open countries of making their homes in
holes and caverns, their mischievousness and prankish good-
nature, all seem to suggest that it was some race like this that
inspired most of the stories of Teuton and Celt regarding a
dwarfish people of quasi-supernatural attributes.   The dwarfs
of the Congo Forest can be good or bad neighbours to the
black people, according to the treatment they receive.   If
their elfish depredations on the banana groves, or their occasional thefts of tobacco or maize are condoned, or even if
they are conciliated by small gifts of such food being left
exposed where it can be easily taken, they will, in return, leave
behind them in their nightly visitations gifts of meat and pro-
ducts of the chase, such as skins and ivory.   I have been
informed by some of the forest negroes that the dwarfs will
occasionally steal their children, and put in their places pigmy
babies of ape-like appearance—changelings, in fact—
bringing up the children they have stolen in the dwarf tribe." [1]

This admirably expresses the view of those who believe that the
idea of fairy spirits had its origin in traditions about dwarfish
aborigines, but Sir Harry took care to add a rider that such an
opinion was capable of being pushed too far.

Robert Hunt, a trustworthy authority on the folk-lore of the
West of England, tells us that in Cornwall " the Small People," or
fairies proper, were regarded as " the spirits of the people who

---

[1] Sir H. Johnston, " Pygmies and Ape-like Men of the Uganda Border-
land," in *Pall Mall Magazine*, Feb., 1902.

I

inhabited Cornwall many thousands of years ago," [1] thus identifying them with the shades of dead aborigines, as did Grant Allen.

But do we discover any actual traditions or vestiges of belief—can we trace any ponderable material remains, or indeed produce other satisfactory evidence—that the fairy superstition had its origin in the former existence of a pigmy race in these islands? I shall place what I have gathered in this connection before the reader precisely as I have found it. In the story of " Llud and Llevelys," contained in the Welsh *Mabinogion*, we are told of certain magicians, the Coranians, who pestered the folk of the isle of Britain by their impish trickeries. Llud, King of the Britons, anxious to terminate their annoyances, concocted a magical fluid by bruising certain insects in water, which he sprinkled indiscriminately over his own people, and the Coranians alike. It had no ill effect upon his subjects, but it annihilated the obnoxious Coranians. These strange folk have been identified by some writers with a tribe alluded to by the Greek geographer Ptolemy as the Coritavi, who dwelt in the area between the river Trent and Norfolk. But Rhys makes it clear that the name " Coranians " is derived from the word *Cor*, " a dwarf," and that the treacherous folk of the legend were fairies is clear from the species of magic ascribed to them, for they were able to hear every word uttered in Britain, and the money they spent returned to them by the ways of sorcery. But the word " dwarf " applied to them here, although it may signify diminutive stature, cannot have any human association in respect of their obviously elfin character, as indeed Rhys appears to conclude.[2]

At the " Butt," or northern extremity, of the island of Lewis, lies an islet, known by the name of *Luchruban*, " the Pigmies' place," or *Eilean Dunibeg*, " the little men's isle." This isle, which is only about 80 feet in length by 70 in breadth, was alluded to by Dean Munro, in the sixteenth century, as a spot where he unearthed a quantity of small bones and " round heads, of wonderful little quantity, allegit to be the baines of the said pigmies." The island also contains a diminutive building, called a " kirk " or chapel by some writers on the subject. The bones of the " pigmies " were collected at the beginning of the present century and examined at the South Kensington Museum, where they were found

---

[1] R. Hunt, *Popular Romances of the West of England*, pp. 80–1.
[2] J. Rhys, *op. cit.*, pp. 674–5; *Hibbert Lectures*, p. 606.

to be the remains of oxen, sheep, lambs, and sea-birds. But the island has all the appearance of a fairy mound, and it was doubtless this circumstance which inspired the adjacent population to name it as they did—for there is a tradition in the neighbourhood that a race of small men actually did reside there in the times before history. The Gaelic name *Luchruban* is cognate with the Irish word *leprechaun*, signifying a species of fairy. The local name by which these pigmies of tradition are described is " Lusbirdan," which is merely a corruption of the Gaelic. There is not the least reason for believing that a pigmy race ever occupied the isle.[1] Any such traditions as are recorded concerning the existence of dwarfish races in Great Britain may, generally speaking, be referred to similar origins, or to the later hypotheses of writers with a theory to serve. Although the general appearance of the population of certain parts of Scotland to-day reveals that their average of stature is not high, it certainly does not fortify the supposition that its ancestry was in any sense dwarfish or stunted in character.

Joseph Jacobs, whose charming adaptations of English, Keltic, and other fairy tales are so widely and deservedly known, regarded MacRitchie's hypothesis in a somewhat favourable light. He thought it proved that traditions about fairies have attached themselves to mounds " which have afterwards on investigation turned out to be evidently the former residence of men of smaller build than the mortals of to-day." These mounds MacRitchie associated with the Picts and other early races, " but with these ethnological equations," remarked Jacobs, " we need not much concern ourselves. It is otherwise with the mound traditions and their relation, if not to fairy tales in general, to tales *about* fairies, trolls, elves, etc." Such occurrences as these tales relate concerning kidnapping, neighbourly assistance, and so forth, may well have actually happened, thought Jacobs, and are not within the sphere of magical occurrence, as are some other incidents in fairy story. If, he declared, a dwarfish race actually dwelt in Northern Europe, and took up its abode in green hillocks, it does not seem improbable " that they should have performed something like the pranks told of fairies and trolls." Jacobs further referred to the resemblance between the mound of Maes How, in Orkney, and the description of a fairy palace in the Scottish story of *Childe Rowland*, which tale he thought exhibited the characteristics of a

---

[1] S. Grieve, *The Book of Colonsay and Oronsay*, I, pp. 84–9; W. C. Mackenzie, *Races of Ireland and Scotland*, pp. 34 ff.

" marriage-by-capture " story in which a dwarfish and non-Aryan dweller in a green hill kidnapped an Aryan maiden, who was later rescued by her brothers. At the same time he felt that Mac-Ritchie's views cannot explain all fairy tales, nor need his identifications of early races with fairies be " necessarily accepted." [1]

Mr. Bertram C. A. Windle also reviewed MacRitchie's theory at considerable length in a temperate and reasonable vein. He regarded it as proved that a pigmy race never inhabited the northern parts of Scotland, and he stated that such excavation as has been effected there makes it clear that ancient human remains discovered in the area approximate at least to average height. The mounds with which the tales about little people are associated " have not, in many cases, been habitations, but were natural and sepulchral in their nature." The " little people (the fairies) are not by any means associated entirely with mounds," but may dwell in stones, under water, in trees, mountains, or on moors. Certain mounds, too, are said to have been inhabited by giants, in this and other countries. " Tales of little people are to be found in countries where there never were any pigmy races "; and particularly is this the case in America, which, he neglected to say, has its own numerous examples of pigmy fairies and fictions. Finally, " the stunted races whom MacRitchie considers to have formed the subjects of the fairy legend have themselves tales of little people "—a significant point.

Windle was thus unable to accept MacRitchie's theory as a complete explanation of the fairy question, although he believed its author had " gone far to show that one of these mythic elements, one strand in the twisted cord of fairy mythology, is the half-forgotten memory of skulking aborigines." [2]

I must now summarize the views of those writers who were more or less unfriendly to the theory that the fairy tradition is wholly explained by the former existence of dwarfish living races or aboriginal folk and their traits. Andrew Lang briefly noticed it in his introduction to Robert Kirk's *Secret Commonwealth*. He wrote: " The gist of Mr. MacRitchie's *Testimony of Tradition* is that there was once a race of earth-dwellers in this island; that their artificial caves still exist; that this people survive in popular memory as ' the legendary Feens ' and as the Pechts of popular

---

[1] J. Jacobs, *English Fairy Tales*, pp. 241–5; *Folk-Lore*, II, p. 126.
[2] B. C. A. Windle, Introduction to Tyson's *Essay Concerning the Pygmies of the Ancients*, pp. lxxxiv–xcvii.

tales, in which they are regarded as dwarfs. . . . There really was, on this showing, a dwarf race, who actually did live in the 'fairy-hills' or howes, now commonly looked on as sepulchral monuments." Lang scoffed at the idea that such traditions as the building of Glasgow Cathedral and other architectural feats of the pechs were a memory of actual occurrences, and made it plain that other legends concerning this mysterious race had their doublets in the Volsunga Saga and the Nibelungenlied. " I cannot believe," he added, " that the historical Picts were a set of half-naked dwarfish savages, hairy men living underground." " The memory of some old race may have mingled in the composite fairy belief, but was at most an element in the whole." [1]

The late E. Sidney Hartland was even more downright in his negation of MacRitchie's views. He admitted that " nothing is more likely than the transfer to the mythical beings of Celtic superstition of some features derived from alien races. This might account for many details that we are told concerning the dwarfs, the Picts, the Finns, or by whatever other names the elvish race may have been known to Scots and Irishmen. But further than this I cannot go with Mr. MacRitchie." His theory, adds Hartland, is founded on too narrow an induction. The truth he does not reckon with is " that no theory will explain the origin of the fairy superstitions which does not also explain the nature and origin of every other supernatural being worshipped or dreaded by uncivilized mankind throughout the world." [2] A statement with which I personally cannot find myself in strict agreement, as it would certainly limit the more precise classification of the different species of supernatural beings, which is surely one of the main endeavours of folk-lore study. For that fairies are, in a measure, different in kind from other supernatural beings as are giants, kelpies, or mermaids is obvious enough. These are certainly all capable of being classed as supernaturals, but they possess well-marked distinctive traits.

MacRitchie endeavoured to prove not only that the Feinne, or heroes of Gaelic legend whom he identified with the Finns of Scandinavia, were either Picts or a people closely allied to them, but that they were also the originals of the *sidhe*, or fairies of Gaelic tradition, whom he regarded as a human folk. Nutt, criticizing this theory, remarks that it is built up on " the semi-

<hr>

[1] A. Lang, Introduction to Kirk's *Secret Commonwealth*, pp. 25–8.
[2] E. S. Hartland, *The Science of Fairy Tales*, pp. 349–51.

literary (Irish) poems of the twelfth century, and lacks all solid basis." This notwithstanding, he thought that MacRitchie's contention that the Feinne were the same as the Picts, and that both were prototypes of the *sidhe*, or fairies, deserved careful attention. He felt, however, that the simplest view to be taken of Fenian literature in Scotland was that the Scots brought the Fenian saga with them from Ireland, so that the notion of MacRitchie and others that the Irish Scots received it from the Picts, instead of the reverse being the case, seemed to him " so opposed to all we know of the growth of the saga, that I cannot hold it worthy of serious discussion." He added that there is nothing to connect the Fenians of Irish saga with the Picts, but the examples which MacRitchie collected from living folk-lore went to prove that " this conception of them has implanted itself in the folk-mind and moreover that it is akin to the popular conception of the fairies." In certain Irish texts of the eleventh and twelfth centuries the word " Fianna," or " Feine," is used as an equivalent for *sidhe* or *sithchuire*, " fairy-like." Nor, he thought, had MacRitchie any difficulty " in adducing instances from the Fenian texts of the close connection between Fion's warriors and the fairy folk."

When " the fairy mythology of the Celts comes to be exhaustively discussed," Nutt declares, " the questions as to its derivation in certain proportions from distorted recollections of alien and inimical races must not be overlooked, and the nature of the mediaeval and modern Scotch traditions concerning the Picts will need the closest scrutiny. The evidence of the Fenian texts, however, in nowise favours an historical basis for the conception of fairydom. Throughout the whole of the saga the Fenians are essentially a mythic folk; the historical element found in the oldest stage known to us is obviously artificial; the historical element in the secondary stage is equally artificial and anachronistic as well." But no historical elements can be brought into line with fairy belief. The latter, he concludes, is much older than any of these literary elements. The Fenian saga, in its earliest " historical " form, consists of tribal mythic tradition euhemerized; that is, tales which were once told of gods or supernatural beings were later told of human heroes. " They contain nothing which could have originated the fairy belief," or to show that this belief " ever had historic fact for its originating cause." [1] We must therefore, I

---

[1] A. Nutt, in D. MacInnes's *Folk and Hero-Tales from Argyllshire*, pp. 399 ff.

assume, differentiate between the earlier character of the Fenian
heroes as expressed in early Irish literature and the much later
folk-lore ideas concerning them as collected by MacRitchie,
though I must admit that in this particular analysis of the question
at issue Nutt does not appear so logically inspired as is his
wont. For, if the Tuatha Dé Danann, who were gods or
supernaturals, developed into fairies, why not the Fenian heroes
as well?

Canon J. A. MacCulloch, whose writings I have quoted on more
than one occasion, has, I think, been more successful in disposing
of the more extravagant elements in MacRitchie's hypothesis than
any other of his critics.   In two remarkable papers, " The Picts of
History and Tradition," and " Were Fairies an Earlier Race of
Men?," he has reviewed the entire question of the historical origin
of fairy spirits with a lucidity which seems to me to make rejoinder
practically impossible.[1]   In the first of these he has rendered it as
clear as the very obscure nature of the subject admits, that the Picts
were a Keltic folk, speaking a form of Keltic speech akin to the
Brythonic, or ancient British tongue, and that they inhabited the
north and east of Scotland and parts of the west.   They were also
responsible for the buildings known as " brochs," or large Cyclo-
pean towers, the remains of which are frequently to be found on
the Scottish eastern seaboard, as well as for the remarkable
sculptured stones enriched by elaborate symbolism which belong
to the north-east of Scotland.

From the consideration of the historical Picts, however, Mac-
Culloch separates the problem of the Picts of folk-tradition, " a
folk akin to trolls or dwarfs."   " The Scottish literary forms of
(this traditional) name were Pegchtis, Pights, Pechtes," while in
colloquial Scots they are represented by the forms Peht, Pecht, and
Pegh.   " From Northumberland to the North of Scotland these
names in folk-tradition became those of a mysterious race, and ·
some of the traditions about this race were borrowed from those
told by Norsemen about their *duergar*, or dwarfs."   They had
become a mysterious folk, half-goblin, half-human, stunted, hairy,
and huge-footed.   All the great architectural works in the land,
castles, and even cathedrals, were attributed to them.   They
brewed the heather ale, the secret of which died with them.   Were

---

[1] J. H. MacCulloch, " The Picts of History and Tradition," *Proc. Scots.
Anth. Soc.*, I, No. 2, pp. 11 ff.; " Were Fairies an Earlier Race of Men?",
Folk-Lore, XLII, pp. 362 ff.

these the same as the Picts of history?   The Picts were certainly
not a diminutive folk.   How is the discrepancy to be explained?
MacCulloch believes that two theories are possible in respect of
such an explanation.   As regards the first of these, the name
" Picts " no longer applied to an existing people, but " lingered in
folk-memory as that of an older race, more or less mysterious."
Floating legends attached themselves to this name, and the Picts
were associated with earth-houses and other structures which
could not be accounted for by later folk.   The subterranean
character of these structures demanded a restricted height, and this
may have helped to form the legend of a dwarfish race of Picts.
These earth-houses came to be confused with burial chambers in
the popular mind as the dwellings of the Picts.   Probably, too,
the dissemination of such works as Thomas de Tulloch's book on
the Orkneys, written in the fifteenth century, which speaks of the
Picts or Peti of these islands as dwarfs, assisted in spreading the
legend.

The second theory which might explain this transformation is
that such words as Picht, Pecht, or Pegh, " may once have been
native names of a mythic dwarf or elfin folk . . . a pigmy people
living underground, and virtually identical with elves and dwarfs."
In many parts of Scotland the word " Pecht " is employed in this
sense, as also in the north of England.   " These names of dwarfs,
resembling that of the historic Picts or Pehts, would inevitably
tend to be confused with the latter.   And when the folk had
forgotten that their ancestral Picts were an actual people, they
would become more and more confused with these traditional
dwarfs or elfins called Peghs."

In his essay " Were Fairies an Earlier Race of Men ? "   Canon
MacCulloch reviews the whole subject of the possible origin of the
fairy superstition from memories of aboriginal races.   Ghosts and
fairies are separate objects of folk-beliefs, he remarks, yet " when
a territory has been conquered, the aborigines are apt to be regarded in course of time as having a kind of spirit form, to which
doubtless, belief in their ghosts contributes."   He cites instances
of this phenomenon occurring among Maories, Melanesians, and
African tribes.   Fairies and ghosts have similar traits, as I have
already remarked.   But to adhere to the consideration of the
aboriginal theory of fairy origin, especially as adumbrated by
MacRitchie, MacCulloch thinks it significant that Lapps, Finns,
and the other races whose traits may have given rise to a belief

in elfin beings, have themselves traditions of dwarfish fairies; while in Africa, where actual pigmies exist, there are legends of dwarfish beings only about two feet in height, but with supernatural qualities, who seem to be creatures apart from the " true " dwarfs of the areas in question.

The various pigmy groups dwelling in many parts of the world—Negrillos in Central Africa, Negritoes in the Malay Peninsula, the Philippines, and New Guinea, and others in the Deccan, Ceylon, and elsewhere—are generally in a low state of culture, living in leaf-shelters, rock-shelters, or beehive huts. These pigmies sometimes rob plantations and steal cattle. If gifts are laid out for them, they return them in kind. Some of them are regarded as " demons " by their larger neighbours. Such pigmy races appear to have existed in prehistoric Europe, and folk-traditions may possibly be traced to such a source. Pigmy tribes are apt to be regarded as uncanny, as spirits or sorcerers. Legends also exist of dwarfs or elves migrating because of the oppression of human neighbours, and this suggests " the expulsion of an aboriginal race by newcomers." But such migrations may be explained by myths of the departure of supernaturals from earth on account of human wickedness, thinks Canon MacCulloch. I may add here that it is significant that the tradition that on the whole the aboriginal pigmies were unfriendly to agriculture, whereas the fairies were notoriously friendly to its operations, seems to reveal a distinction between them. I have also indicated that many dwarfish traits, such as kidnapping, stealing, and borrowing, which might conceivably reflect occurrences in the contact of stronger races with weaker or smaller peoples, are also told of the fairies. But, as Canon MacCulloch remarks, the habit of kidnapping was also ascribed to beings who had no possible human status, such as water-spirits and demons.

Canon MacCulloch lays stress on the fact that MacRitchie's tales of fairies dwelling in mounds and tumuli, and resenting interference with their abodes, could scarcely have reference to the habits of a mortal race. " Tumuli were not dwellings; even had they been, they were too small for houses to be built on them, nor are there any traces of dwellings on the top of mounds." Here, he says, " we are evidently dealing with forms of the widespread belief that earth-spirits—whether earth personified, or spirits and demons, or later, dwarfs and fairies—resent men's opening up the earth, ploughing it, building on it, defiling it. . . .

The reference is primarily one concerning spirits; it had nothing to do with aboriginal inhabitants dwelling underground." Nor need the fairy dislike of iron, he believes, imply that the elves were an early non-metal using folk, but only that " a well-known human fear of metal was transferred to supernatural beings by those who used it." Similarly, " the association of elfins with (stone) arrowheads must have arisen when the use of stone weapons by men was forgotten." It must indeed be evident that the stone arrowhead which he did not himself use, might, when found by iron-using man, appear as a supernatural or uncanny weapon for which he could not account.

In conclusion, MacCulloch inclines to the opinion that " while some traits of fairies and dwarfs suggest an earlier race of men, others, when traced back, are found to be purely animistic in origin." Even when some of the traits posited of dwarfish races in Melanesia, Africa, and elsewhere seem to imply the presence of an earlier race, many of the things told of them are non-human in their character, especially those concerning their dimensions, supernatural powers and spirit appearance. " With every allowance for the facts, the existence of a pigmy or dwarfish race cannot be the sole cause of the belief. Probably the belief in the manikin soul, no less than general animism," had great influence in the formation of the idea of fairy spirits. There has probably been interaction " between animistic belief in groups of imaginary beings and folk-memory of earlier races, regarded always more and more from an animistic and mythical point of view."

My own belief is that the word " pech," " paikie," and its other forms found in Scotland, are local expressions for a very ancient type of rough fairy familiar to many parts of Britain, and known in some of its areas as pixie, piskie, buckie, Puck, and so forth. The descriptions we have of the pechs from modern folk-lore—" wee, wee fouk, but unco' strang," with shaggy bodies and red hair—make it plain that they are of the same class as brownie and the *urisk*, as the English and Frisian Puck, the hairy sprite of Milton and Ben Jonson, and the buckie of Aberdeenshire and Ireland, who has a bad habit of jumping on the backs of travellers and scaring them. All these names, I believe, hark back to a very ancient root which both the Teutonic and the Keltic tongues accepted from an earlier common lingual ancestry, as is revealed by the fact that in Irish, Icelandic, and German we find the word in the forms of *puca*, or *phooka*, *puci*, and *spuk* respectively—all implying an elf, sprite, or hobgoblin. It has thus no connection with the term " Pict," which, after all, is not a word native to Britain, but a mere slang expression invented by the Romans to denominate those British folk who painted or tattooed themselves, and whose correct racial title was *Cruithne*, and not Picts. This nomenclature, then, makes it perfectly clear that the pechs of North Britain were creatures of indubitably elfin or goblinesque race, and it does even more. For the German and Dutch forms of the word, *spuk*, and *spook*, more closely imply ghost form, thus associating it with a time when fairies and the spirits of the dead were practically regarded as one and the same, and even the Old English form " pook " is translatable as " spirit," as well as " elf."

"The Pict of Scottish tradition," declared Mr. Alexander Hutchison, a practised collector of tradition, " always appears as Pech or Pecht. . . . I have heard in my time many old people in Scotland speak of the ' Pechs,' never once did I hear from them the term ' Pict.' "[1] This testimony I can substantiate from my own experience, lasting over a period of more than half a century. I cannot recall a single instance in which I have heard country people in Scotland allude either to the Picts of history—which they seemed to know little about—or to those of tradition by any other term than that of " pech." I understand, too, from competent authorities, that the word " pixey " is seldom or never used in the West of England, " piskey " being the form invariably employed by the folk of the soil.

I should like to add that I believe one rather important consideration concerning the legend of the pechs has been lost sight of by the majority of those who have written upon it. I refer to the circumstance that most of the tales relating to the pechs are to be found not in the more northerly parts of Scotland, as most people appear to believe, but in the Lowlands of that country. By the very simple expedient of marking the localities associated with these legends on a map of Scotland I have found that by far the greater number of them are connected with Stirlingshire, Fife, Midlothian, Peebles-shire, Lanarkshire, and Angus; while in the north the bulk of them are confined to the Orkney and Shetland Islands. With the exception of Angus, these were decidedly areas in which the historical race of the Picts was not

---

[1] A. Hutchison, *Stories in Stones*, pp. 103–9.

nearly so numerously or so continuously settled at any time as in the north and north-central portions of Scotland, particularly in Perthshire, Inverness-shire, and Ross-shire, the Lothians and Fife being only occasionally under their influence, especially in later times. This might seem to suggest that the pechs of tradition, but certainly not the Picts of history, were more intimately associated with the Lowland portions of Scotland than with the Highland, though such an implication may be subject to criticism because of the well-known fact that two distinct portions of the historical Pictish race are known to history—the Southern and the Northern. Even so, we are dealing with tradition and not with history, and in the face of an overwhelming mass of evidence that the legendary material dealing with the pechts, or pechs, is chiefly attached to Lowland areas, we may safely regard it as associated with spirits, fairies, or goblins known more intimately to the Lowland population. Indeed, I find myself wellnigh driven to the conclusion that the " standard " fairy population of the Lowlands of Scotland is merely the pechs under another and later name, the word " fairy " not having been adopted in Scotland until about the thirteenth century at least.

As regards the larger hypothesis that the existence of diminutive or stunted races of aboriginal character in many parts of the world gave rise to the general belief in fairies, I incline to the opinion that it utterly fails to explain such a belief more than partially. In the first place those communities, savage as well as semi-civilized, who regard fairies as spiritual creatures are much more numerous than those who consider them to be dwarfish but tricksy mortals. Indeed, it may safely be said that no race known to science actually does think of them as entirely of human origin, and even those who incline to believe that their dwarfish neighbours partake of elfin habits notoriously think of them as gifted with supernatural attributes. It is upon the fact that the great majority of superstitious mankind believe their fairies to be supernaturals that I chiefly rely in rejecting the theory that elfins are merely aboriginals disguised. At the same time I cannot, and indeed do not wish to deny, that such a belief is one of the strands which go to make up the fairy superstition *as we know it*. In most fairies, as depicted in genuine folk-lore, we surprise a vein of such primitive savagery as may well descend from stories depicting the deeds of men in a barbarous state of existence. As men are, so will their gods or fairies be. But, as the great majority of specialists in fairy-lore

ave declared, no merely human conditions will explain the fairy
gend in its entirety.   And if the elves reveal at times the un-
leasant traits of our early ancestors, this, I believe, is to be
ccounted for by the circumstance that they very frequently
escribe such conduct as might be expected from the ghosts of
rimitive folk.

CHAPTER VIII

ARE FAIRIES DERIVED FROM GODLIKE FORMS?

GREAT is the diversity of the strands of fairy origin; yet I believe that my readers, when they come to the end of this chapter, will agree that, as a part of the fairy tradition is derived from ideas concerning the dead, another portion of it from beliefs concerning elementary spirits, and yet another from reminiscences of aboriginal races, so a goodly portion of it is descended from memories of the gods of vanished races. In one or two cases, indeed, the proof is so clear as to invite, if not to compel, immediate acceptance. In others it is, as we shall see, reasonably apparent; while in certain important instances, particularly those of the " reluctant " Queen Mab and the highly mysterious Morgan la Fay, it remains tantalizingly obscure.

Much, of course, depends on the sum and quality of the evidence. It must be understood that in some cases the process by which a god or goddess degenerates into a fairy may occupy centuries, and that in the passage of generations such an alteration may be brought about in appearance and traits as to make it seem impossible that any relationship actually exists between the old form and the new. This may be accounted for by the circumstance that in gradually assuming the traits of fairyhood the god or goddess may also have taken on the characteristics of fairies which already existed in the minds of the folk, the elves of a past age, who were already elves at a period when he or she still flourished in the full vigour of godhead. For in one sense Faerie represents a species of limbo, a great abyss of traditional material, into which every kind of ancient belief came to be cast as the acceptance of one new faith after another dictated the abandonment of forms and ideas unacceptable to its doctrines. The difference between god and fairy is indeed the difference between religion and folk-lore.

Sir Walter Scott was of opinion that the fairy superstition owed much to the influence of classical mythology. " An absurd belief in the fables of Classical antiquity," he wrote, " lent an additional feature to the character of the woodland spirits of whom we treat. Greece and Rome had not only assigned tutelary deities to each province and city, but had peopled with peculiar spirits the Seas, the Rivers, the Woods, and the Mountains. Hence we find the elves occasionally arrayed in the costume of Greece and Rome, and the Fairy Queen and her attendants transformed into Diana and her nymphs, and invested with their attributes and appropriate insignia." [1]   This is rather putting the cart before the horse, for Diana and the rest were transformed into fairies, and not the reverse.

As I have already indicated, some of the old English poets identify certain of the figures of classical mythology with the Fairy folk. Chaucer, for example, speaks of " Pluto that is king of fayrie," and " Proserpine and all her fayrie," while the old Scottish poet Gawain Douglas compares the fairies to nymphs:

> " With nymphis and faunis apoun every side,
> Qwhilk Farefolkis or than Elfis clepen we."

In France, too, as early as the fourteenth century, it seems to have been recognized that the word *fée* had been adopted from the Latin *fata*.[2]   Regarding this etymology from the mediaeval point of view, it would appear to have had a decidedly classical tinge in Italy. Thus in the *Pentameron* we find the Italian *fate* to be three in number, while in Spain and France the *fada* and *fées* are sometimes, though not invariably, seven. Cervantes, in his *Don Quixote*, alludes to " the seven castles of the seven *fadas*," while in the Spanish romance of *The Infantina* one of the characters remarks that " seven *fadas* have predicted " such-and-such an occurrence. In the French tale of *The Sleeping Beauty* the number of the *fées* are seven.   On the other hand, in some French fairy tales of older provenance, and in at least one old French romance, *Guillaume au Court-nez*, we discover the *fées* as a triad, like the classical Fates, while in a Provençal romance, *Folquet de Romans*, we also read of them as " three sisters."   Alfred Maury, indeed, uncompromisingly remarks that in France those *fées* who endow children and preside over birth are invariably a sisterhood of three members, like the classical Fates.

Grimm obviously wrestles with the question of the resemblance between the classical Fates and the fays. But he comes at length to realize that the fays do not spin the cord or cut the thread of life, like the classical Fates or the Norse *Norns*, whom they resemble.[3] He believed that both *Norns* and fays are " domestic motherly divinities," and that this is revealed in their faculties for spinning

---

[1] W. Scott, *Border Minstrelsy*, II, p. 325.
[2] A. Maury, *Les Fées du Moyen Âge*, p. 24 *note*.
[3] J. Grimm, *Teutonic Mythology* (trans. by Stallybrass), p. 413.

and bestowing boons on children. Especially among the Kelts, he thought, was this idea current respecting their maternal propensities.[1] If this was so in Europe proper, I can find little or no vestige of it among the Kelts of Scotland and Ireland; nor can I trace an obvious association between the act of spinning and maternity. That the fairies were associated with the business of human birth I should be the last to deny. But I believe that such is the case, so far as some Keltic peoples were concerned, in a very different sense from that alluded to by Grimm. The Keltic fairies were, I believe, human spirits awaiting rebirth, and that in quite a mechanical way. It was rather in the Latin lands that they came to be thought of as *presiding* over human birth, as did the classical Fates. In Scotland, particularly, every effort was made to ward them off from a newly-born infant, whereas in mediaeval France the reverse was the case. One would have to prove that the Scottish dread of fairies approaching the natal bed was post-Christian before it could be admitted that this fear was not original but acquired.

That the fays were the lineal descendants of the Fates of classical mythology is a widely accepted belief. It is obvious that the *fatuae* of the older Latins, the *fate* of later Italy, and the *fées* of mediaeval France, were beings whose names at least all descended from one common form. But were these three classes of spirit one and the same, or did they differ in type, even though their names had so close a resemblance the one to the other? It was the conviction of Henry Charles Coote, who wrote on the question towards the end of last century, that, though fay and *fatuae* were one and the same, the *fatuae* were by no means related to the Fates of classical belief.

Coote compared the *fatuae* with the fays of mediaeval times. " The *fatuae*," he wrote, " were beautiful and ever young." They dwelt on earth in places inaccessible to man, near lakes, woods, and fountains. There were males of the species, known as *fatui*. Like men, they died after a long life, but were the possessors of magic powers. But these beings, he insists, are not the Fates of Roman myth. They are nymphs and not *Parcae*.[2] As we shall see, however, a good deal of evidence exists to the contrary.

The theory that the fairies were to some extent derived from the old maternal divinities of whom we find traces in many European

[1] J. Grimm, *op. cit.*, p. 416.
[2] H. C. Coote, " The Neo-Latin Fay," *Folk-Lore Record*, II, pp. 1 ff.

countries has much to recommend it. In Wales a certain type of fairy, or rather group of fays, is known as *Y Mamau*, or " the Mothers," and vestiges of a belief in such forms have been discovered on various inscribed monuments, in Britain and the Continent. These, in the Roman inscriptions which describe them, are usually alluded to as *matrae, matres* and *matronae*. They generally take the form in sculpture, or bas-relief, of three women of benevolent appearance clad in long robes, who frequently carry baskets of fruit, symbolical of agricultural prosperity. Occasionally their worship appears to have been localized. That these shapes in course of time shaded gradually into those of fairies was the belief of Rhys, who was of opinion that the numerous spots where they were wont to preside in pagan times—forests, mountain-tops, rocks, and lakes—were later regarded as the haunts of fays, and this is a conclusion at which numerous other writers on the subject have arrived.[1]

As most readers of folk-lore and myth are aware, a certain class of spirit is regarded as presiding over human birth. In ancient Egypt the goddess *Hathor* is known to have assumed this office, as did the Greek *Moirai* and *Nereids*, the Roman *Fatae* and *Nymphae*, and the *Norns* of Scandinavian belief. The older fairies of France also presided over the child-bed in almost precisely the same manner as did their classical predecessors, and were in the habit of endowing new-born infants with good or evil qualities. The Egyptian *Hathors*—this goddess was occasionally multiplied into seven—brought human souls to birth. The association of the above-mentioned goddesses with human birth links them in some degree with later fairies who were thought of as presiding over child-birth and endowing infants with various virtues or vices. The *Hathors* and *Moirai* played the part of fairies at human baptisms. Indeed, the *Hathor* of a family seems to have represented an ancestral form, like the *Banshee*.

The manner in which fairies came to be confused with the Fates in some European areas is strikingly revealed by Mr. F. S. Copeland, who says that " in the Slovene parts of Jugo-Slavia, the Sojenice or Rojenice (Fates) . . . preside over the birth of the child and then decide its fate and the time and manner of its death. Sometimes they are popularly confused with the Fairies or White Ladies," although he believes that they were originally distinct from them.[2]

[1] J. Rhys, *Hibbert Lectures*, pp. 101 ff.
[2] F. S. Copeland, " Slovene Folk-Lore," *Folk-Lore*, XLII, p. 429.

K

Mab, the " fairy queen " of literature, appears to have presided over birth.   Respecting her origins there seems to be more than a little dubiety.   Some authorities have traced her to Maeve, the Irish queen famous for her association with the saga of *The Cattle-raid of Cooley,* while others connect her name with that of Habundia, evidently an early pagan goddess, who later became, like Hecate and Diana, a patroness of witches in mediaeval times. That Maeve was certainly associated with faerie is revealed by the mention of her in an ancient Irish tale, *The Fight of Castle Knock,* as " Maeve the *Sith*-queen." [1]   Miss E. Hull says that " she is remembered by the Irish as Queen of the Fairies," and that she is " probably the Queen Mab of Spencer's *Faerie Queene.*"   Her first husband, Conacher, was a fairy man.[2]   Rhys remarks that the name of another of her husbands, Ailill, seems to be the Irish equivalent of the Welsh *ellyll,* " an elf or demon."   He believed her to be " a dawn-and-dusk goddess." [3]   Some writers think the name Mab is simply the Cymric for " a small child," and that it may have reference to Mab's maternal characteristics.[4]   Mab as a fairy may have been known in Shakespeare's Warwickshire, as the local phrase " Mab-led " (pron. Mob-led) shows.   It meant being led astray by the will-o'-the-wisp.[5]

Mab, says Voss, a German translator of Shakespeare, is not the fairy queen.   As regards the actions of Mab, they do not appear to differ much from those of Habundia, or Abundia, seemingly a maternal spirit, for whom feasts were spread in the houses which she frequented.   " Abundia " is mentioned by William of Auvergne, Bishop of Paris, who died in 1248, and she is also alluded to in the *Roman de la Rose* of the same century.   George Henderson, in his introduction to J. F. Campbell's *The Celtic Dragon Myth,* suggests that Maeve " may have been a sort of sea-mother " who perhaps formerly took shape " as a sort of serpent or water monster." [6]

We certainly have not a sufficiency of material to arrive at any decision concerning the theory that the Mab of later tradition was derived from the mediaeval Habundia.   On the other hand, as regards her association with Queen Maeve, we find that this personage was herself of fairy nature and that she is " remembered

---

[1] P. Kennedy, *Fictions of the Irish Celts,* p. 191.
[2] E. Hull, *The Cuchullin Saga,* pp. lv ff.
[3] J. Rhys, *op. cit.,* p. 138.   [4] Wirt Sikes, *British Goblins,* p. 14.
[5] J. Brand, *Popular Antiquities,* p. 799.
[6] G. Henderson, *The Celtic Dragon Myth,* pp. xl, xlii.

by the Irish as Queen of the Fairies."   There is, however, nothing to show that in the latter connection she has any association with child-birth, as the traditional Mab is said to have had.   Habundia, however, is distinctly mentioned in the *Roman de la Rose* as entering houses at night, tieing horses' manes into knots, and indulging in other elvish pranks.   For tnat reason she equates more readily with the Mab of tradition than does Maeve, though I must confess that the philological associations of the name appear to lead nowhere.

Alfred Maury summarizes the natal influence of the French fairies with lucidity.   He says that at a birth they dispense the good qualities and defects of the infant, as well as its lucky and unlucky fortunes.   These, he considers, are the attributes of the *Parcae*, or Fates, and he shows how these Fates visited the " natal couches " of the heroes of ancient Hellas precisely as did the fairies of old France the cradles of Ogier the Dane, Bruno de la Montagne, Maillefer, and Yseult.   At the spot known as the Roche-aux-Fées, in the canton of Rhetiers, he tells us, the peasants still believed in his day (1843) that the local fays guarded small children and prognosticated their future.   They entered houses by way of the chimneys.   In Brittany a repast was served in a room close to that in which a woman was in labour.   This was an offering to the fairies to ensure their placation and enlist their goodwill.   These fairies appear to have had a definite rôle as obstetricians.   In the legend of St. Armentaire, written in the year 1300, mention is made of sacrifices to the fairy Esterelle, who made women fecund. These sacrifices were made at a stone named " the *Lauza de la Fada*," or " the Fairy Stone." [1]

Maury, in his delightful work, continues his antique but valuable disquisition upon the fairies and human birth by indicating the importance of the number three in connection with those who presided over accouchements.   As with the classical Fates, the number, he says, is constant in its association with such beings in France, not only in respect of the natal function, but in many other circumstances, although, as I mention elsewhere, the number seven does not seem to have been unknown.

I turn now to an authority no less delectable in his treatment of the affairs of Elfin, Canon J. A. MacCulloch, to whom students of folk-lore are deeply indebted for many a refreshing volume and essay.   He believes the French fays of whom Maury has treated to

---

[1] A. Maury, *op. cit.*, pp. 29–32.

be " the product of Celtic, Teutonic, and Latin traditions.   They
have traits of the *Matres*, the *Norns*, the *Parcae*, and other demi-
goddesses. . . .   They act as fairy godmothers, attending on
infants and prophesying their fate or giving them gifts.   As such
they may have been the objects of a cult."   He alludes to the
mediaeval spreading of a table for the *Parcae* mentioned by
Burchard in his *Corrector*, and equates it with the table set for
Habundia and the *bonæ res* which I have already mentioned.   For
one of these matron-like fays, named Maglore, no knife was set,
for she bestowed ill-fortune on the folk of the house, while her
companions were beneficently inclined.   She may thus be the
prototype of the " wicked fairy " of nursery legend.   " Similar
instances occur in other romances, in the Norse sagas and in the
poetic Edda." [1]

The goddess Diana or Artemis of classical lore appears to have
been particularly identified with the fairy tradition.   In both the
early and later Middle Ages she was regarded as one of those
darker divinities who, as the wild huntress, wandered through
the air with evil spirits, Herodias, Holda, and others.   Diana,
at a later time, became the leader and protectress of the mediaeval
witches, especially in Italy, but plenty of evidence exists that
she is one and the same with Titania, the " Fairy Queen."   In
the thirteenth-century tale of *Sir Lancelot of the Lake* we are
told that the lake in which the fairy Lady of the Lake dwelt
was " the Lake of Diana."   She is, indeed, " that fourth kind of
spirit ";   as James I says, in his *Demonologie*, " quhilk by the
gentilis was called Diana, and her wandering court, and amongst
us called the Phairie."   Ovid, in the third book of his *Metamorphoses*, styles Diana " Titania."   At the same time, I am
convinced that it is an error to regard the name Titania as a mere
corruption of that of Diana, as some writers have done.   It was,
indeed, an honorific or poetic title conferred upon such goddesses
as belonged to the Titan race.   For example, Pyrrha, daughter of
Epimethius and Pandora, was so called because of her Titanic
ancestry.

In the *Vecchia Religione*, or " Old Religion," of modern Italy,
a remnant of pagan faith which existed among the peasants in
Tuscany and in the region of Naples up to the end of last century,
and which is perhaps not quite extinct even now, Diana was known
as " the fairy " *par excellence* and was regarded as the mother of

---

[1] J. A. MacCulloch, *Mediaeval Faith and Fable*, pp. 38 ff.

Aradia, or Herodias, the immediate protectrix of the worshippers of that cult.   It is said of her in the secret book or gospel of that rather amusingly innocent cultus:

> " Therefore thou dost belong unto the race
> Of witches or of fairies,"

for the *folletti*, or fairies, were considered as the familiars or emissaries of the goddess Aradia, or Herodias, although this Herodias was evidently not the same as that sanguinary-minded young woman of the New Testament who demanded the head of John the Baptist on a charger, but a replica of Lilith, " the first wife of Adam," on whom he begat a legion of spirits.   The Diana of the Italian peasant, however, does not seem to be the Latin goddess of that name, but an imported form of the Greek Artemis.[1]

The worship of these witch-mothers, derived in part from the goddesses of classical times, is denounced in many of the decrees of the old Church Councils of the early Middle Ages.   It is not generally realized that Diana, or more properly her Greek form of Artemis, the virgin huntress, had a darker side to her character. For she cannot be dissociated from Hecate, the goddess of Hades and gloom.   She is also, in one of her several forms, the moon, and even in that guise was terrible enough, for anciently she was described as having serpents for feet and snakes for hair.   It was only in the verses of later poets that she came to be associated with the calm luminary of night in a more celestial form.   Nor was she particularly merciful, as the story of Acteus makes evident, and she was certainly, in her form of Hecate, the patroness of sorcerers in ancient Greece.   In Wallachia and Dacia, Diana was still recognized as a species of goddess in the early nineteenth century;[2] while in Portugal, as has been made evident by Violet Alford and Rodney Gallop, she has left behind her a cult much the same as that of Aradia in Italy, and which stretches into the confines of Catalonia.   In this area fairies and witches seem to have become confused, being known indiscriminately as *fados*, *hadas*, and *encantados*, while the souls of the dead are also identified with them.   Vestiges of the god Janus, the Roman double-faced deity of gates and entrances, and so of divination, are also to be found to the west of the Basque country, along with certain spirits which are known as *Jana*; while, in old Italian, *Gana* means " witch " or

<hr>

[1] C. G. Leland, *Aradia, or the Witches of Italy*, pp. 101–31.
[2] A. Schott, *Walaschiche Sagen*, p. 292.

" fairy," and in old French *Gene* has the same implication.   In the Asturias *Dianu* means devil.[1]   The above statements are fortified by the remark of a reviewer, in *Folk-Lore*, that " the Diana of mediaeval lore is, of course, not derived from the aboriginal Italian divinity, but from the Graeco-Roman Diana-Artemis-Hecate."

On the conversion of the European tribes to Christianity the ancient pagan worship was by no means incontinently abandoned. So wholesale had been the conversion of many peoples, whose chiefs or rulers had accepted the new faith on their behalf in a summary manner, that it would be absurd to suppose that any general acquiescence in the new gospel immediately took place. Indeed, the old beliefs lurked in many neighbourhoods, and even a renaissance of some of them occurred in more than one area. Little by little, however, the Church succeeded in rooting out the public worship of the old pagan deities, but it found it quite impossible to effect an entire reversion of pagan ways, and in the end compromised by exalting the ancient deities to the position of saints in its calendar, either officially, or by usage.   In the popular mind, however, these remained as the fairies of woodland and stream, whose worship in a broken-down form still flourished at wayside wells and forest shrines.   The *Matres*, or Mother gods, particularly those of Celtic France and Ireland, the former of which had come to be Romanized, became the *bonnes dames* of folklore, while the *dusii* and *pilosi*, or hairy house-sprites, were so commonly paid tribute that the Church introduced a special question concerning them into its catechism of persons suspected of pagan practice.   Nevertheless, the Roman Church, at a somewhat later era, reversed its older and more catholic policy, and sternly set its face against the cultus of paganism in Europe, stigmatizing the several kinds of spirits and derelict gods who were the objects of its worship as demons and devils, whom mankind must eschew with the most pious care if it were to avoid damnation.

The *nereids* of Modern Greece have a strong resemblance to Keltic fairies.   They have their queens, they dance all night, disappearing at cock-crow; they indulge in shape-shifting, " take " children in death, make changelings, and fall in love with young men, quite in the manner of the Highland and Irish *leannan sidhe*.[2]

---

[1] V. Alford and R. Gallop, " Traces of a Dianic Cult from Catalonia to Portugal," *Folk-Lore*, XLVI, pp. 350 ff.

[2] J. C. Lawson, *Modern Greek Folk-Lore and Ancient Greek Religion.*

Professor H. J. Rose is none too positive, however, that they are one and the same with the *nereids* of classical mythology. It is not certain, he thinks, that the modern name is philologically derived from the ancient Greek appellation, and he gives reasons for this doubt which I need not specify here. They closely resemble the nymphs of classic times, but there has been a great deal of Slavonic influence in modern Greece, and such forms are commonly found among the South Slavonian *vilas* and the Russo-Bulgarian *russalkas*. " Instead therefore of simply calling the modern beliefs survivals," he concludes, " I should say that there existed at any time during the last couple of millennia, probably longer yet, a vast mass of beliefs concerning the existence of creatures of fairy- or nymph-like type common at least in general features to several populations who in that time have inhabited or entered the Balkan Peninsula and the adjacent islands; that immigrants into any part brought with them a readiness to believe in such beings and found them waiting for them when they arrived." [1]

The American folk-lorist, Charles Godfrey Leland, demonstrated that at least a few of those spirits which the modern Tuscan peasant regards as fairies are certainly forms descendant from ancient pagan deities. The old Etruscan goddess Turanna, a form of Venus, is still thought of by the country folk of Tuscany as a fairy. She assists the poor in true fairy fashion, bestowing prosperity and good fortune on the meritorious.[2] The fairy Corredoio is a modern form of Juno, but scarcely resembles that dignified goddess, so full of frolic is he—or she, for the sex of this spirit is a matter of dispute.[3] The ancient Tuscan nymphs, the *Virae*, are now represented by the fairy known as Vira, who dwells in the forests, and who appears to handsome young wood-cutters and charcoal-burners as a beautiful girl, who either finishes their work for them or reveals to them a portion of the abundant treasure of Faerie.[4] The fairy Albina appears to hopeless lovers at dawn and punishes girls who betray their sweethearts. She is none else than a reminiscence of the goddess Aurora, the deity of the dawn.[5]

That the fairies of Ireland, or at least a considerable proportion of them, are in direct descent from the old gods worshipped in that

---

[1] H. J. Rose, *Folk-Lore*, XLVI, pp. 350 ff.
[2] C. G. Leland, *Etruscan Roman Remains*, pp. 38 ff.
[3] C. G. Leland, *op. cit.*, pp. 72 ff.   [4] C. G. Leland, *op. cit.*, pp. 109 ff.
[5] C. G. Leland, *op. cit.*, pp. 123 ff.

island is, of course, a fact so widely accepted and vouched for by authorities of such standing that it would be difficult even to imagine a reasonable argument which might be advanced in opposition to it. Here, then, I intend to deal with the tradition of these gods, the Tuatha Dé Danann and their elfin associations, as affording one of the most complete and definite of those proofs which illustrate fairy descent from godlike forms. Practically every authority of rank who has investigated this question agrees that the descent of the Irish fairies from the Tuatha Dé admits of no question whatsoever, and the circumstance that the modern elves of Ireland are still known to the peasantry by the same name as formerly described the ancient gods of the Green Isle is perhaps the best evidence of an unbroken tradition which has survived for centuries, and which is perhaps the most remarkable of its kind in the whole range of European folk-lore.

I am not concerned here with the history of the Tuatha Dé otherwise than as it serves to reveal their metamorphosis into fairy form. Briefly, it would appear that soon after the introduction of Christianity into Ireland, and certainly before the period of Norse invasion (the eighth century), the tradition of the Tuatha Dé Danann was cast by the ancient annalists of the country into that kind of history which not infrequently develops out of myth, as in the case of the Danish history of Saxo-Grammaticus, or the Japanese *Nihongi*. These gods, the Tuatha Dé Danann, were conceived as kings, to whom definite dates were attached. This early humanizing of the gods was a process similar to that by which Arthur and his knights came later to be conceived as men. But as we find it in manuscript form, this pseudo-history belongs to the tenth and eleventh centuries; that is, it is subsequent to the period of Norse invasion. On the first coming of the Tuatha Dé, we learn, they were confronted by the Firbolgs, then the dominating race in Ireland, whom they conquered at the battle of Moytura, after which they are described as ruling in the island until the appearance there of the Milesians.

From the pages of Keating we learn that the salient feature of the Tuatha Dé as a race was their expertness in the art of magic. Anciently, we are told, they dwelt in Greece, and when the Athenians were attacked there by the Syrians, the Tuatha Dé aided their allies by means of their necromantic powers, for they sent demons into the bodies of those Athenians who had been slain, so that they might engage once more in the combat. At a later time they migrated to the North of Europe, where they sojourned in the four cities of Falias, Gorias, Finias, and Murias. Thence they took ship for North Britain and Ireland, bringing with them four magical talismans—the *Lia Fail*, a stone which acknowledged the king of the race by roaring under him at his election, the sword of the sun-god Lugh, his spear, and the cauldron of the god known as the Dagda. Throughout this account the magical character of the Tuatha Dé is insisted upon.

In his *Voyage of Bran* Alfred Nutt has made it plain that the Tuatha Dé, as deities, were regarded as givers of life and as the patrons of growth and fertility, and anything I might say here could only be a repetition of what he has already made self-evident. But it is also obvious that the pantheon of which they were the gods is reflected in the myths and tales of the ancient British as they have come down to us through Welsh sources, and we know that, despite local differences, the Tuatha Dé Danann and the British " Children of Don," as revealed in the *Mabinogion* and elsewhere, are one and the same in essence as in origin.

As Miss Eleanor Hull has indicated, " the most ancient god-names [in Ireland] were impersonations of qualities." Some of the names of the older Tuatha Dé Danann were taken from verbal roots signifying " the Good God," " Knowledge," " Prosperity," and the like. Others personified the healing art, Eloquence, Poetry, and metal-working. When, at last, the Tuatha Dé were overborne by the invading Milesians they were dispossessed of the upper earth and took counsel as to where they should dwell in the future. One part of them resolved to quit Ireland for ever and to seek refuge in the overseas paradise, but the greater number resolved to dwell in subterranean retreats, or *sidhe*, which were allotted to them by their chief, the Dagda. These underground strongholds were situated under barrows or hillocks, and were merely the vestibules to extensive realms stretching far and wide, where every delight and material amenity existed.

Some writers have found it difficult to believe that the majestic gods of the Irish Kelts should have been transformed into the fairy sprites, to whom the Irish peasantry allude with such intimate freedom. Yet so it is. " The fairies," says Alfred Nutt, " are the lineal descendants of the Tuatha Dé Danann. Name and attributes can be traced, and yet the result is so different. . . . In spite of identity of name and attribute, can these beings be really the same as the courtly amorous wizard-knights and princesses of the romances? The difference is as great as that between the Oberon and Puck of Shakespeare. And yet, as we have seen, the historical connection is undeniable."[1] As the reader will recollect, I have briefly described the fairy descendants of the Tuatha Dé and indicated their spheres of influence in modern Eire in the first chapter.

I have already said that the Cymric races in Britain, the Brythonic folk, possessed gods of similar derivation to the Tuatha Dé, and I should like to indicate that traces of these still exist in English as well as Welsh folk-lore, as the evidence will have a certain bearing upon what I shall have to say farther on. In Ireland we find very numerous references to a fairy-like population known to tradition as " the Danes," whose dwellings are usually pointed out as those " forts," or raths, which are of such common incidence in that island. More than one writer on the subject has not hesitated to identify these " Danes " with the traditions respecting the Norse invaders of Ireland, but that the name " Danes " has reference to the Tuatha Dé Dannan alone is plain enough. We find similar " Danes " in Cornwall. There is a " Danes' Castle " near Penzance, another in St. Columb, and still another in Perran-Zabuloe. All are constructed from great stones and their building is referred to Scandinavian pirates who landed on the Cornish coasts.[2] But that these Danes were a folk-memory of the Tuatha Dé Danann, and not of Scandinavian invaders, is obvious enough. The expression is merely a corruption of " Danann." As Miss E. Andrews remarks: " Their name appears to identify them with the Tuatha Dé Danann, whose necromantic power is celebrated in Irish tales, and of whom, according to O'Curry, one class of fairies are the representatives."[3] In a cave in the Dane Hills in Leicestershire, says tradition, dwelt a terrible " Black Annis," who devoured lambs and children, and, taking the topographical name into consideration, I believe this legend may refer to the old Keltic goddess Danu, sometimes known as Anu, the mother of both the Tuatha Dé Danann and the British " Children of Don."[4] That the strife between Fenian and Norsemen, or the " Lochlanners," which figures so largely in later Fenian saga and the floating legends of Finn MacCoul, induced this confusion

[1] A. Nutt, *The Fairy Mythology of Shakespeare*, p. 19.
[2] R. Hunt, *Popular Romances of the West of England*, pp. 307–8.
[3] E. Andrews, *Ulster Folklore*, p. 11.
[4] E. Hull, *Folklore of the British Isles ;* Edwardes and Spence, *Dictionary of Non-Classical Mythology*, p. 57.

between the names of Danann and Danes appears so probable that it seems to explain everything, but that the more ancient appellation is the true source of the tradition of the Danes of the Irish and Cornish forts is, I believe, unquestioned. There certainly exists in the *Leabhar na Feinne,* or " Book of the Fenians," a statement that the fairy subterranean strongholds were plundered by " Denmarkians," whose magic led them to these spots; but this can only imply that the invading Scandinavians sought for treasure in the Irish burial-mounds, and not that they took the places of the Tuatha Dé in Irish folk-lore, as has been suggested. Professor Macalister, however, ventures the statement: " I pass over . . . the theory that the word ' Danes ' in such traditions refers not to the Scandinavians, but to the legendary Tuatha Dé Danann. Conceivably there is such a popular confusion, but the hypothesis is unnecessary." [1] In Scotland, remarks Miss E. Hull, " most of these Gaelic gods are unknown." But I would point out that in the romance of *Thomas the Rhymer* the Fairy Queen, in her general appearance, recalls the great ladies of the Tuatha Dé Danann. Like these, she is accompanied by greyhounds, her horse-furniture and apparel are reminiscent of those of the princesses of the Tuatha Dé, and she lures Thomas into a subterranean land which faithfully reflects the scenery of the underground portion of the fairy mounds of Ireland. It may well be that this romance is not of Scottish provenance, as has been ably argued, but the *mise en scène* of other Scottish tales, particularly that of *Childe Rowland*, collected by Jamieson, would appear to claim an Irish origin. And if the numerous accounts of fairy hunting on horseback known to Scottish folk-lore do not mirror similar " meets " of the Tuatha Dé, I cannot imagine whence they proceeded. This is not to say, however, that they represent a very definite Irish influence, and that they are not due to late acceptances, the entire fairy tradition of Scotland revealing a rather striking difference to both Irish and English notions, except in the West and the Western Isles, where literary influences from Ireland were potent until comparatively modern times, more particularly, however, in respect of Fenian saga than that which deals with the traditions of the Tuatha Dé. It is also true that the Irish goddess Brigit took hold of the imagination of the folk of Western Scotland, where she was until recently regarded as a patroness of the harvest, and that several of the old Scottish witch-

---

[1] R. A. S. Macalister, *The Archæology of Ireland*, p. 331, note 1.

mothers, such as the Cailleach Bheur, reveal strong resemblances to Danu or Anu, who in later Ireland may have become a similar figure, the " witch " or *banshee* Ainé. Brigit, too, may have been known in the North of England as the goddess Brigantia, the eponymous deity of the tribe of the Brigantes, who dwelt beyond the Humber and the Mersey.

The fays of old France are occasionally somewhat baffling as regards their immediate origins. D'Aussy, in his *Fabliaux*, provides us with some insight into their characteristics. He tells us that there were two kinds of French fays, one a species of nymph or divinity, and the other sorceresses, women instructed in magic, who are found in the romances which deal with Morgan la Fée, Vivien, and other fairy dames of the type. These latter had at their command all the marvels and evils capable of causing good or ill to humanity. Yet " they could not absolutely control the demons with which they had commerce." [1]

In the old romance of *Lancelot* we read that " in these times there were fairies who had knowledge of enchantment and charms, and these were more numerous within the bounds of Great Britain than in any other land. They were acquainted with the powers of words and of stones and herbs, for by means of these they were able to retain their youth and beauty." [2]

Gregory Lewis Way, in his notes to the *Fabliaux, or Tales Abridged from French Manuscripts*, remarks of these old French fays, that the first class alluded to by D'Aussy resembled the nymphs, naiads, and dryads of classical mythology, while the others, such as Morgan la Fée and Vivien, were merely witches who " conducted their operations by the intervention of demons." [3] So it would certainly appear to have been in later French romance; but when we come to examine more closely the nature of such fairies as Morgan and Vivien we certainly discover the attributes of ancient goddesses beneath the mantle of the sorceress. Gower seems to allude to female wonder-workers of the sort in his *Confessio Amantis*, when in the Eighth Book of that poem he says:

> " And that was Circes and Calipse,
> That cowthen do the Mone eclipse,
> Of men and change the likenesses,
> Of Artemagique Sorceresses."

---

[1] Legrand d'Aussy, *Fabliaux ou Contes*, I, p. 153.
[2] *Roman van Lanzelet*, ed. K. A. Hahn, X.
[3] G. L. Way, *Fabliaux*, pp. 231–2.

Equally mythological with Morgan la Fée is Vivien, or Viviana, the fairy who stole Sir Lancelot du Lac from his mother and brought him up from infancy beneath the waters of her lake, whence he derived his surname, although other authors name her Nimüe. She it was, too, who beguiled the enchanter Merlin into a magic slumber in the enchanted forest of Broceliande. But, like the Egyptian Osiris, Merlin has more graves than one, and Scotland can show a site of the kind at the Pausayl burn where it flows into the Tweed. Vivien would, indeed, appear to have emerged from the romances of that outpost of the ancient British race which was formerly situated in the south of Scotland, and to have been the "Hwimleian," or "Chwifleian," of Merlinus Sylvestris, the historical Merlin of that people, rather than a Breton spirit. She is repeatedly alluded to in the poems associated with this actual or legendary bard. Her name, in its more ancient British form, has allusion to that species of apparition which suddenly appears and disappears; that is, she may represent the mists which shift and veer above a lake.[1] Rhys, however, believes that the name, in its earlier form, was Nimüe, but that through a series of mis-copyings on the part of Norman scribes it became Vivien. Now Nimüe is undoubtedly the same as the British goddess Rhiannan, who was almost certainly a moon-goddess, so that, according to the great Welsh critic, the fairy Vivien is a direct derivation of a Brythonic lunar deity.[2]

Miss Jessie Weston made it clear in her study of the legend oi Sir Gawain that some fairy ladies possessed attributes which seem to identify them with goddesses of love. On one of his adventures, as recounted by Chrètien and Wolfram, Gawain is led to a castle under the conduct of a lady whom he encountered sitting beside a spring or fountain. This castle is situated on an island, and Miss Weston was of opinion that it represented a later idea of the ancient Isle of Women, a part of the Land of the Gods so frequently encountered in Irish literature, especially in the legend of *The Voyage of Bran*. The lady who dwelt in this retreat is nameless, and Miss Weston considered that it was not till, at a later date, certain attributes of the Goddess of Love had been passed over to the Queen of the other-world that she received a name. "Elsewhere we find it distinctly stated that Gawain's love was a fairy"; for instance, in the romance of *Saigremor*. Thus the contact

---

[1] T. Price, *Literary Remains*, I, p. 144.
[2] J. Rhys, *Arthurian Legend*, p. 284 and *note*.

between the shapes of Faerie and those of pagan mythology becomes fairly obvious.[1]

It is a little difficult to find a point of departure in discussing the myth of Morgan la Fée. In more than one old book we are told in a desultory way that she was associated with the phenomenon of the *Fata Morgana*—a mirage so called by the fishermen of the southern coasts of Italy, near the ancient city of Rhegium, and seen only during the summer months. The mirage which went by her name appears to have been almost entirely confined to the Straits of Messina.

In the romance of *Ogier the Dane*, one of the Paladins of Charlemagne, Morgan la Fée figures prominently as a sort of Fairy Queen of the other-world. This French romance must certainly have drawn its inspiration from an older British story which told how Morgan la Fée was the sister of Arthur and spirited him away to Avalon after the battle of Camelot. In the thirteenth-century romance of *Sir Lancelot of the Lake* she is described as a malicious fairy, the sister of Arthur.

In the romance of the *Green Knight* Morgan is alluded to as " the mistress of Merlin," a position she seems to have shared with Vivien. She is spoken of as if she had acquired her magical training from Merlin, and one gathers that it was from .this circumstance that she came to be known as " Morgan la Fée," or the Enchantress. In this romance she is alluded to as " Morgne the goddess," and it seems not impossible that the author of the tale confused her with Viviana, the Lady of the Lake, as the *amie* of Merlin.[2]

In clearing such dubious ground it is necessary to use pick and spade rather roughly at times. In *The Prophecies of Merlin* a story is related of a trial of skill between four fairy ladies—Morgan, the Lady of Avalon, Sibile the enchantress, and the Queen of North Wales. Now, according to Malory, this latter personage is one of the three queens who bore Arthur away in a mystic barge after the battle of Camelot, the other two who attended him being the Queen of the Waste Lands and Morgan herself. It seems likely, therefore, that in both passages we are dealing with the self-same personages, though Sibile may be a composite memory of the Sybils of classical tradition. " If," says the author, " the Lady of the Lake (that is Nimüe) had been there, all the subtility of the world would have

---

[1] J. L. Weston, *Sir Gawain*, pp. 32–48.
[2] G. L. Kittredge, *The Green Knight*, Early English Text Society.

been present." [1]　This remark goes to show the nature of the class to which these magical women belong, and that they are actually goddess-sorceresses who have dwindled to fairies.　Morgan conjures up a legion of fiends to carry away the Lady of Avalon (who in this particular case is not Morgan herself), but they are repulsed. The Lady of Avalon is the possessor of a ring which changes her wishes into acts, and Morgan finds herself stripped of her apparel. The point is that the exposure revealed her as an old woman, a hag, a witch.　In the *Green Knight* Morgan is also changed into Aggteb, a witch, who has the power of transforming other people. [2]

The Urganda of Spanish romance has been confused with Morgan, but we must be careful concerning such analogies.　Rhys makes it pretty clear that the " Morgawse " mentioned by Malory was that goddess known to earlier Welsh myth as Gwyar, who was the sister of Arthur and the wife of the sky-god Llud, metamorphosed by Malory into King Lot.　The name Gwyar means " shed blood," or " gore," and reminds us of the relationship of the Morrigan, the war-goddess of the Irish Gaels. [3]

I am of opinion that Morgan la Fée and this goddess, the Morrigan, a kind of Irish valkyrie, who hovered over the battlefield as a raven, and who revealed such enmity to the Irish hero Cuchullin, may, indeed, be derived from a common source, for it seems improbable that Morgan la Fée is the mythical descendant of the Morrigan.

The word " Morgan " in some Celtic languages would appear to connect certain spirits called by it with the sea.　Thus the Bretons call their mermaids " Morgan "—that is, " sea-women," as Villemarqué says—while near Glasfryn, in Wales, Morgan is a lakespirit who seems to carry off naughty children into the neighbouring lake.　In Irish, says Rhys, the word is Muirgen, one of the names of the lake-lady Liban, and in France is that of a waterlady, while in Wales it becomes masculine, because Morgan is a common male name there. [4]

Now in Scottish folk-lore we encounter a figure not altogether unlike the Italian and Breton guises of Morgana.　She is Muireartach, or spirit of the Eastern Sea, who is " ill-streaming, bald-red, white-maned, terrific and with open roaring mouth."　She is converted by the fancy of poets into an old woman, and is called " a spectre, a film of vapour."　She is spoken of in connection with the

---

[1] F. Madden, *Sir Gawaine*, p. 332.　　[2] G. L. Kittredge, *op. cit.*
[3] J. Rhys, *op. cit.*, p. 169.　　[4] J. Rhys, *Celtic Folk-Lore*, p. 373.

Fians. She appears to me to be a Caledonian, and therefore rougher and fiercer type, of the more southern mirage spirit.[1]

Morgan is held by some Welsh etymologists to signify " Born of the Sea." In German legend, says Grimm, Morgan is Femurgan, Famorgan, or Feimurgan, or Marguel; also Morguein de elwinne. Walter Scott rather insists upon a Persian derivation for her name, which he received from Herbelot, who cites such names from Oriental romance as the Peri Mergian Banou, over which we need scarcely linger here. In any case Herbelot .confounds Morgana with Urganda, and he has been imitated in his error.

Miss J. L. Weston, reviewing in *Folk-Lore* the *Studies in the Fairy Mythology of Arthurian Romance* of Miss Lucy A. Paton, asks if Morgan is *ab origine*, a Celtic fay. " And if certain qualities of the fay have been postulated of her, are we therefore bound to believe that *all* the essential characteristics must, at one time or another, have been hers? That is a question which must be proven and not assumed." Miss Paton seems inclined to equate her with the Irish Morrigan. But the reviewer believes the data concerning that figure to be too scanty to found upon and that they do not offer the material necessary for transition to the conventional fay. Five traits, she thinks, are postulated of Morgan in early lore. (1) She lives in the Isle of Avalon; (2) she is the chief of nine queens; (3) she can change her shape and fly through the air; (4) she possesses a magic ointment which will heal all wounds; (5) she carries off the wounded Arthur to her home in Avalon. These, Miss Weston says, are traits connected with the Scandinavian Valkyrie. In fact she thinks that Morgan, in her relation to Arthur, is a loan from Scandinavian tradition. She modifies this statement by adding that " the final identification was brought about by confusion between the Arthurian Morgan and an independent and powerful fairy being bearing a similar name. The belief may have been brought from the East by the Crusaders, and a careful examination of the fairy traditions of Sicily and the East might reveal that if the Crusaders absorbed traditions of Arthur and his sister, they also borrowed stories of a powerful fairy queen." [2]

But the very points cited by Miss Weston as being the implicits associated with Morgan in early lore serve to shake her analysis considerably. If Morgan was chief of nine queens, so was the

---

[1] K. Grant, *Myth, Tradition, and Story from W. Argyllshire*, pp. 13 ff.
[2] J. L. Weston, *Folk-Lore*, XIV, p. 437.

Banshee, who is sufficiently Celtic. And if Morrigan was not a Celtic " Valkyrie," what indeed was she? The Tuatha Dé Danann line of goddesses, to which the Morrigan belonged, all developed into fairies, as Nutt pointed out in a covering note to the aforesaid review. Morrigan, he also indicates, belongs to the earliest and rudest stage of Irish saga, " a survival from an older and more savage world." But he thinks it " untenable that the Morrigan story, as we know it in Irish tales of the seventh–twelfth centuries, could originate or account for the Morgan story in the twelfth-century French and Latin romances."

But is Nutt correct in his mythical diagnosis? That some members of the Arthur group are associated with the raven or chough as a symbol, as was the Morrigan, seems clear enough. Cornish tradition says it brings ill-luck to shoot a raven or chough, " as King Arthur is still alive in the form of that bird,[1] " and in the fifth chapter of the second book of *Don Quixote* a statement to the same effect is made. The name Arthur is said to be derived from " Arddhu," very black, evidently applied to a surrogate of Bran, " the Raven,"[2] while the name of Gawain, Arthur's nephew, is merely a Normanized form of Gwalchmai, which in Old British means " the Falcon of May." The Morrigan of Irish lore also appears in her " battle-dress " as a carrion-crow. At other times she is, as revealed by the spiteful trick of the Lady of Avalon, " a lean hag." The resemblance between Morgan la Fée and the Morrigan is therefore rather patent. Both were queens, for the Irish form of the name simply means " Great Queen," while Morgan la Fée was the wife of King Lot, or Lludd.

I must not press the analogy too far, but I believe that we are dealing here with a group of very ancient deities related one to the other, who may have been developed from bird-form through totemic or other processes. And if I have dwelt at some length upon the subject of Morgan's origins, it has been in an endeavour to display the difficulties which beset the student of folk-lore in tracing back the fay to the divinity in some instances. I must add, however, that the evidence that Morgan has a maritime association seems strong, and that this does not appear consonant with those other attributes of her which I have already described. But an entire volume might easily be written respecting these differentiations. In any case it seems fairly evident that Morgan

---

[1] *Choice Notes*, p. 70.
[2] R. Briffault, *The Mothers*, III, pp. 432–3, note.

la Fée stands in much the same relationship to Arthur as does the Morrigan to Cuchullin, and analogies have been drawn between the myths of both heroes. (See also J. Curtin, *Hero-Tales of Ireland*, xli–xliii.)

Gwyn ap Nudd—that is, son of Nudd, the heaven-god—was himself a British deity of battle and of the dead, who conducted the slain into the other-world and ruled over them there. Later he came to be regarded as the King of the Welsh fairies, the *Tylwyth Teg*, and the wild huntsman of Welsh folk-lore and that of the West of England. Here, then, we have a very clear case of the god who has later been metamorphosed into the fairy.[1]

There is some reason to think that Puck, in his particular guise of Robin Goodfellow, may be the later representative of a forgotten deity. Nutt believed that deities of growth were gradually elaborated out of primitive spirits of vegetation, who are essentially amorous and endowed with the power of transformation or reincarnation (as indeed is the grain they represent). " A vivid form of expressing this idea," he says, " is to represent the god amorous of a mortal maiden, and father by her of a semi-divine son whose nature partakes of his own, and who is at times a simple reincarnation of himself." He proceeds to consider the contents of the tract entitled *Robin Goodfellow, His Mad Pranks and Merry Jests*, which dates from the year 1628. This " doggerel chapbook," thinks Nutt, provides a " worn-down form of the same incident found in the legends of Arthur and Merlin, Cuchullin and Morgan, told also in Greek mythology of no less a person than Dionysus, son of Zeus and Semele." [2]

The tract, which is to be found in Hazlitt's *Fairy Tales and Romances Illustrating Shakespeare*, tells how a fairy king or " governor " had a son by a country girl. He was named Robin, and turned out a mischievous lad enough. In time King Oberon revealed himself to the youngster, calling him by the name of " son," and bearing him off to Fairyland, where he did " shew Robin Good-fellow many secrets, which hee never did open to the world." As Nutt remarks, the incident certainly finds its reflex in many a passage in pure mythology, and appears to illustrate a connection between fairy tradition and myth proper.

But yet another circumstance seems to fortify the assumption that Robin Goodfellow may represent a forgotten deity. The fairy

---

[1] C. Squire, *Mythology of the British Islands*, pp. 254–5.
[2] A. Nutt, *op. cit.*, pp. 30 ff.

of that name has been considered by some authorities to be identical with another character in folk-lore, now proved to be more fabulous than actual—bold Robin Hood. A May-time drama in celebration of the " forester of Sherwood " was certainly represented over the length and breadth of Britain until the end of the sixteenth century, and this evidently had reference not to a mortal archer, but to some deity of vegetation. A critical examination of Robin Hood's legend has made it plain that he never was "Earl of Huntingdon," as is alleged, and that the circumstances of his festival display all the characteristics of a ritual drama associated with a deity or spirit of vegetation or of the wild wood, a god of the spring-time.

A recent examination of the rolls of the Manor Court of Wakefield has made it clear that a forester named Robin Hood actually did exist, who appears to have been born about the year 1290; but as the Scottish historian, Fordun, writing in 1340, speaks of Robin Hood as a famous figure in drama and tradition at a time when the Wakefield Robin could not have been more than fifty, it is obvious that the Yorkshire forester could not have been one and the same with the legendary hero. The Robin of tradition was indeed King of the May, and his lady-love, Maid Marian, as certainly the May, or Spring Queen. He is obviously the shadow in legend of a ritual king who reigned from one May Day to the next, when, like the priest of the Golden Bough at Aricia, whose history has achieved world-fame through the studies of Sir James Frazer, he was compelled to fight for his title and his life, as the ballads concerning him reveal. In these he is usually defeated by a rival. He was, indeed, the human counterpart of a " king," or spirit of fertility whose waning vigour made it essential to put him to death and replace him by a stronger human representative. His alleged tomb, near Halifax, is described as a standing stone, or monolith, surrounded by a grove of sacred trees—such a spot as might well have been a centre of pagan worship—and miracles are said to have occurred there.[1] And it is significant that he is said to have been slowly bled to death by a treacherous abbess.

Jacob Grimm remarks upon the resemblance of Robin Goodfellow to Robin Hood. The name Robin is associated with " the devil " in British witchcraft, and I can find little difficulty in connecting the horned and hoofed satyr-like figure round which the

---

[1] L. Spence, "The Supernatural Character of Robin Hood," *Hibbert Journal*, XL, pp. 280 ff.; Lord Raglan, *The Hero*, pp. 47–56, 244 ff.

witches dance, which adorns the frontispiece of the tract of his *Merry Pranks*, with Robin, the spirit of vegetation, whom Lord Raglan in his book *The Hero* identifies as a spirit of the woodland, like " Jack-of-the-green." The distance between Robin Hood, the deity of springtime, and the fairy Robin Goodfellow, is by no means so great as that betwixt the Tuatha Dé Danann and the fairies of modern Ireland, and the causes which brought about such a degeneration were remarkably similar.[1]

At times, Shakespeare and the Elizabethan dramatists appear to confound fairies with classical forms. Shakespeare calls his fairy queen Titania, which, as we have seen, is a title of Diana, and in one of his songs Campion calls her Proserpina. To Reginald Scot, also, she was known as Diana. Mr. Henry B. Wheatley remarks on this particular head that " the fundamental difference between the folk-lore tradition and the literary treatment of fairies, mixed up with classical learning, is that in the latter case they are part of a system of evil spirits as opposed to the folk-lore assumption of mischievous soulless creatures."[2] So much can scarcely be said of Shakespeare's fairies, which, however disguised, accurately reflect the old English notion of rural spirits presiding over agriculture and public morals, as Nutt maintains. And I should like to add here, as I have already mentioned in passing, that fairly recent criticisms of certain Elizabethan descriptions of the fairies as exceedingly diminutive, such as those of Drayton and Lilly, are based upon a total misapprehension of the facts, not only antique evidence, but more modern folk-lore providing abundant testimony respecting the almost minute proportions of many ancient British elfin types, both in the south and west of England and in some parts of Wales and Ireland.

As I have said, to link the tradition of fairy spirits with older god-like forms is, in certain instances, a comparatively simple matter, while in others the process is frequently a perplexing one. It follows that if we are able to identify certain fairies with the gods of a discarded religion, as in the case of the Tuatha Dé Danann, a reasonable certainty exists that the same process has taken place in respect of other elfin types. Even so, we must not by any means assume that all fairy spirits are the " lineal descendants " of ancient gods, or even that some of the latter who reveal fairy

---

[1] Lord Raglan, *op. cit.*, p. 54.
[2] H. B. Wheatley, "The Folk-Lore of Shakespeare," *Folk-Lore*, XXXII, p. 379.

characteristics are so " descended." Wherever the proof is clear and sufficient it is competent to do so; otherwise it is rash and unscientific to assume such an origin. It is, for example, obvious that Morgan la Fée may well have been derived from a spirit of the elements. There appears to have been nothing in the nature of a cultus associated with her, which, after all, is the supreme test of original godhead; whereas in the case of Mab certain elements of cult-practice are indicated. We may conclude that some fairies are the degenerate representatives of gods, but we may do so only when their genealogy is capable of being entered in what might be described as the " Debrett," or " The Almanach de Gotha " of Fairyland.

CHAPTER IX

FAIRIES AS TOTEMIC FORMS

As is well known, many peoples in a primitive state of existence believe themselves either to be descended from, or to have kinship with, certain animals or plants. This belief is associated with the condition generally known as totemism, which has extensive social as well as religious significances which need not be touched upon here. The question before us is whether the animal, semi-animal, or human forms associated with the belief in totemism have contributed anything to the stock of fairy tradition. That they actually have done so to some extent is, I think, borne out by the evidence afforded in this chapter.

We have not to proceed very far before we encounter a plenitude of animal shapes in fairy lore. But these are indeed animals of a most unusual kind, gifted with powers of speech and magic, such as that Puss in Boots which attended the Marquis of Carabas. Jacob Grimm assures us that many of the house-spirits of old Germany have animal forms or associations. These are the *heinze* or *heinzelmann*, the *polterkater*, the *katermann*, the boot-cat, the squirrel, who dwell in the cellar or stable of the person whose society they have chosen,[1] and the same may be said of brownie, who possesses certain animal characteristics.

In the tales which recount the circumstances in which friendly fairies in animal shape come to the timely assistance of the sorely beset hero or heroine, we encounter forms which almost undoubtedly reveal their identity with the totemic ancestor or kinsman. Such stories, as I have already said, are not over-abundantly represented in British folk-tale, and those which have been officially recorded are mainly Scottish and have reference to Northern versions of the Cinderella theme, in which the friendly fairy bulks so largely. In one of these, *The Red Calf*, collected in Aberdeenshire, the neglected daughter is sent to herd the cattle, and gets only porridge and whey for her diet. But a red calf leads her through a wood to a fine house, where she feasts sumptuously. Later, the calf presents her with gorgeous clothes in which to go to church, where she meets with a prince.[2] In a similar

---

[1] J. Grimm, *Teutonic Mythology* (trans. by Stallybrass), p. 509.
[2] *Folk-Lore Journal*, II, pp. 72–4.

story from Inverness-shire the heroine is the daughter of a king by a sheep (a distinctly totemic trait), the animal being a princess in disguise.[1] To her great work *Cinderella*, a monument of personal devotion to the science of folk-lore, the late Miss Cox appended a long list of the tales in which helpful animals aid human beings to cut a figure of importance (p. 526), though few of these are of British provenance. Some friendly animal tales are furnished by Larminie in his *West Irish Folk-Tales*.

The astonishing facility for transforming themselves into animal shapes exhibited by the nymphs of classical mythology would appear to argue a distant connection between these fairy-like spirits and totemic forms. An analogous instance comes from Wales, for the fairy bride of Corwrion, when she leaves her husband, flies away in the shape of a wood-hen.[2] The very large number of tales relating to swan-maidens and seal-women collected by the industry of the late E. Sidney Hartland reveal many traits and incidents which can only be attributed to a totemic origin. It is needless once more to traverse ground which has been so admirably covered by a master of his subject in a work readily accessible to all and easily procured. Not a few of the tales he recounts are indubitably to be referred to a totemic origin.[3]

It is principally from native Australian and other primitive evidence that the connection between totemic spirits and fairies becomes manifest. I have already drawn attention to those savage tales which deal with the common origin of man with animals and plants. These are connected, so far as primitive Australia is concerned, with what is known as the *Alcheringa*, or " dream-time," of early human mythology—the age of man's first self-knowledge, when as yet all species were one and humanity had not separately developed from other forms of life; and they indeed present a saga of the savage notion of evolution.

These composite human-animal-plant creatures, we are told, deposited in the ground in certain spots a number of spirit-individuals who became men and women, and so founded the first totem-groups, or clans. Since that time, according to the tribes of North-eastern Australia, these spirit-individuals have been undergoing continual reincarnation. When a native man

---

[1] M. R. Cox, *Cinderella*, pp. 534–5.
[2] E. S. Hartland, *The Science of Fairy Tales*, p. 269.
[3] E. S. Hartland, *op. cit.*, pp. 255–332.

incarnating one of these spirits dies, the spirit which ensouled him returns to the spot where the original deposit of " spirit "-individuals was made and there awaits reincarnation or rebirth as a human infant. He chooses his next mother. Among the Arunta Blackfellows a very large number of places are associated with these *Alcheringa* spirits in respect of totem-groups connected with the kangaroo, emu, or certain plants. When a woman conceives, it is thought that one of these spirits has entered her, and the child, when born, is regarded as a reincarnation of one of the spirit-ancestors associated with the spot where she first so conceived; therefore it belongs to the totem-group connected with that spot.

The ancestor-spirits which inhabit these haunted localities (which are known as *okanikilla*) are always ready to pounce on any likely woman who may pass their abodes. Among the Arunta these spirits are associated with a stone or wooden oval slab, inscribed with totemic symbols, which object is known as a *churinga*, and this they are thought to leave behind at the spot where they enter a woman. Search is made for this object, and by its markings and the symbols it bears, it identifies the spirit, after which the child is duly named. The spots where these ancestor-spirits reside are usually marked by some natural feature —a tree, a rock, or a pool of water—and this spot where the spirit has awaited rebirth is known as the *nanja*.[1]

Among some Australian tribes these ancestral spirits are regarded as mischief-makers and workers of evil. They can make people sick or send madness upon them. These *Iruntarinia*, as they are called, says Wentz, " offer an almost complete parallel to the Celtic belief in fairies . . . they are a spirit race, inhabiting an invisible or fairy world. . . . Only certain persons, medicine-men and seers, can see them, and these describe them as thin and shadowy and, like the Irish *sidhe*, as always youthful in appearance. Precisely like their Celtic counterparts in general," they haunt certain spots " as in Ireland demons are believed to frequent certain places known to have been anciently dedicated to the religious rites of the pre-Christian Celts, and, quite after the manner of the Breton dead and of most fairies, they are said to control human affairs and natural phenomena."[2] The Celts,

---

[1] E. S. Hartland, *Primitive Paternity*, pp. 236 ff.; J. G. Frazer, *The Belief in Immortality*, I, p. 93 ff. See also M. F. Ashley-Montagu, *Coming into Being Among the Australian Aborigines* (*passim*).

[2] W. Y. E. Wentz, *The Fairy Faith in Celtic Countries*, p. 227.

as we know, both in ancient and modern times, have regarded themselves as incarnations or reincarnations of ancestors and fairy beings. Moreover, the Arunta of Australia think of the *Iruntarinia*, or spirits, as Celts think of fairies—as beings who must be propitiated, and as protecting and guardian entities, unless offended or neglected.

Now do we find any of these " totemic " beliefs reflected in Britain? We certainly do. I shall furnish some evidence of them as revealing that totemistic ideas must have existed among our primitive forefathers and that their notions of fairy-spirits may have been coloured by them. Moreover, where totemic ideas formerly prevailed, such beliefs as those presently held by the native Australians may also have been current. We have already seen that certain groves of trees were regarded as sacred in Scotland. Near the chapel of St. Ninian, in the parish of Belly, there formerly stood a row of trees which were regarded as sacred and from which no branch nor any fruit might be taken. In the Island of Skye, some two hundred years ago, there was a holy lake surrounded by a wood which none might cut or injure in any fashion. That these were the Scottish representatives of *nanja* trees, as found in Australia, and that they were originally regarded as the repositories of the spirits of the dead awaiting rebirth, seems most probable in view of the Australian and other evidence. As we shall see later on, when we come to deal with the evidence for the existence of fairy spirits in stones once associated with the burial of the dead, there is every reason to believe that these, too, were soul-repositories of those spirits awaiting reincarnation—*nanjas*, in fact. I must beware of pressing the analogy too far, but I cannot refrain from the belief that the peculiar spiral markings to be observed upon many sculptured stones in Scotland, and especially those which are of that class known as " cup-and-ring " stones, may have been developed from patterns of the same type as those to be seen on Australian *churingas*.

If we seek for evidence of early totemic belief in Britain and Ireland we shall not be altogether disappointed. In our ballads we frequently find that the soul may be transformed into a plant, an animal, a bird, a fish. or into some inanimate object.[1] There was formerly in Ireland an ancient belief that certain races or families were endowed with the power of assuming the forms of

[1] L. C. Wimberley, *Folk-Lore in English and Scottish Ballads*, p. 33.

wolves whenever they so pleased. In the Irish *Annals of the Four Masters* it is soberly set down that in the year A.D. 690 a wolf was heard speaking with a human voice. In Irish lore we also read of a king who was the son of a woman who was wooed by a suitor in the form of a bird. In consequence of this avian origin he was throughout his life debarred from hunting birds. The inference is obvious. " He was," says Professor Macalister, " a member of a bird totem, and the story has grown up at a late date when the nature and restrictions of totemism were being forgotten. Many of the ' population groups ' of ancient Ireland were called after animals, fire, the ploughshare, and other things which are pressed into the service of totemistic heraldry elsewhere." [1]

Walter Johnson thought that the shape of the gigantic British animal figures cut on hills—the " white horses " at Uffington and Bratton, for example—were at least partly of the nature of totemic memorials.[2] Some years ago Mr. H. MacColl pointed out in a newspaper correspondence that " the ancient totem-mark of the MacColls was a crescent moon with a five-pointed star caught between the horns. . . . As far as one can judge, this clan practised totem-worship or some features of it long after it had ceased to become generally practised. Thus it was unseemly for a MacColl to marry outside his own name "—which, by the way, is a direct reversal of most totemic practice.[3] In detailing the events which occurred previously to the death of Cuchullin, the great Irish hero, we are told that the three daughters of the wizard Calatin had cooked a hound on spits of the rowan tree. It was *geas*, or taboo, for Cuchullin to eat his namesake's flesh, for his name is associated with the dog. They jeered him into partaking of the mess, and he ate of the shoulder-blade of the hound and placed the bone under his left thigh. The hand that took it and the thigh under which he put it were stricken with palsy.[4] Ossian, the Gaelic bard, might not eat of deer's flesh, as his mother had been metamorphosed into a deer. His name means " Little Fawn," and when rallied because of his abstention from venison he was wont to remark: " When everyone picks his mother's shank-bone I will pick my own mother's slender shank-bone." [5]

R. A. S. Macalister, *The Archæology of Ireland*, p. 93.
W. Johnson, *Folk-Memory*, p. 332.
H. MacColl, in *The Scotsman* of May 25, 1936.
E. Hull, *The Cuchullin Saga*, pp. 254–5.
J. G. Campbell, *Superstitions of the Scottish Highlands*, p. 126, note.

A tribe of Cat-folk seem to have given their name to Caithness. The Gaelic name of *Cataibh*, given to Sutherland, appears to indicate an extension of the territory of this people, and the Duke of Sutherland was known as *Diuc Chat*, as a Sutherland man is still known as a *Catach*. In the same way the Orkneys are called *Inse Orc*, or the "Boar Islands."[1] The families of the Lees and the Coneelys in Ireland, and the MacCodrums in Scotland, are supposed to be descended from seals.[2] In some instances drawn from savage totemism the souls of men are thought of as migrating into their totemic animals after death, and when the animal in turn dies, its spirit enters that of a newly born infant.[3] This may explain the tradition of the friendly animal and that of the fairy taking animal form, as in later times these separate ideas would seem to have become confused in the tribal consciousness.

We see, then, that the general idea of totemic belief, with its notions of the interchange of spirit betwixt human and animal bodies and the approximation of the spirits of the dead, as recognized by those who entertain totemic beliefs, to fairy forms, can scarcely be separated from those ideas generally current concerning fairies or fairy-like spirits in many parts of the world. The likelihood is that the belief in totemic spirits derives from times considerably remote, and that their adaptation to the tradition of Faerie is part of a later process. Conversely, belief in totems and fairies may have been contemporaneous in their origin, as in Australia. The ancestral character of fairies certainly fortifies the assumption of their original totemic nature very considerably. The ideas concerning the Australian *Iruntarinia*, their reincarnation, their occasional spitefulness, their interim existence in trees, rocks, stones, and ponds, gives me the impression that they may represent an early substratum of ideas which, in conjunction with other beliefs, went to make up the general and original idea of fairy spirits. If I am right in my conclusions it becomes necessary to assume that beliefs so widely accepted over an area stretching from Australia to Northern Europe must indeed be of great antiquity, and that they must have radiated from a common centre.

[1] E. Hull, *Folk-Lore of the British Isles*, pp. 142–3.
[2] E. Hull, *op. cit.*, p. 155.
[3] J. G. Frazer, *Totemism and Exogamy*, II, pp. 551 ff.

CHAPTER X

OTHER THEORIES ABOUT FAIRY ORIGINS

IN this chapter I intend to deal with several of the minor and less important theories concerning the origin of the belief in fairies which at one time or another have made their appearance. Some of the older writers on folk-lore were of the opinion that the British fairy superstition was almost exclusively of Scandinavian provenance, and these claimed that certain of the myths of Norse mythology sufficiently accounted for the origin of the fairies in British tradition.

Grimm pointed out that the *Elder Edda*, one of the repositories of Norse mythology, in more than one passage associates the Aesir, or Northern gods, with the Alfar or Elves " as though they were a compendium of all higher beings," and states that the Anglo-Saxon words *es* and *ylfe* stand to each other in a relationship similar to that of the Norse denominations referred to. Alfar and Dvergar, or Elves and Dwarfs, are mentioned in the *Alvismal*, another Norse compilation, as beings apart, while in Norway elves and dwarfs are regarded as distinct species of spirits.[1]

It is true that in Norse mythology gods and elves are regarded as having the same divine character. But we have found that the Tuatha Dé Danann of Ireland, once gods, later degenerated into elves, and we have no evidence to show that much the same process did not come to pass in Scandinavian mythology. It seems probable that the elves of Scandinavia were at one time gods, perhaps the deities of an older race, who lost much of their pre-eminence and whose worship was superseded by that of a later people. For we certainly have proof that the elves were worshipped and sacrificed to in Scandinavia within historical times. Not only were such offerings made to them as we find in the case of British fairies, but a definite *alfablot*, or blood-sacrifice of animals, was devoted to them. In one passage in the *Kormaks-saga* we read of such a sacrifice being offered up on an elf-hill, where the gore of a bull slain to placate the elves is spilt on the soil, the animal's flesh being devoured by the spirits themselves

---

[1] J. Grimm, *Teutonic Mythology* (trans. Stallybrass), p. 442.

and not by men.[1] We must here recall the warning of Alfred Nutt that it is unwise to discriminate between the folk-lore beliefs of races which are both of " Aryan " origin, as the ideas of all Aryan races are susceptible of being traced to a common source. He particularly discredits those theories which seek to attribute British fairy origins solely to a Teutonic or a Celtic source on the score that both of these races possessed early common traditions concerning the spirit world and its denizens.

One Scandinavian legend relating to the origin of the elves has relationships with a class of story concerning their beginnings which I intend to discuss at some length. This tells us that when God visited Adam and Eve he requested Eve to allow him to see their children. He asked her if she had no more than those he saw, and she replied that she had not. The truth was that some of them had not been washed and that she had hidden them, as they " were not fit to be seen." Aware of her subterfuge, the Creator declared that those who had been hidden from him should also be hidden from mankind. So the dirty children became invisible and dwelt in the woods, on the heaths, in knolls, and in stones, and from them are the elves of the Northland descended.[2]

This rather amusing story brings us to the question of the influence of the Christian Church upon fairy belief. That this influence, from the point of view of the student of folk-lore, was of the most disastrous description is rather a sad commentary upon Christian liberality of thought. True, many a Christian minister has laboured strenuously to make good the deficiencies in our tradition which have been caused by the stupid and wrong-headed attitude of the Church to folk-tradition from its inception until " the day before yesterday." But my purpose here is not to castigate the Church for its narrow-minded attitude to folk-belief, or for the ignorant and perfectly absurd manner in which it confounded Fairyland and the Celtic Land of the Gods with the Jewish Hell, but to make it plain in what manner it influenced the belief in fairy spirits.

The earliest Christian missionaries, notably those sent to Britain by Pope Gregory the Great, turned a blind eye to rites associated with the fairies at their shrines in woodland and by water-side; and it seems probable that, as is certainly the case in Brittany, not a few of the less official saints of the Roman Church

<hr>

[1] J. Grimm, *op. cit.*, pp. 448, 1411; Meyer, *German Myth*, pp. 175 ff.
[2] W. A. Craigie, *Scandinavian Folk-Lore*, p. 142.

are merely fays disguised.   But when the Church found firmer ground beneath her feet in Britain and Ireland she began to stigmatize the fairy as a " devil " and to thunder forth threats of the most appalling kind against the spiritual condition of such as dared submit their offerings at elfin shrines.   Doom in the lowest abysses of Hell would be their part without recall.   Equally uncompromising was the attitude of early Protestantism.   Luther literally scoured the countryside in search of fairy changelings, and at least in one instance was only prevented from drowning an unhappy child through the intervention of the Elector of Saxony.   The great reformer then requested the people of Dessau to pray in the church that " the blessed God might take the imp away."   " This," Luther assures us in his *Table-Talk*, with evident satisfaction, " was done *daily*," and as a result the unhappy " changeling " died within a year's time.

There formerly existed in Scotland a fairly general belief that the fairies quitted North Britain at the time of the Protestant Reformation, a view which is recorded in the *Effigies Clericorum* of the Scottish poet Cleland.   Indeed, we seem to trace a similar belief in the well-known verses of Bishop Corbet, beginning " Farewell, Rewards and fairies."   The elves, he assures us, were " of the old profession " :—

> " Their songs were *Ave Maries*,
>   Their dances were procession."

Nevertheless we have the evidence of Chaucer that the Roman Church had done its zealous utmost to sweep England clear of the elvish " demons," a task in which it had succeeded, or thought it had, which is sometimes the same thing in the case of very anxious people.

But to the Dissenters of Wales, or some of them, the fairies were every bit as taboo as to monk and friar.   Edmund Jones, in his unconsciously amusing *Account of Aberystwyth*, produced at Trevecca in 1779, observes that the Episcopal Ordinance known as *The Book of Sports*, a harmless enough compilation legalizing certain games and holidays, roused all the devils in Wales.   " All Hell rejoiced in it, for there was a dreadful harvest of souls prepared for it.   Now did the Fairies frisk and dance and sing their hellish music, for the darkness of ignorance and vice in which they delighted returned again and feasts of sin were made for them."

Robert Kirk, the minister of Aberfoyle, who wrote *The Secret Commonwealth of Elves, Fauns, and Fairies*, expressed a more liberal view when he aired the opinion that the elves lived in expectancy of " a higher and more splendid state of Lyfe." [1]   A Ross-shire story tells how a beautiful green lady appeared to an old man who was reading the Bible, seeking to know if the Scriptures held out any hope of salvation for such as she.   The old man admitted that the sacred book made no mention of salvation for any but the seed of Adam, whereat she screamed loudly and plunged into the sea. [2]   Numerous versions of this tale are to be found in nearly all European countries.   Only one, I think, extended the wished-for hope.   It recounts how an Irish priest broke a chalice whilst saying mass.   To him appeared a little man wearing a red jacket, who asked if the Good People would reach Heaven at the end of the world.   The priest replied that they would if the " full writing of a pen of blood were to be found among the whole of them."   In some versions, however, the conclusion alludes to the impossibility of gathering even so small a quantity of blood from a phantom folk.

The general opinion in Wales, remarks Rhys, is that the fairies had been exorcised or banished from the Principality for a generation or more. [3]   The remarks of Reginald Scot, in his *Discovery of Witchcraft*, appear to make it clear that he at least believed that the Reformation had made a clean sweep of the fairies, along with witches, dwarfs, giants, and imps, and supernaturals of all sorts and species.   " Well, thanks be to God," he ejaculates, " this wretched and cowardly infidelity, since the preaching of the Gospel, is in part forgotten." [4]   " It is a common remark," observes Mr. Wirt Sikes, formerly American Consul at Cardiff, " that the Methodists drove them [the fairies of Wales] away from the district of Craig y Dinas in Glamorganshire, where their last court was held." [5]

In his beautiful little treatise on the fairies of old France, Alfred Maury humorously alludes to the anxious manner in which the writers of mediaeval romances assure their readers of the impeccable Christianity of the fays of whom they tell.   Thus Melusina impresses upon her husband Raymond that she is a

[1] R. Kirk, *Secret Commonwealth.* p. 113.
[2] J. F. Campbell, *Popular Tales of the West Highlands*, II, p. 75.
[3] J. Rhys, *Celtic Folk-Lore*, pp. 221, 228.
[4] R. Scot, *The Discovery of Witchcraft*, Bk. VII, ch. 15.
[5] Wirt Sikes, *British Goblins*, p. 6.

good Christian; while Melior, another fairy lady, recites to Parthenopex of Blois the profession of her faith. Maury adds, however, in a sly vein of mischief, that the fairies of Lower Brittany nourished a mortal hatred for the clergy, as for the Virgin. Days consecrated to her are non-days to them. In the seventeenth century a mass was actually celebrated at the church of Poissy in order to avert the wrath of evil fairies from the land.[1] One recalls that Oberon, King of the Fairies, as he appears in the romance of *Huon of Bordeaux*, so admirably translated by John Bourchier, Lord Berners, about the year 1544, expresses the most sublime sentiments respecting the Christian faith.

But the " blackguarding " of the fairies proceeded from age to age, sect vieing with sect in the most absurd manner in blackening the elfin record. Sir Laurence Gomme remarks that " Grimm's observation that the witches' devils (or familiars) have proper names so strikingly similar to those of elves and kobolds that one can scarcely think otherwise than that nearly all devils' names of that class are descended from older folk-names for those sprites," strikingly confirms the explanation he (Gomme) has " ventured to give as to the connection between witchcraft and fairycraft." [2]

The legend that the fairies were the proud angels who, with their chief Lucifer, fell from heaven, has a Christian, or more probably an anterior Jewish origin. In Ireland the fairies were thought to be Fallen Angels who were " not good enough to be saved nor bad enough to be lost," as the peasantry phrased it.[3] The Scandinavians formerly believed that when the Devil raised rebellion in heaven, he and all those who fought on his side were driven into outer darkness. Those who joined neither party were cast down to earth and doomed to live in knolls, fells, and stones, and they are called elves or huldu-folk.[4] The following rhyme on the genealogy of the fairies, translated from the Scottish Gaelic, is interesting as revealing the presence of the legend in Scotland :—

> " We are not of the seed of Adam,
> And Abraham is not our progenitor;
> But we are the offspring of the Haughty Father,
> Who out of Paradise was driven." [5]

---

[1] A. Maury, *Les Fées du Moyen Age*, pp. 50 ff.
[2] G. L. Gomme, *Ethnology in Folk-Lore*, p. 56, note 2.
[3] W. B. Yeats, *Irish Folk and Fairy Tales*, p. 1.
[4] W. A. Craigie, *op. cit.*, p. 431.
[5] W. Mackenzie, *Gaelic Incantations*, p. 51.

In the Anglo-Saxon dialogue of Satan and Solomon the answer to the question: "Whither went these angels?" is given as follows: "They were divided into three companies. One of these God placed in the vortex of the air, another in the vortex of the water, and a third in the abyss of Hell." In Jutland there is a tradition that when the Fallen Angels were cast out of heaven some of them fell on the mounds or barrows and became Mound-folk. Others descended into the elf-moors and became elves, while others dropped into human dwellings, and from these last were descended the domestic sprites resembling the brownies.[1] In the poem known as *Altus Prosator*, attributed to St. Columba, the story of the fall of the angels from heaven is told. "The idea is still prevalent in Ireland," says Miss Eleanor Hull, "that the meddling and malicious fairies are the angels who fell with Lucifer, and who were on their way down to hell when our Lord held up his hand, which caused them to remain stationary wherever they happened to be at the time." This, she adds, seems to find an echo in the poem in question, which narrates that "the spaces of the air are closely crowded with a disordered crew of rebel satellites, held invisible lest man should become infected by their evil examples and their crimes, if there were no wall or screen between him and them." [2]

In Cornwall the Small People are believed by some to be the spirits of those who inhabited that country many thousands of years ago, and who, being pagans, were not worthy to merit the joys of heaven, yet were too good to be condemned to eternal flames. When they first came into the Duchy they were much larger than they are now, but ever since the birth of Christ they have been getting smaller and smaller.[3] We may compare the latter part of this statement with the Irish tradition that the Tuatha Dé Danann, when no longer worshipped and fed with offerings, "dwindled away in the popular imagination and are now only a few spans high." [4]

The legend of the apostasy of the Rebel Angels and the Scriptural and Apocryphal accounts of them, are, I believe, merely late versions of the classical legend of the fall of the Titans, or giants, and their expulsion from Olympus. The statement that these apostate spirits were "angels" does not make its appearance

---

[1] W. C. Mackenzie, *The Races of Ireland and Scotland*, p. 48.
[2] E. Hull, *Folk-Lore*, XXI, pp. 424 ff.
[3] R. Hunt, *Popular Romances of the West of England*, pp. 80–1.
[4] W. B. Yeats, *op. cit.*, p. 1.

M

until they are so described in the Book of Enoch, and Josephus, who was himself a Jew, identifies these " angels " with the Greek Titans.   The story was embraced by the early Christian writers, who gave full currency to it.   In the Book of Genesis the spirits in question are alluded to as " Sons of God," and no mention of angels is made there.

Lastly, in seeking among the more fantastic origins for the fairy superstition, we come to that which asserts that the elves are really a species of human beings.   This theory was upheld by Johannes Prætorius in his *Anthropodemus Plutonicus*, and by a venerable Icelandic pastor, Einar Gudmund, who is quoted by Torfæus in his preface to the Hrolf Krakas saga.   " I believe," said this divine, " that this people are the creatures of God, consisting of a body and a rational spirit; that they are of both sexes; marry and have children; and that all human acts take place among them as with us; that they are possessed of cattle, and of many other kinds of property; have poverty and riches, weeping and laughter, sleep and wake, and have all other affections belonging to human nature; and that they enjoy a longer or shorter term of life according to the will and pleasure of God." [1]   This is quite a useful if unsolicited testimonial to the acumen of those who are of opinion that the superstition regarding the fairies originated in the beliefs of primitive people respecting the dead, whom they thought of as living a life underground almost in every way similar to that which they had pursued while they were alive.

[1] T. Keightley, *The Fairy Mythology*, pp. 157-8.

CHAPTER XI

VESTIGES OF CULT IN FAIRY TRADITION

WRITERS upon the subject of the fairy tradition have frequently suggested that much of the material concerning fairy practice and belief which has come down to us is suggestive of the former existence of a cultus of worship of which the fairies were the objects or governing spirits. This theory, to which I will draw attention in the present chapter, has received its most important demonstrations at the hands of foreign students of tradition, particularly in France, Germany, and Scandinavia. But I do not wish to infer that most valuable hints have not already been thrown out as to the cult-like character of much British fairy lore by some of our native exponents of it. The suggestions of Nutt and Gomme can certainly not be overlooked in assessing what has been accomplished in this particular field of elfin study. But cogent as are their arguments, they are to a great extent unsupported by adequate research and unfortified by collected material; nor has such evidence as they present been classified in such a manner as to illustrate sufficiently the opinions of these gifted critics of a vexed and complicated theme and render them of definite value. My endeavour in this place will be to present, as fully as my space permits, the evidence forthcoming from the British area in support of the theory that the fairy tradition is to a large extent the broken-down folk-memory of a definite and far-reaching cultus or system of worship which must, at a distant epoch, have had sanctions in practically every part of the British insular group. The collection of this evidence has occupied the better part of a lifetime; but here I may employ only its more salient and important examples, as to review the whole in its entirety would necessitate the publication of at least another volume of a bulk equal to this.

The association of fairy spirits with certain days of the week and times of the year is eloquent of the former existence of religious festivals with which they must have been identified. In many parts of the world we find the worship of gods associated with certain weekly or seasonal occasions; indeed, this relationship is so familiar as scarcely to need more than passing reference. The connection of fairies with certain times of the year in Britain, especially with the seasonal festivals of Bealltainn or May Day, and Samhain (Hallowmass, or November 1), is significant. It is to be remarked, however, that they are by no means the only supernatural beings active at these seasons, practically all supernaturals being associated with the events in question. Whether or not this connection is one of late acceptance is for the moment beside the question. The Scottish elves, says one authority, came out of their dwellings on Rood Even (May 2), when they enjoyed their first dance of the year, their last taking place on October 31; that is, Hallowe'en, or Hallow Eve.[1] In Scottish ballads, such as *Tam Lin* and *Alison Gross*, we have a picture of the elves roaming about on the eve of Hallowe'en, the last night of the Celtic year, when they appear to make a world-wide tour.

So far as the association of the fairies with the days of the week is concerned, we find it regarded as unpropitious to make mention of them on Mondays and Thursdays in some parts of Ireland.[2] In other parts of that island it was ominous to speak of them on Wednesdays and Fridays, particularly upon the latter day.[3] Wednesday, says evidence hailing from the North of England, " is the fairies' Sabbath or holiday." [4] A Scottish Highland tradition states that the fairy host were powerless for evil on Thursday.[5] " When you speak of them you should always say the day of the week " was the earnest advice proferred by an old Irish woman to Lady Gregory.[6] In the Western isles of Scotland it is not considered lucky to call Friday by its proper name. It should be spoken of as " the day of yonder town "; that is, the danger of allusion to it should be transferred to some imaginary spot.[7] From the above it will be seen that no uniformity exists concerning such days as were thought of as associated with the fairies, and that Tuesday, Saturday, and Sunday are omitted from the catalogue. This, however, does not seem to me to detract from their significance, as local practice may have been a ruling factor in their selection.

It appears that, if there is anything of value in the theory of an " official " fairy cultus, we may expect to find it associated in some manner with the seasonal religious festivals of the Celtic

---

[1] *British Calendar Customs, Scotland* (Folk-Lore Society), II, p. 245.
[2] L. Duncan, " Fairy Beliefs from Leitrim," *Folk-Lore*, VIII, p. 174.
[3] Lady Wilde, *Ancient Legends of Ireland*, p. 72.
[4] *Denham Tracts*, II, p. 115.
[5] A. Carmichael, *Carmina Gadelica*, II, p. 240.
[6] Lady Gregory, *Visions and Beliefs in the West of Ireland.*
[7] J. G. Campbell, *Superstitions of the Scottish Highlands*, p. 19.

race, which for centuries were recognized in these islands, and the names of which in some areas still refer to our quarterly periods. These were the annual high points of an ancient solar and agricultural religion, side by side with which the remains of a much older nature-worship of trees, stones, and waters still proceeded.

This Celtic worship, the rites and circumstances of which were quite as definitely fixed and as formally conducted as any recorded in religious history, centred around the four days in the year which mark the rise, progress, and decline of the sun, and therefore of agricultural and vegetable growth and animal bringing-forth. These were Bealltainn, on May 1; Midsummer Day; the feast of the sun-god Lugh, in August, when the sun's turning-point has been reached; and Samhain, or Hallowmass (November 1), when the great luminary was regarded either as banished or imprisoned by the forces of winter. Of these the first and last were the more important. The first day of May was notoriously a season when supernatural beings of all kinds held high revel, whilst the Hallowmass festival had an equal notoriety for the proximity of uncanny spirits.

At Bealltainn, or May Day, every effort was made to scare away the fairies, who were particularly dreaded at this season. In the West Highlands charms were used to avert their influence.[1] In the Isle of Man the gorse was set alight to keep them at a distance.[2] In some parts of Ireland the house was sprinkled with holy water to ward off fairy influence.[3] These are only a mere handful out of the large number of references available, but they seem to me to reveal an effort to avoid the attentions of discredited deities on occasions of festival once sacred to them. The gods duly return at the appointed season, but instead of being received with adoration, they are rebuffed by the descendants of their former worshippers, who have embraced a faith which regards them as demons.

In like manner the fairies in Ireland were chased away from the midsummer bonfires by casting fire at them.[4] At the first approach of summer, the fairy folk of Scotland were wont to hold a " Rade," or ceremonial ride on horseback, when they were liable to tread down the growing grain.[5] This celebration has,

[1] J. F. Campbell, *Popular Tales of the West Highlands*, II, p. 63.
[2] E. Hull, *Folk-Lore of the British Isles*, p. 251.
[3] Lady Wilde, *op. cit.*, p. 108.   [4] Lady Wilde, *op. cit.*, p. 141.
[5] R. H. Cromek, *Remains of Nithsdale and Galloway Song*, p. 239.

I think, all the appearance of such processional rides as we read of in connection with the remains of the cult of " Godiva," at Coventry and the neighbouring villages, and which have been so ably discussed by Gomme and Hartland.[1] I should add, however, that, particularly on the occasion of Samhain, bonfires were lit with the express intention of scaring away the demonic forces of winter, and we know that, at Bealltainn in Scotland offerings of baked custard were made within the last hundred and seventy years to the eponymous spirits of wild animals which were particularly prone to prey upon the flocks—the eagle, the crow, and the fox, among others. Indeed, at these seasons *all* supernatural beings were held in peculiar dread. It seems by no means improbable that these circumstances reveal conditions arising out of a later solar pagan worship in respect of which the cult of fairy was relatively greatly more ancient, and perhaps held to be somewhat inimical.

W. B. Yeats, in his notes to Lady Gregory's *Visions and Beliefs in the West of Ireland*, remarks that she tells a story of " the crying of new-dropped lambs of faery in November," and some evidence seems to exist that an idea prevailed that in the fairy sphere there is a reversal of the seasons, our winter being their summer. Some such belief seems to have been known to Robert Kirk, for he tells us that " when we have plenty they [the fairies] have scarcity at their homes." In respect of the Irish fairies they seem to have changed their residences twice a year: in May, when the ancient Irish " flitted " from their winter houses to summer pastures, and in November, when they quitted these temporary quarters.

Even until recently offerings were made in Ireland to the fairies at Samhain, or Hallowmass. W. B. Yeats says that " the offering to the *Sidhe* is generously made at Hallowe'en, the old beginning of winter (October 31), and upon that night I was told when a boy *the offering was still made in the slums of Dublin*." [2] At Waterford, says Miss E. Hull, Hallowe'en was known as " the night of mischief and confusion, partly, no doubt, because the fairies made it so." [3] The old Irish tale of the adventures of Nera reveals how risky it was to go out-of-doors on that night,

[1] G. L. Gomme, *Ethnology in Folk-Lore*, pp. 36–40; E. S. Hartland, *The Science of Fairy Tales*, p. 76.

[2] W. B. Yeats, in notes to Lady Gregory's *Visions and Beliefs in the West of Ireland*.

[3] E. Hull, *op. cit.*, p. 232.

when all the fairy raths were open.[1] Fairy hills in Perthshire were also to be entered on that date, for if anyone went alone round one of these eminences nine times, keeping towards the left hand, a door would open and he would be admitted to the elfin realm.[2] Lads with torches paraded round the farms in Scotland at Hallowe'en to protect land, steading, and cattle from the fairies.[3] On the twenty-fourth night of Yule in Shetland, an event formerly held in November, the trows, or fairies, were driven out of the house in pantomime.[4] At that time children might be kidnapped by the elves, unless care was exercised. These examples, I think, make it clear that throughout Celtic Britain a very definite belief obtained until comparatively recent times that the fairies had an extraordinary influence at certain seasons once associated with religious ritual occasion, either as discredited deities, or because they were regarded as unfriendly to a still later pagan faith.

If we turn now to such vestiges of cult as are associated otherwise than with time and season, we discover a definite recognition of the survival of these nearly a century ago. Keightley, the old fairy mythologist, who did such yeoman service in the collection of much valuable elfin lore, says, as long ago as 1850, when referring to the confused nature of his subject: " Indeed it could not well be otherwise, when we recollect that all these beings (the larger and greater fairies) once formed part of ancient and exploded systems of religion and that it is chiefly in the traditions of the peasantry that their memorial has been preserved." [5] Long before his time, Burton, in his *Anatomy of Melancholy*, alluding to the fairies, said that some placed them in the rank of demons " which have been in former times adored with much superstition."

We have already seen that fairy cults have survived in Italy, as that of Aradia, described by Leland, and in other European areas. Why not also in Britain? Elf-worship was certainly indulged in in ancient Scandinavia, for we find in the Kormak Saga that the hill of the elves is to be reddened by the blood of a slaughtered bull, the flesh of which is to be offered to its denizens.[6] This is further attested to, says Jacob Grimm, by the former

[1] E. Hull, *op. cit.*, pp. 246–7.
[2] P. Graham, *Sketches of Perthshire*, pp. 249–50.
[3] A. MacGregor, *Highland Superstitions*, p. 44.
[4] Edmondston and Saxby, *The Home of a Naturalist*.
[5] T. Keightley, *The Fairy Mythology*, p. 13.
[6] J. Grimm, *Teutonic Mythology* (trans. Stallybrass), p. 447.

existence of a rite known as the *Alfablot*, or " elf-blood," which was performed in one's own house.[1] The jinn of Arabia, who so closely resemble our own fairies in almost every respect, have a rite paid to them known as *sufra-sabzi*; that is, " the table spread on the greensward," which is also known as " the feast for the Daughter of the Fairy King." Its purpose, says Professor R. A. Nicholson, " is to propitiate the jinn whose anger has been aroused " and who have in consequence smitten someone with sickness. For the feast three sacrifices are provided—a fowl, a sheep, and a pigeon—and the rite is held in "a fairy-haunted glade." [2]

" I would urge," declared Alfred Nutt, " that the love of neatness and orderly method so characteristic of the fairy world is easily referrible to a time when all the operations of rural life formed part of a definite religious ritual, every jot and tittle of which must be carried out with minute precision." He proceeded to say that the ritual of the fairy cultus, rapid dancing and other orgiastic circumstances, recall the rites of Dionysus. " These deities," he concludes, meaning the fairies in their earlier state, " gradually developed out of primitive spirits of vegetation, who were essentially amorous." In the tract of *Robin Goodfellow*, to which I have already drawn attention, he thinks we have the memory of a British myth about Faerie referrible to a period when it had a religious aspect. Robin is the son of a fairy king by a mortal maid. His father endows him with powers of shape-shifting, and tells him that if he obeys his behests he will one day see Fairyland.[3]

In an early Irish hymn attributed to St. Fiacc, and dedicated to St. Patrick, we find the worship of the *sidhe* actually alluded to. " On Erin's folk lay darkness," proclaims this ancient strain, " the tribes worshipped the *Sidhe*." [4] Now this is among those instances in which the word *sidhe* does not imply supernatural beings in general, but particularly the *Fir Sidhe* or people of the mounds. It thus reveals a very definite tradition of the worship of the fairies in ancient Ireland, before the advent of St. Patrick. Further evidence of such a cult of the *sidhe* is to be found in the strange yet prepossessing fragment known as *The Sick-bed of*

---

[1] J. Grimm, *op. cit.*, p. 1411.
[2] R. A. Nicholson, " Some Notes on Arabian and Persian Folk-Lore," *Folk-Lore*, XLI, p, 355.
[3] A. Nutt, *Folk-Lore*, XXXII, p. 47.
[4] Whitley Stokes, *Gaedelica*, p. 131.

Cuchullin, which describes his love-affair with Fand, and in which we are informed that that hero was given a drink of forgetfulness so that he should be " destroyed by the People of the Mound; for the power of the demons was great before the advent of the faith; so great was that power that the demons warred against men in bodily form, and they showed delights and secret things to them; and that those demons were co-eternal was believed by them. So that from the signs that they showed, men called them the Ignorant Folk of the Mounds, the People of the *Sidhe*." [1]

This passage, it is known, was added by the early editor or compiler of the romance in question. As Cuchullin was undoubtedly one of the forms of the Irish sun-god, it cannot but have reference to a myth which tells of the baneful manner by which the sun was " destroyed " or rendered powerless during the winter months by the subterranean forces. The fragment is, of course, deeply tinged with Christian bias against the *sidhe* or fairy folk, but it casts light on the reason why the fairies were so dreaded on the occasions of the Irish solar festivals. At the festival of Samhain they evidently succeeded in applying a draught of forgetfulness to the sun-god, who consequently remained in a comatose condition throughout the winter. In one version " Druids " are spoken of as having administered the draught, but we must suspect this as a late interpolation. It is indeed strange that this passage in the Cuchullin saga has not before been recognized as explanatory of the disappearance of the sun-god at Samhain. Its very title, *The Sick-bed of Cuchullin*, seems to have reference to a myth which in its pristine entirety must have narrated the weakness or infirmity of the sun-god during the winter months. The older cultus here manifests its hostility to the solar pagan institution. Or have we to do with a pantheon of the underworld powers in dualistic opposition to the luminary of day? The Tuatha Dé Danann and the fairies were one and the same. More than one of the Tuatha Dé is a god of brightness and solar light. It was the insistence of Christian scribes and other meddlers with the ancient manuscripts of Ireland which transformed them into " demons." Nevertheless, I think we have here a fragment of a myth which tells of a discredited race of gods acting as demons of darkness in a hostile manner against the sun-god of a newer cultus, probably that of

[1] A. H. Leahy, *Heroic Romances of Ireland*, p. 184, note.

the Milesians, who banished the gods of the Tuatha Dé Danann into the mounds or *sidhe*. Cuchullin is described as the "son" of Lugh, the sun-god of the Tuatha Dé. Sonship is a circumstance notorious in the case of supplanting deities. Throughout the whole Cuchullin Saga, in short, we find that hero in opposition to the fairy, or folk of the *sidhe*. At the period of his story, the events of which are usually attributed to the first century of the Christian era, it may perhaps be inferred, his cult had partially superseded that of the *sidhe*.

Miss Eleanor Hull has given it as her convinced opinion that the Tuatha Dé Danann, later the Irish fairies, were formerly an older pantheon of native deities. They were, she says, "the *dii terreni*, or spirits of the earth. They were, no doubt, the god-powers of whom the Kings of Tara were the reincarnation," and rites associated with the inauguration of the kings of Ireland were held at that place in connection with them. A study of the taboos imposed on these kings strengthens this view. They were the repositories of god-like powers incarnated in them, and in whose preservation the well-being of the people at large was involved. [1]

Let us examine a little more particularly such rites and ceremonies as would appear to confirm the former existence of a fairy cultus. Certain cups and chalices said to have been stolen from the fairies seem to have enshrined traditions of a sacrificial character. Hartland devotes several pages to this aspect of the fairy cultus which I cannot elaborate here, tempting though it is to do so. [2] We have already seen that oblations of milk were offered to some Scottish fairies, particularly the *gruagach* and the *glaistig*, who tended the herds. "In every district," wrote Brand, "there is to be met with a rude stone consecrated to *Gruagach* or Apollo." [3] "There are two hills in the Highlands of Aberdeenshire," says Wentz, "where travellers had to propitiate the *banshee* by placing barley-meal cakes near a well on each hill; and if the traveller neglected the offering, death or some dire calamity was sure to follow." [4] Wood-Martin, writing of the *sidhe* hills of Ireland, says that "in and around them the family or clan . . . assembled for worship." [5]

At a place known as "Wilkie's Knolls," two burial mounds

<hr>

[1] E. Hull, *op. cit.*, pp. 271 f.
[2] E. S. Hartland, *op. cit.*, Chapter VI, *passim*.
[3] J. Brand, *Popular Antiquities*, II, p. 16.
[4] W. Y. E. Wentz, *The Fairy Faith in Celtic Countries*, p. 437.
[5] W. G. Wood-Martin, *Pagan Ireland*, p. 85.

near Pier o' Wall, Westray, Orkney, libations of milk were made daily by the inhabitants little more than a century ago, and this offering was poured into a hole in the centre of one of the tumuli. If the practice were not carried out daily the people believed that " Wilkie," the presiding spirit of the knolls, would steal their clothes, haunt their houses, and inflict disease upon the cattle.[1] Such damage is precisely that which the fairies notoriously visit upon those who tempt their displeasure, and I have no doubt that " Wilkie " was of the elfin strain. Food was left for the fairies in many parts of Britain, and water in which they might wash themselves. In 1649 the Kirk Session of Humbie, in Haddingtonshire, dealt with a certain Agnes Gourlay, who poured milk down a drain, saying: " God betuch us to, they are under the yird [earth] that have as much need of it as they that are above the yird." [2]

Offerings of cheese were made to the fairies on the summit of Minchmuir, a height in Peebles-shire where there is a spring known as " the cheese-well." [3] An old dame in Northumberland, we are told, nightly set aside " a loake of meal and a pat of butter " for the good folk, as lately as the third quarter of last century, claiming that " she got a double return from them." [4] Until recently, Norwegian peasants on the eve of a holiday were wont to visit the mounds of the elves and make offerings of cake and porridge.[5] An old woman in the Isle of Man remembered seeing a live sheep burnt " for a sacrifice " on May Day—a day, remarks Rhys, referring to this incident, " when systematic efforts were made to protect man and beast against elves and witches." [6] A " magical stone " at Altagore, County Antrim, was famous as the site of food-gifts offered to " the Grogan," the name for a fairy in the North of Ireland.[7] Even human sacrifice to the fairies is occasionally hinted at. A fairy man in Leitrim informed a cottager that elfin treasure could be acquired, but that to gain it a life must be lost: " a dog or a cat would do." The seeker was to raise his hearthstone and place the victim beneath it. The man followed his instructions, found a crock of gold in the cavity, and

---

[1] MS. letter by J. Paterson, dated 1833, in Library of Society of Antiquaries, Edinburgh.

[2] J. G. Dalyell, *The Darker Superstitions of Scotland*, p. 193, note.

[3] W. Scott, *Minstrelsy of the Scottish Border*, II, p. 309.

[4] *Denham Tracts*, II, p. 143.

[5] G. Henderson, *Folk-Lore of the Northern Counties*, p. 2.

[6] J. Rhys, *Celtic Folk-Lore*, p. 307.

[7] W. G. Wood-Martin, *op. cit.*, p. 307.

near Pier o' Wall, Westray, Orkney, libations of milk were made daily by the inhabitants little more than a century ago, and this offering was poured into a hole in the centre of one of the tumuli. If the practice were not carried out daily the people believed that " Wilkie," the presiding spirit of the knolls, would steal their clothes, haunt their houses, and inflict disease upon the cattle.[1] Such damage is precisely that which the fairies notoriously visit upon those who tempt their displeasure, and I have no doubt that " Wilkie " was of the elfin strain. Food was left for the fairies in many parts of Britain, and water in which they might wash themselves. In 1649 the Kirk Session of Humbie, in Haddingtonshire, dealt with a certain Agnes Gourlay, who poured milk down a drain, saying: " God betuch us to, they are under the yird [earth] that have as much need of it as they that are above the yird." [2]

Offerings of cheese were made to the fairies on the summit of Minchmuir, a height in Peebles-shire where there is a spring known as " the cheese-well." [3] An old dame in Northumberland, we are told, nightly set aside " a loake of meal and a pat of butter " for the good folk, as lately as the third quarter of last century, claiming that " she got a double return from them." [4] Until recently, Norwegian peasants on the eve of a holiday were wont to visit the mounds of the elves and make offerings of cake and porridge.[5] An old woman in the Isle of Man remembered seeing a live sheep burnt "for a sacrifice" on May Day—a day, remarks Rhys, referring to this incident, " when systematic efforts were made to protect man and beast against elves and witches." [6] A " magical stone " at Altagore, County Antrim, was famous as the site of food-gifts offered to " the Grogan," the name for a fairy in the North of Ireland.[7] Even human sacrifice to the fairies is occasionally hinted at. A fairy man in Leitrim informed a cottager that elfin treasure could be acquired, but that to gain it a life must be lost: " a dog or a cat would do." The seeker was to raise his hearthstone and place the victim beneath it. The man followed his instructions, found a crock of gold in the cavity, and

---

[1] MS. letter by J. Paterson, dated 1833, in Library of Society of Antiquaries, Edinburgh.
[2] J. G. Dalyell, *The Darker Superstitions of Scotland*, p. 193, note.
[3] W. Scott, *Minstrelsy of the Scottish Border*, II, p. 309.
[4] *Denham Tracts*, II, p. 143.
[5] G. Henderson, *Folk-Lore of the Northern Counties*, p. 2.
[6] J. Rhys, *Celtic Folk-Lore*, p. 307.
[7] W. G. Wood-Martin, *op. cit.*, p. 307.

a twelvemonth later, still footing it with the elves, or ghosts, they are amazed when told that they have been tripping it for an entire year without cessation.

Frequently the fairies seem to adopt the style of dancing engaged in by the natives of the country they inhabit, precisely as they sometimes adopt its costume. Thus in Britain we may expect to find them engaging in our native "hornpipes, jigs, strathspeys, and reels," and country dances generally, and the best proof of this is that they frequently employ local pipers or fiddlers as their musicians, who would normally be ignorant of any other species of melody. But tales which describe such a condition may well be late and locally inspired. Have we any dependable data which may give us to realize the nature of a genuine fairy dance, apart from late rustic inventions concerning elfin terpsichorean fashions? Alfred Nutt has, with insight, compared the fairy dance with that frenzied measure which inspired the wild-haired devotees of Bacchus, to whom Robin Goodfellow bears so close a resemblance in certain of his characteristics. " A psychological reason (for the tripping of the elves by moonlight) may be sought in the opinion that night is essentially (in savage philosophy) the time for growth, vegetable and animal." [1] Thus the fairy dance may be associated with the growth of the crops, as was that of Bacchus with the growth of the vine and fruit generally, and as the wild orgiastic measures danced at the festival of the Mexican goddess Tlazolteotl were connected with the bringing-forth of vegetation. As Canon MacCulloch has it, the fairy dance may connect the fairies with actual rites of an orgiastic character among the folk, performed for purposes of agricultural magic. [2] It seems to me that precisely as Britons of the twelfth, seventeenth, or eighteenth centuries thought of fairy dancing in terms of their own rustical jiggings or reelings, so earlier British man must have regarded elfin capers as the reflex of his own more primitive " footwork," imitative of the symbolic or magical measures he employed in the dancing-out of fertility rites.

" Till of late years," says Miss Eleanor Hull, " Derbyshire men believed that Morris-dancing was borrowed from the fairies." [3] A survival of a dance which traditionally may have been borrowed from alleged fairy practice is that of " Green Garters," which,

---

[1] A. Nutt, *The Voyage of Bran*, II, p. 224.
[2] J. A. MacCulloch, Article on " Fairy " in Hastings' *Encyclopedia*, Vol. V.
[3] E. Hull, *Folk-Lore*, XIII, p. 426.

says Miss M. A. Murray, " was throughout England, the customary introduction to the Maypole rites." [1] Witch-dances were usually performed by the participators, men and women, placing themselves alternately with their backs to the centre and tripping in a circle, and the English edition of Olaus Magnus provides a picture of elves disporting themselves much in this manner. The frontispiece to the chap-book of *Robin Goodfellow,* frequently alluded to in these pages, shows the fairy folk dancing round that spirit in this fashion, the sexes placed alternately, with Robin himself, horned, and footing-it like a very Bacchus, in their midst. The " Horned Dance," still celebrated at Abbot's Bromley, in which the dancers are tricked out in deer's antlers, and some other ancient measures, may be survivals of very ancient fertility dances which afford us some general idea of the kind of movement which fairy dancing was supposed to reflect.

The " fairy rings " so commonly seen in our fields, and which are probably caused by a species of mushroom spawn, were regarded as the results of fairy midnight trippings; and as old Olaus Magnus remarks, " they [the elves] make so deep an impression on the earth that no grass grows there, being burned with extreme heat." [2] The cumulative evidence, I think, especially that which bears upon its resemblance to the dances of fertility rites, makes it plain that fairy dancing had a ritual complexion, and was no mere expression of elfin joyousness and vitality. Especially does this seem so when we consider the very extensive volume of proof of the ritual character of the dances of the dead in barbaric folk-lore, which I have no space to describe here, the literary references to which are scattered over a generous tract of bibliographical and journalistic citation in the annals of anthropological research.

We now approach that class of evidence which alludes to traditions of fairy association with standing stones and other rude stone monuments. As I have said, but little has been accomplished in British folk-lore in this particular department of the subject, though in France a quite respectable literature has grown up around it since the beginning of this century. It is, however, to such data concerned with this topic as applies to our own islands that I must confine myself. The amount of material I have gathered respecting this part of the fairy tradition is very

---

[1] M. A. Murray, *The God of the Witches,* p. 111.
[2] Olaus Magnus, *History of the Goths,* III, p. 10.

considerable. But here I must restrict it to such limits as will serve to support my main hypothesis that the fairy belief has intimate associations with religious rite and practice.

The theory that the spirits or ghosts of the dead take up their dwelling in standing stones which mark their places of sepulture is a venerable one, and is familiar to readers of folk-lore chiefly through the admirable conclusions of the late Grant Allen in his *Evolution of the Idea of God.* Here I need not stress it farther; but if we can substantiate the tradition that fairies also reside in standing stones, we shall have gone far to prove their general resemblance to the spirits of the departed. It may be thought that if fairies haunt the monuments of the New Stone Age the belief in them must necessarily have had its origin in the Neolithic period. But in support of such a supposition we have no evidence, and we do know that they also haunt structures of a much later period—brochs, barrows of the Iron Age, and so forth, as temporal and local superstitions dictate—to say nothing of churchyards. Indeed, the elves appear to be associated with the sepultures of almost every period.

Now, in some parts of the British Isles we find standing stones still regarded as the effigies, or " statues," of the dead persons, who are frequently, if not invariably, buried underneath or beside them. In Ireland and the Southern Highlands of Scotland such standing stones are known as *Fear Breagach*—that is, " false men "—and such " statue menhirs " are fairly widely known in France.[1] Martin tells us that in the Island of Lewis, in his time, people believed that monoliths were men turned by enchantment into stones, and that these were known as *Fir Chreig*, or " false men " (Martin mis-spells the second word). All over Britain stones are to be found which were once believed to be men or women transformed into boulders or monoliths by the sleights of some malignant enchanter. A mere list of such stones would occupy several pages. Some of these stones, too, are thought to have the power of motion at midnight, and to dance on certain occasions. The point is that these monoliths, sometimes free-standing, sometimes associated with stone-circles, were regarded as " statues," or representations of folk either deceased or petri-fied by enchantment, and that the spirits of these folk were thought of as occupying such stones or boulders is, I think, clear enough

---

[1] R. A. S. Macalister, *The Archæology of Ireland*, p. 105; W. G. Wood-Martin, *op. cit.*, pp. 302–3.

from the circumstances of fairy tradition. That is, for one reason or another, the spirits of the dead, or the dead-alive and enchanted people who ensouled these stones, came to be classed in many cases as " fairies " rather than as ghosts. " I am struck by the fact," wrote Sir John Rhys, " that the fairies are not infrequently located on or near ancient sites, such as seem to be Corwrion, the margin of Llyn Indyn, etc., on which, I am told, there are hut foundations." [1] In other parts of Wales, too, similar traditions exist. " At Banwan Bryddin, a few miles from Neath, a stone pillar long stood on a tumulus which by the peasants was considered a fairy ring. The late Lady Mackworth caused it to be removed to a grotto she was constructing on her grounds. An old under-gardener on her estate told the Rev. Mr. Williams, of Tir-y-Cwm, that this act would not go unpunished by the guardian of the stone. He had seen the fairies dancing in the rings of Banwan Bryddin. Lady M.'s grotto, which had cost thousands of pounds to erect, was no sooner finished than a terrific thunderstorm swept the estate, and the next morning the grotto was gone. The hill had fallen over it and hidden it for ever. That night the gardener and his friends heard the fairies laughing loud after the storm had cleared away." [2]

Cromlechs in Wales are associated with the fairies. A shepherd of Frennifawn saw them dancing about an old cromlech there, and it is thought that they protect the cromlechs. When farmers attempt to remove the standing stones from their fields, storms interrupt the work, or swarms of bees, which are thought to be fairies in disguise.[3]

At Tara, in Ireland, is a stone of red sandstone about five feet above ground, which has a figure sculped upon it. " The figure stands out in fairly high relief. . . . It resembles one of those strange fertility and luck-bringing figures which are seen occasionally on the walls of churches." It is much worn, its legs are crossed, it seems to have a torque round its neck, " and at the sides of the head are two great projections which can hardly be ears, and are much like horns." [4] There is no doubt in my mind that the figure is that of a fairy, or elf, as its general appearance reveals. It gives me the impression of a fairly late superimposition upon an Iron Age stone monument. The " Blue

---

[1] J. Rhys, *op. cit.*, p. 674.   [2] Wirt Sikes, *British Goblins*, pp. 374–5.
[3] Wirt Sikes, *op. cit.*, pp. 380 ff.
[4] R. A. S. Macalister, *Tara*, pp. 52 ff.

Stone " just outside the town of St. Andrews, in Fife, was said to be a haunt of the elves; [1] and the favourite meeting-place of the fays of Chillingham, in Northumberland, was the " Hurle Stone," around which they danced to the strains of elfin music. [2] Near Granna, in County Galway, there is an inscribed stone, known to the peasantry as " the Stone of the Fruitful Fairy." It is a boulder of very irregular form, measuring 46 inches by 32 inches, and presents water-worn hollows. [3] A few miles from the old boundaries of Wychwood Forest, in Oxfordshire, lies a circle of monoliths known as the Rollright Stones. It is said that the fairies dance round the " king," or principal stone, and that " they were little folk, like girls to look at." [4] Mr. T. J. Westropp remarks that stone monuments all over Ireland are found to be connected with the phooka, or puca, " the malignant prototype of Puck." [5]

" In the Parish of Pembray, near Llanelly, Wales, is a Holy Stone, around which the young people of the district assemble every Good Friday. Not far away is a village known as Cwm Verman, where the *Bobl Bach*, or Little People, are said to live. They are also known as the *Bendith y Mamau* (' the Mothers ') in the same district, an unusual circumstance. Near this place is a farmhouse called *Ty Gwyn*, or ' the House of Gwyn,' who is the son of (the British god) Nudd, and who is King of the Fairies. At the top of the valley is a large mound surrounded by a deep ditch where the fairies danced. This burial mound is situated on the side of a hill on the top of which is a large rectangular camp, whilst less than a mile away is the stone circle of Cilmaenllwyd so that we have close together the residential camp, the stone circle for worship and the burial mound." [6]

Mr. J. W. Lukis has asserted, with regard to the cromlechs, tumuli, and other ancient sites in Glamorganshire, Wales: " There are always fairy tales and ghost stories connected with them, some fully believed by the inhabitants of these localities." [7] In the Island of North Ronaldshay, Orkney, at the beginning of the year

---

[1] J. Wilkie, *Bygone Fife*, pp. 372–3.
[2] G. Tate, *History of Alnwick*, I, p. 438.
[3] W. G. Wood-Martin, *op. cit.*, p. 56.
[4] A. J. Evans, *Folk-Lore*, VI, pp. 6 ff.
[5] T. J. Westropp, " A Folk-Lore Survey of County Clare," *Folk-Lore*, XXI, p. 183.
[6] G. Arbour Stephens, *Folk-Lore*, I, pp. 385–6.
[7] J. W. Lukis, in *Archæologia Cambrensis*, 4th series, VI, p. 174.

N

the people formerly " circled round in fairy dance " a perforated standing-stone nine or ten feet in height.[1]

The " spriggans," a species of Cornish fairies, are to be found only in the neighbourhood of " the cairns, coits, or cromlechs, burrows, or detached stones, with which it is unlucky for mortals to meddle." [2]

Wentz, quoting Borlase, says that in ancient Ireland the Tuatha Dé Danann were approached by a pilgrimage made to their abode, a spirit-haunted tumulus, around which they remained during three days and three nights, fasting. Later, the Tuatha Dé were expected to appear and grant the pilgrim's prayer. Near Lough Gair, in Munster, Ireland, is a hill known as Knoel-lainy, where on the night of St. John, people used to gather from all quarters. They made a procession round the hill, says Nutt, carrying poles to which wisps of straw were fixed. But the fairy Ainé, who with her host inhabited the hill, appeared on one occasion and courteously suggested that they would depart, as the fairies " wanted the hill to themselves." The ceremony gives the impression as having been anciently associated with the fairy cultus.

For the sake of comparison, and because some foreign instances fill up gaps in British tradition, I add a brief paragraph relative to these. The *korregs* and *courils*, fairies of Brittany, invariably haunt its stone circles. The dolmen of Manné-er Hrock, at Locmariaquer, in Brittany, is said to have been built by a fairy.[3] In the legend of St. Armentaire we read of a fairy called Esterelle, to whom barren women were wont to sacrifice at a certain stone.[4] Another fairy built the Tioul de las Fadas, in Haute Auvergne, to shelter herself from the wind and rain.[5] A fay is said to have buried her husband at the cromlech of Roque Brun, in the Canton of La Double, Perigord. It was taboo even to touch the crom-lech.[6] Fairies inhabit the dolmen known as the Maison des Fées at la Sauvagère, near Domfront, and steal straying cattle— perhaps a memory of an ancient teind or tithe of bestial once offered up to them.

[1] *The Old Statistical Account of Scotland*, VII, p. 489.
[2] R. Hunt, *Popular Romances of the West of England*, p. 81.
[3] B. C. A. Windle, Introduction to Tyson's *Pygmies of the Ancients*, p. lxxii.
[4] M. Cambry, *Monuments Celtiques*, p. 342.
[5] M. Cambry, *op. cit.*, p. 232.
[6] T. Keightley, *op. cit.*, p. 472 and note.

The Scandinavian story of Thorsten tells how the dwarfs had their dwelling-places in stones.[1] The Edda describes how the *duergar*, or dwarfs, dwelt in the ground and in stones, and in the Norse " Alvis-Mal " an elf is made to say: " I possess, under the stone, my seat."   Wherever cromlechs are to be found in India, traditions that they were dwarfs' houses are attached to them.[2] Grimm says that in the Netherlands hills containing sepulchral urns are called *alfenbergen*, or " elfs' hills." [3] In the Faroe Islands dwarfs are supposed to dwell in stones, which are numerous all over the archipelago.[4]   In Sweden the elves recline in little stones of a circular form, called " elf-mills." [5]

Barren women in many places have contact with idols and rough stones in the hope that these may render them fruitful. This seems to me a reminiscence of the notion that the spirits of those awaiting rebirth dwelt therein. It will be recalled that the rock, tree, or pool where the Australian Blackfellow believes that a spirit awaiting rebirth takes up its dwelling is known as the *nanja*. Were not such fairies as we have been dealing with, and who dwelt in stones, the British equivalents of these antipodean " fairies " awaiting reincarnation? As regards the French examples of such *nanja* stones, as we may conveniently call them, Hartland has given it as his opinion that " these facts are only explicable on the supposition that they were the object of a very ancient cult, too deeply rooted in the popular affections to be wholly supplanted by the Church "—which presently, indeed, tolerates them, and even in certain instances recognizes them to some extent.

The dwarfish proportions of the fays who inhabit these stones is to be accounted for by the ancient belief in the comparatively diminutive size of the human soul, when apart from its earthly tenement. The soul, primitive man believed, could hardly be of the same size as the body, otherwise the latter could not contain it. It appears to have been normally regarded as about two-thirds of the bodily bulk in size, though its alleged proportions differed according to tribe and locality.

Some of the megaliths of which I have been speaking were certainly associated with ritual in the form of human sacrifice, as the survival of many ancient customs makes clear. I merely

---

[1] Joske, *International Arch. für Ethnographie*, VIII, p. 254.
[2] Meadows Taylor, *Folk-Lore*, p. 401.   [3] J. Grimm, *op. cit.*, p. 449.
[4] W. A. Craigie, *Scandinavian Folk-Lore*, pp. 138–41.
[5] Afzelius, *Svenska Folk-Viser*, III.

indicate the fact, having no space for its discussion. The early Christians in Britain were hard put to it to extirpate the worship of standing stones among the native population. The Roman emperors Constantine, Valentinian, and Theodosius did their best to destroy worship at standing stones, and in the year A.D. 657 the Council of Tours banished all such worshippers from the Church. Even in the time of Canute it was found necessary to forbid the worship of stones, trees, and fountains.

I have already said something concerning fairies in trees, and so will merely summarize the rest of what I have to record on this subject. The Irish fairies regard the hawthorn as their favourite resting-place, and no peasant will cut it down.[1] The thorn was also the favourite gathering-place of the Northumberland elves.[2] In the ballad of *Sir Cawline* a lady dares the hero to go to " Eldridge Hill," where a thorn grows, to await the coming of an elfin knight. Elder trees are chiefly inhabited by the fairies of the Isle of Man.[3] W. B. Yeats wrote that if an Irish farmer cut down a fairy bush, the elves would place a black lamb in his flock as a warning. This happened to a relation of his own in Sligo![4] When fairy bushes in County Leitrim were cut down, says L. L. Duncan, " the fairies pelted the miscreant's house with stones, like poltergeists."[5] A fairy in the Western Isles of Scotland, says Dr. Carmichael, dwelt in a tree and came forth occasionally to give " milk of wisdom " to local women. There was formerly in the park of Sir Robert Vaughan, in Wales, a celebrated old oak tree, named " the Elf's Hollow Tree."[6] In the ballad of *Tam Lin* the hero forbids his sweetheart to pluck roses from a bush, or to break it at the fairy site of Carterhaugh. I will add one foreign instance only of " fairies " dwelling in trees, but it is a cogent one. Mr. G. D. Hornblower, an Egypto-logist, writing of an acacia grove at the Egyptian village of Nezlet Batran, near Gizeh, says that it is sacred to " the Inhabitants of the Acacias," who live underground. The local tradition has it that when the Egyptian gods were displaced, first by Christian and then by Moslem saints, the trees were allotted to them. So, like the Tuatha Dé Danann of Ireland, and under the same

---

[1] Lady Wilde, *op. cit.*, p. 39.   [2] *Denham Tracts*, II, p. 136.
[3] W. Y. E. Wentz, *op. cit.*, p. 126.
[4] W. B. Yeats, *Folk-Lore*, X, p. 123.
[5] L. L. Duncan, " Further Notes from County Leitrim," *Folk-Lore*, V, p. 178
[6] B. C. A. Windle, *op. cit.*, p. lxxviii.

conditions, the old gods were relegated to the earth and the tree-trunks, and took on the status of " fairies." [1]   What I have said above respecting the possible *nanja* status of stones applies equally in the case of trees and bushes.

I must also briefly refer to a few of the outstanding instances in which fairies are believed to inhabit wells. I have already mentioned the Minchmoor Well, or Cheese Well, in Peebles-shire, which is thought to be in charge of a fairy, to whom some offering must be made—a piece of cheese, or a pin—and wells at Brayton, Harphan, Holderness, and Atwick, in Yorkshire, and Wooler, in Northumberland, are presided over by fairies or " spirits." In Inverness a fairy well existed. Women whose babies did not thrive sufficiently, and were suspected of being changelings, brought them there, together with some small offering, left the infants on the spot all night, and in the morning found their own children in place of the interloper.[2] In East Yorkshire the Robin Round Cap Well is haunted by a brownie.[3] At St. Mungo's Well, at Huntly, as lately as 1883, the people assembled on the First of May and carried away bottles of its water as a charm *against* the fairies, who were supposed to hold their revels at the Elfin Croft hard by.[4] Anyone who drank the waters of a well called Tobar Bhile na Beinne, in Argyll, left some equivalent to the fairy who guarded it. In France hundreds of wells are under the tutelage of " saints," who are either fairies or other spirits disguised by later piety.

The fact that certain tracts of ground were regarded as " sacred " to the fairies, and that no spade or plough might disturb their surface, or no bush or tree which grew thereon might be damaged, makes it abundantly clear that such spaces were regarded as the precincts of spirits to whom some kind of worship was offered and that these spots were regarded as taboo, or sacrosanct. Examples of the existence of such sacred demesnes abound on British soil. The first castle of Glamis, the childhood home of our Queen, might not be built on the hill of Denoon in that neighbourhood, because it was associated with traditions of the fairy race, and its foundations were nightly overthrown by the outraged elves.[5] A similar tale is told of the castle of Melgund,

<hr>

[1] D. A. Mackenzie, *The Folk-Lore of Scotland*, p. 214.
[2] Frazer, *Northern Folk-Lore*, p. 17.
[3] J. M. Mackinlay, *Folk-Lore of Scottish Lochs and Springs*, p. 164.
[4] C. F. Gordon Cumming, *In the Hebrides*, p. 212.
[5] J. C. Guthrie, *The Vale of Strathmore*, p. 33 ff.

in the parish of Aberlemno.[1]   Richard Corbett, Bishop of Oxford, in his collected poems, edited by Gilchrist, says :—

> " If ever you at Bosworth would be found
> Then turn your cloaks, for this is fairy ground."

The allusion is to Chorley Forest, near Bosworth, evidently an elfin preserve. To turn the cloak, or coat, was a sure safeguard against fairy enmity, making the sprite visible to the lonely wayfarer, so that he could be struck at, when he would refrain from annoyance.

In Tipperary is an oddly shaped hill, which was known to be fairy ground. A certain herdsman insisted upon grazing his cattle there, whereupon the Queen of the Fairies appeared to him by night in divers terrible shapes and stampeded the beasts, many of which fell into pits, or were drowned in neighbouring lakes.[2] A man in the Loch Awe district, while travelling over a hill, seated himself on its summit to rest, but two fairies appeared and tried to push him over the cliff. He escaped, but, on revisiting the site later, was sadly mishandled by the enraged elves, who warned him that worse would happen to him did he ever return.[3] An old woman in Devonshire, who had a beautiful bed of tulips in her garden, found that the pixies were wont to repair to it with their infants. She left them unmolested, but at her death her heir converted the spot into a parsley bed, whereupon everything in the garden withered.[4] Two lads in Galloway, who were ploughing in a field, described a circle round a fairy thorn, the space about which was regarded as sacrosanct. On ending the furrow they found a green table heaped with fairy viands. One of them partook of the fare and throve greatly afterwards.[5] The burn of Invernauld, and the neighbouring hill of Durcha, in Sutherland, were haunted by fairies, who once chased a man into the sea and destroyed a new mill because the earth for the embankment of the mill-dam had been taken from the side of their hill. In the Isle of Man it was believed that to pasture sheep on ground which contained a stone circle would certainly bring disease to the flock.[6]

---

[1] J. C. Guthrie, *op. cit.*, pp. 316 f.
[2] F. J. Olcott, *The Book of Elves and Fairies*, pp. 20 ff.
[3] MacDougall and Calder, *Fairy-Tales and Folk-Lore*, p. 191.
[4] Mrs. Bray, *Letters on Devonshire*.
[5] R. H. Cromek, *op. cit.*, p. 301.
[6] Tyack, *Lore and Legend*, p. 36.

An old Scottish rhyme assures us of the misfortunes which will attend any infringement of fairy territory:—

> " He wha tills the fairies' green,
> Nae luck again shall hae,
> And he who spills the fairies' ring,
> Betide him want and wae.
> For weirdless days and weary nights
> Are his till his deein' day."

Though we are also told that

> " He wha cleans the fairies' ring
> An easy death shall dee." [1]

Writing on fairy beliefs in County Clare, Ireland, Mr. T. J. Westropp says: " The son of a farmer, called Nihill, told me in 1892 that, after some days' wreckage and removal of the outer wall of the fine triple stone fort of Cahercalla, near Quin, his father was stricken with acute pain, and only recovered from his illness when work was stopped. A certain landlord nearly lost the use of an eye from an explosion when blasting a rock in an earth-fort, and a local astronomer had his hand injured by a similar cause. A workman, employed to level the earthworks at Dooneeva, fell to all appearance dead and was only brought back to life by the ministrations of a wise woman of the neighbour-hood." [2]

We have seen that Robert Kirk put it on record that the Highlanders of his time (1691) refused to remove earth or timber from a fairy knoll. In Ireland one might not remove timber or stone from a fairy rath, or the elves would blind him or give him a crooked mouth.[3] An affliction was said to be caused by treading on fairy grass. It was a weakness, the result of sudden hunger which came upon one during a long journey, or in particular places, in consequence of treading on this grass, which, in England, is known as shaking-grass (briza) and is said to be good for the ague.[4]

I think I have brought sufficient evidence to prove that fairy ground was formerly regarded as of peculiar sanctity in many British localities. I have not here drawn upon that considerable body of Scottish evidence which is associated with those untilled

---

[1] R. Chambers, *Popular Rhymes of Scotland*, p. 324.
[2] T. J. Westropp, " Folk-Lore Survey of County Clare," *Folk-Lore*, XXI, pp. 194 ff.
[3] Lady Wilde, *op. cit.*, p. 142.
[4] J. Cameron, *Gaelic Names of Plants*, p. 120.

unsubstantial. In a word, they are as much human as spiritual; they reveal an association with that early doctrine of spirit which held that the spirit-body of man had a certain material and ponderable quality. If there is any confusion between them and the dead it is in respect of more modern ideas of the dead.

In my opinion the association of British fairies with rocks, trees, and lakes, or wells, reveals them not so much as " elemental " or nature-spirits, as human souls lurking in these and, like their modern Australian counterparts, awaiting reincarnation in human form. That, I believe, was the original form which the superstition concerning them assumed. The persistent tradition respecting fairy changelings and of infant kidnapping, too, appears to be related not so closely to the idea of human sacrifice, as Alfred Nutt and others conjectured, as to the notion of the dead human soul seeking reincarnation. The bodies of kidnapped children are unquestionably thought of as ensouled by aged spirits (the ancestors), and this I cannot interpret otherwise than as symbolic of reincarnation. The soul of the infant is spirited off to the abode of the fairy horde. The superstition, distorted as it is in certain of its features, is a memory of the doctrine of the reincarnation of human spirits in human bodies, and the physique of the changeling notoriously reveals at times the traits of senility.

Among the ancient Irish a tradition existed that divine personages and national heroes who were members of the Tuatha Dé Danann, or who were otherwise celebrated or honoured, underwent reincarnation. Miss E. Hull, Alfred Nutt, and Professor Macalister, have brought the whole battery of their erudition to bear upon this aspect of Irish religious tenet. Miss Hull thought that " there is no doubt that all the chief personages of this cycle [the Cuchullin cycle of Irish literature] were regarded as the direct descendants, or, it would be more correct to say, as avatars or reincarnations of the early gods. . . . There are indications in the birth-stories of nearly all the principal personages that they are looked upon simply as divine beings reborn on the human plane of life." [1]

Now the Tuatha Dé Danann degenerated into the later fairies of Ireland, who dwelt underground. Like all subterranean powers, they busied themselves in the task of stimulating the growth of the crops and vegetation and the increase of herds and flocks. We have here a divine caste not only reincarnating in the kings and

[1] E. Hull, quoted by Wentz, in *The Fairy Faith in Celtic Countries*, p. 368.

heroes of Ireland, but stimulating the national food supply by magic, precisely as did the gods of Egypt, who were reincarnated in the Pharaohs and who presided over vegetable growth. The difference is, apparently, that in the case of Ireland the transition was from the god to the fairy spirit, whereas in Egypt development seems to have taken place from the spirit of growth to the god. There is no question, however, that, as Alfred Nutt has indicated, the Tuatha Dé Danann were originally developed from mere spirits of growth, which later assumed godhead, and which returned at a still later time to something resembling their primitive humble status, doubtless because of a more popular and primitive conception of them.   That they also came to be regarded as the souls of the dead, in virtue of the association of the deceased with growth, it seems impossible to doubt.

We discover, then, the point of departure of the idea that the fairies were ancestral in their nature. They were the dead ancestors, man-gods, or celebrities, who later returned to earth-life in a reincarnated form.   As such they were revered in a species of cultus, and received food-offerings.   In the same way, what may mildly be stigmatized as the fallacy that the fairies were in some cases " elementary " or nature-spirits may be explained.   The elves may at first sight seem to compose a class of nature-spirits because of their residence in rocks, trees, and wells, but their en-soulment of these *nanja* spots is accounted for by the tradition of a time when they were thought of as occupying them as places of vantage whence they might the more readily achieve reincarnation through a mortal mother.   In my view the Australian and other evidence reveals the whole process and makes it impossible to adopt any other explanation.   The proof, too, that the belief in reincarnation existed and still exists in the mind of the Irish peasant is pressed down and running over, and the existence of fairly numerous *nanja* localities in ancient Scotland, the traditions of which have survived to some extent, makes it clear that a similar belief formerly existed in North Britain as well.   Nor is Wales destitute of similar localities.   And, as I have made it clear, many of these spots are associated with the fairies.   At the same time, I hope that I will not be conceived as implying that *no* fairy types were ever derived from nature-spirits pure and simple.   Indeed, in some foreign areas such have actually been identified.

The notion that a belief in fairies is to be accounted for by a memory of aboriginal or dwarfish races, and by no other means, several different epochs of the distant past are frequently mingled in tales concerning the fairy folk—a process eloquent of their sustained antiquity in our island.

As we have seen, the terms of certain ritual survivals reveal the existence of a fairy cultus in which spirits regarded as reincarnating at intervals were also thought of as powers exercising their fertilizing magic upon the growth of vegetation, of the crops and of flocks and herds. To my way of thinking, the picture we receive of them scarcely gives us any option but to regard them as the folk-lore or mythic equivalents of that class of spirits which the Central Australian natives and other primitive folk consider to be the souls of their departed ancestors, ever ready to reincarnate in the bodies of newly conceived infants and returning to their spirit nuclei when at last they die, there to await a fresh reincarnation. I believe that the proof I have adduced in respect of this theory, and the parallel illustrations I have furnished, will bear the strain even of the most searching examination, although the Australian part of the evidence would seem to refer to a somewhat more primitive outlook than any forthrightly expressed in British fairy tradition. I am not positively concerned here with the origins of other European fairy systems, but from what I know of these, their general identity with the principles of the Australian and other savage and barbarous spirit-cults appears indisputable. In all likelihood the Australian cult represents a former, and now " embalmed," body of early belief which spread from a common centre.

In my view the theory of the multiple origin of the fairy superstition, so long respected, requires partial restatement. The hypothesis that ideas respecting fairies were developed from several different sources—beliefs about nature-spirits, classical forms such as gods, nymphs, or Fates, the memory of aboriginal races, or fallen angels—and that these came to be gradually combined into one well-defined corpus of belief, should be tempered by the much more reasonable and acceptable view that these hypotheses of origin are merely the sequels and consequences of the original legend respecting the fairies that they were the spirits of the ancient dead awaiting reincarnation. These " sources " or " strands," so called, appear to me as inferences which arose out of that belief, as ideas which were inherent in it and which issued from it, being rather implications from its original legend, basic factors belonging to and embedded in that legend. Thus the fairies were thought to resemble elementary or nature-spirits because, like those of Australia, they dwelt in natural objects during the period when they awaited reincarnation; they give the impression of aboriginal races simply because they were originally the ghosts of aborigines or primitive folk, and because the traits of such folk have traditionally adhered to them; they are generally diminutive, or even microscopic, because primitive peoples had slightly differing conceptions of the dwarfish proportions of the human soul, most of which appear to have survived. Lastly, they give the impression of a humanity somewhat altered by enchantment, or the conditions of a magical environment, for the reason that early man was under the impression that death was a consequence of magic, and that magic governed the circumstances of his after-life. In short, I believe these varying conceptions of fairy origin did not gradually build up a composite idea of elfin spirits, as so many folk-lorists aver when they speak of " the numerous threads that have gone to make up the web of fairy tradition," or when they state that interaction has taken place " between animistic beliefs in groups of imaginary beings and folk-memory of earlier races." I prefer to accept the view, developed during many years devoted to the careful examination of the fairy problem, that the seemingly disconnected theories respecting fairy origins actually represent ideas which naturally issued from the main body of fairy tradition because they were implicit therein, and which later received the illusory status of separate contributory sources to that tradition not only because they seemed superficially to have the sanction of popular credit, but for the reason that this view of separate traditional strands or sources received powerful advocacy from students of traditional science. Each and all of these so-called " contributory sources of belief " were, I am persuaded, already embedded and apparent in the fairy tradition ages before they came to be regarded by students of folk-lore as worthy of consideration as separate hypotheses of fairy origin. The " aboriginal," and especially the ancestral, views of the elfin race are obviously of very remote acceptance. That of its dwarfish stature is manifestly implied in its earliest idea as the condition of the human soul apart from the body. That which would link the fairies to nature or elementary spirits is readily explained not only by their environmental conditions, but by the primitive notion, still accepted by many peoples of low culture, that the spirits of the dead take up their abode in the wilderness. The persuasion that they represent in part the gods, nymphs, or fates of classical myth is certainly a later one, and perhaps out of this alone can a case be made for regarding it as a " contributory source " of fairy tradition, though it applies to more or less restricted areas and has only a limited application to British fairy beginnings. With this possible exception, I maintain that all these hypotheses of a multiple origin are merely themselves myths embryonic in the earliest conception regarding fairy spirits, and explanatory of certain traits in the original legend concerning them. Those who daily deal with the problems of myth realize only too well its propensity to exaggerate or lay stress upon certain circumstances inherent in its original nuclei. In this particular instance, students of folk-lore, in an endeavour to account for fairy origins, have, I think, confused the issue, and have erected as hypotheses of these origins ideas inherent in the nucleal tradition of Faerie.

BIBLIOGRAPHY OF WORKS CONSULTED

(*N.B.* Essays and articles are referred to in the paginal notes only.)

ALLIER, RAOUL, *The Mind of the Savage*, 1929.
ALLIES, J., *The Antiquities and Folk-Lore of Worcestershire*.
ANDREWS, ELIZABETH, *Ulster Folklore*, 1913.
AUBREY, JOHN, *Miscellanies*, 1784.

BLACK, G. F., *Examples of Printed Folk-Lore Concerning the Orkney and Shetland Isles* (Folk-Lore Society), 1903.
BOTTRELL, W., *Traditional and Hearthside Stories of West Cornwall*, 1870, 1885.
BOVET, RICHARD, *Pandæmonium, or the Devil's Cloister*, 1685.
BOWKER, J., *Goblin Tales of Lancashire*, N.D.
BRAND, JOHN, *Observations on Popular Antiquities*, 1900.
BRAY, MRS., *The Borders of the Tamar and the Tavy*, 2 vols., 1879.
British Calendar Customs, Scotland (Folk-Lore Society), 1937, 1939.
BURNE, C., *Shropshire Folk-Lore*, 1883–85.
BURTON, ROBERT, *The Anatomy of Melancholy* (New edn.), 1887.

CAMERON, ALEXANDER, *Reliquiæ Celticæ*, 2 vols., 1892–94.
CAMERON, JOHN, *The Gaelic Names of Plants*, 1900.
CAMPBELL, J. F., *Popular Tales of the West Highlands*, 4 vols. (New ed.), 1890. Extra vol. published by the Anthropological and Folk-Lore Society of Scotland, 1940.
CAMPBELL, J. G., *Superstitions of the Highlands and Islands of Scotland*, 1900.
—— *The Fians* (in *Waifs and Strays of Celtic Tradition*, Argyllshire Series No. IV), 1891.
CARMICHAEL, ALEXANDER, *Carmina Gadelica*, 2 vols., 1912.
CHAMBERS, ROBERT, *Popular Rhymes of Scotland*, 1841.
—— *The Picture of Scotland*, 2 vols., 1828.
CHILD, F. J., *The English and Scottish Popular Ballads*, 2 vols., 1882.
Choice Notes, from *Notes and Queries*, 1859.
CLODD, E., *Tom Tit Tot*, 1898.
COLLIER, J. PAYNE, *The Mad Pranks and Merry Jests of Robin Goodfellow*. (Reprinted from the edn. of 1628. Percy Society Publications, Vol. II.) 1841. Reprinted also in Joseph Ritson's *Fairy Tales, Legends, and Romances Illustrating Shakespeare*, pp. 173 ff., 1875.
COX, MARIAN ROALFE, *Cinderella* (Folk-Lore Society), 1895.
—— *An Introduction to the Study of Folklore*, 1897.
CRAWLEY, A. E., *The Idea of the Soul*, 1909.
CROKER, T. CROFTON, *Fairy Legends and Traditions of the South of Ireland*, 3 vols., 1828.
CROMEK, R. H., *Remains of Nithsdale and Galloway Song*, 1810. New edition, 1880.
CURTIN, JEREMIAH, *Myths and Folk-Lore of Ireland*, N.D.; *Hero-Tales of Ireland*, 1894.

DALYELL, J. G., *The Darker Superstitions of Scotland*, 1834.
D'AUSSY, LEGRAND, *Fabliaux ou Contes* 1829.
DIXON, JAMES, *Ancient Poems, Ballads and Songs of the Peasantry of England*, 1857.
DIXON, JOHN H., *Gairloch*, 1886.

O

Examples of Printed Folk-Lore Concerning Fife (ed. J. E. Simpkins, County Folk-Lore Series, Vol. VII), 1912.

FISON and HOWITT, *The Kamilaroi and Kurnai*, 1880.
Folk-Lore (from 1890 to date); *Folk-Lore Journal*, 1883–9; *Folk-Lore Record*, 1878–82.   (Organs of the Folk-Lore Society.)
FRAZER, J. G., *Taboo and the Perils of the Soul*, 1917.
—— *The Magic Art and the Evolution of Kings*, 2 vols., 1917.
—— *Spirits of the Corn and of the Wild*, 2 vols., 1917.
—— *The Belief in Immortality*, 3 vols., 1924.

GAIDOZ, H., and ROLLAND, E., *Melusine, Recueil de Mythologie*, 1878.
Gentleman's Magazine Library.   (Ed. G. L. Gomme.)   English Traditions and Foreign Customs, 1885.
GERVASE OF TILBURY, *Otia Imperialia* (Rolls Series), 1875.
Giraldus Cambrensis.   (Ed. T. Wright.)   Bohn's " Antiquaries Library," 1863.
GOMME, G. L., *Ethnology in Folklore*, 1892.
GORDON CUMMING, C. F., *In the Hebrides*, 1883.
GRAHAM, P., *Sketches Descriptive of the Picturesque Scenery of Perthshire*, 1810.
GRANT, K. W., *Myth, Tradition, and Story from Western Argyll*, 1925.
GRANT (Mrs., of Laggan), *Essays on the Superstitions of the Highlanders of Scotland*, 1811.
GREGOR, W., *Notes on the Folk-Lore of the North-East of Scotland* (Folk-Lore Society), 1881.
GREGORY, LADY, *Visions and Beliefs in the West of Ireland*, 1920.
GRIEVE, SYMINGTON, *The Book of Colonsay and Oronsay*, 2 vols., 1923.
GRIMM, JACOB, *Teutonic Mythology*, 4 vols. (trans. by J. S. Stallybrass) 1880–8.
GUEST, LADY CHARLOTTE, *The Mabinogion*, 1877.

HADDON, A. C., *Magic and Fetishism*, 1910.
HARLAND, J., and WILKINSON, T. T., *Lancashire Legends*, 1873.
HARTLAND, E. SIDNEY, *The Science of Fairy Tales*, 1890.
—— *English Fairy and Folk-Tales*, N.D.
HALLIWELL, J. O., *Nursery Rhymes and Nursery Tales of England*, N.D.
HAZLITT, W. C., *The Fairy Mythology of Shakespeare*, 1875.
—— *Fairy Tales*, 1878.
HENDERSON, GEORGE, *Survivals in Belief Among the Celts*, 1911; *The Norse Influence on Celtic Scotland*, 1910.
HENDERSON, W., *Folk-Lore of the Northern Counties* (Folk-Lore Society), 1879.
HIBBERT, S., *A Description of the Shetland Isles*, 1822.
HOWELLS, W., *Cambrian Superstitions*, 1831.
HULL, ELEANOR, *Folklore of the British Isles*, 1928; *The Cuchullin Saga*, 1898.
HUNT, ROBERT, *Popular Romances of the West of England*, 1923.
HYDE, DOUGLAS, *Beside the Fire*, 1910.

JACKSON, J., *The Originall of Unbelief*, 1625.
JACOBS, J., *Celtic Fairy Tales*, 1892.
—— *More Celtic Fairy Tales*, 1894.
—— *English Fairy Tales*, 1890.
—— *More English Fairy Tales*, 1894.
JAMES I and VI, KING, *Dæmonologie*, 1597.
JAMIESON, JOHN, *Illustrations of Northern Antiquities*, 1814.
JOHNSTON, A. W., and JOHNSTON, A., *Old Lore Miscellany of Orkney, Shetland, Caithness, and Sutherland* (Viking Club), 1907–8.

JOHNSON, WALTER, *Folk-Memory*, 1908.
JOYCE, P. W., *Old Celtic Romances*, 1920.

KEIGHTLEY, THOMAS, *The Fairy Mythology*, 1850.
KENNEDY, PATRICK, *Legendary Fictions of the Irish Celts*, 1891.
KIRK, ROBERT, *The Secret Commonwealth of Elves, Fauns, and Fairies*, 1933.
KITTREDGE, G. L., *A Study of Gawain and the Green Knight*, 1916.
KRAPPE, A. H., *The Science of Folklore*, 1930.

LAING, D., *Early Popular Poetry of Scotland*, 2 vols., 1895.
LANG, A., *Custom and Myth*, 1893.
LARMINIE, W., *West Irish Folk-Tales and Romances*, 1893.
LELAND, C. G., *Etruscan–Roman Remains in Popular Tradition*, 1892.
—— *Aradia, or the Gospel of the Witches of Italy*, 1899.
LESCURE, M. DE, *Le Monde Enchanté*, 1883.
LEYDEN, J., *The Complaynt of Scotland* (Intro. to), 1801.

MACALISTER, R. A. S., *Tara*, 1931.
MACCULLOCH, J. A., *The Childhood of Fiction*, 1905.
—— *Mediaeval Faith and Fable*, 1932.
MACDONALD, J., *Religion and Myth*, 1893.
MACDOUGALL, J., *Folk and Hero Tales* (Waifs and Strays of Celtic Tradition, No. III), 1891.
MACDOUGALL, J., and CALDER, G., *Folk Tales and Fairy Lore in Gaelic and English*, 1910.
MACGREGOR, A. A., *The Peat Fire Flame*, 1937.
MACGREGOR, A., *Highland Superstitions*, 1901.
MACKENZIE, W., *Gaelic Incantations, Charms, and Blessings of the Hebrides*, 1895.
MACKINLAY, J. M., *Folklore of Scottish Lochs and Springs*, 1893.
MACINNES, D., *Folk and Hero Tales* (Waifs and Strays of Celtic Tradition, No. II), 1890.
MACLEOD, R. C., *The Island Clans during Six Centuries*, N.D.
McPHERSON, J. M., *Primitive Beliefs in the North-East of Scotland*, 1929.
MACRITCHIE, DAVID, *The Testimony of Tradition*, 1890.
—— *Fians, Fairies, and Picts*, 1893.
MANNHARDT, W., *Wald- und Feld-Kulte*, 2 vols., 1875–7.
MAP, WALTER, *De Nugis Curialium* (trans. by F. Tupper and Marburg Bladen Ogle), 1924.
MARTIN, M., *A Description of the Western Islands of Scotland* (new ed.), 1934.
MAURY, L. F. A., *Les Fées du Moyen Age*, 1843.
MILLAR, HUGH, *Scenes and Legends of the North of Scotland*, 1872.
MITCHELL, ARTHUR, *The Past in the Present*, 1880.
MOORE, A. D., *The Folk-Lore of the Isle of Man*, 1891.
MORGAN, *Phœnix Britannicus*, 1732.
MURRAY, M. A., *The God of the Witches*, N.D.

NAPIER, J., *Folklore, or Superstitious Beliefs in the West of Scotland*, 1879.
NICHOLSON, J., *Folk Lore of East Yorkshire*, 1890.
NUTT, A., *The Voyage of Bran*, 2 vols., 1895.

O'GRADY, STANDISH H., *Silva Gadelica*, 2 vols., 1892.
OWEN, E., *Welsh Folk-Lore*, 1896.

PARKER, K. L., *Australian Legendary Tales*, 1896.
PATON, L. B., *Spiritism and the Cult of the Dead in Antiquity*, 1921.
PENNANT, THOMAS, *A Tour in Scotland and Voyage to the Hebrides*, 2 vols., 1790.

PERCY, THOMAS, *Reliques of English Poetry*, 3 vols., 1775.
PERRAULT, *Contes du Temps Passé*, 1697.
PITCAIRN, R., *Criminal Trials in Scotland*, 1833.
POLSON, A., *Our Highland Folklore Heritage*, 1926.
PUGH, J., *The Physicians of Myddvai*, 1861.

RAGLAN, LORD, *The Hero*, 1932.
RALPH OF COGGESHALL, *Chronicum Anglicanum* (ed. Stevenson, Rolls series),
    1875.
RADIN, *Primitive Religion*, 1938.
RICHARDSON, M. A., *The Local Historian's Table-Book*, 3 vols., 1846.
RIVERS, W. H. R., *The Todas*, 1906.
ROGERS, C., *Scotland, Social and Domestic*, 1869.
RHYS, J., *Celtic Folklore, Welsh and Manx*, 1901.
—— *Lectures on the Origin and Growth of Religion as Illustrated by Celtic
    Heathendom* (Hibbert Lectures), 1888.
RITSON, J., *Fairy Tales*, 1831.

SAXBY, JESSIE M. E., *Shetland Traditional Lore*, 1932.
SCHEBESTA, PAUL, *With Congo Pygmies*, 1933.
SCOTT, REGINALD, *The Discoverie of Witchcraft*, 1584.
SCOTT, SIR WALTER, *Minstrelsy of the Scottish Border*, 4 vols., 1873 and 1902.
—— *Letters on Demonology and Witchcraft*, 1868.
SHARPE, CHARLES KIRKPATRICK, *A Historical Account of the Belief in Witch-
    craft in Scotland*, 1884.
SIKES, WIRT, *British Goblins*, 1880.
SPENCER, B., and GILLEN, F. J., *Northern Tribes of Central Australia*, 1904.
SINCLAIR, GEORGE, *Satan's Invisible World Discovered*, 1746.
STERNBERG, T., *The Dialect and Folk-Lore of Northamptonshire*, 1851.
STEWART, W. G., *The Popular Superstitions of the Highlands of Scotland*,
    1823.
SUTHERLAND, G., *Folk-Lore Gleanings and Character Sketches from the Far
    North*, 1937.

TAYLOR, ELIZABETH, *The Braemar Highlands*, 1869.
TRAIN, J., *Historical Account of the Isle of Man*, 1845.
TYLOR, *Primitive Culture*, 2 vols., 1929.
The Book of Bon-Accord, 2 vols., 1839.

WALDRON, G., *A Description of the Isle of Man*, 1865.
WAY, GREGORY LEWIS, *Fabliaux, or Tales Abridged from French Manuscripts
    of the XI and XII Centuries*, 2 vols., 1800.
WENTZ, W. Y. E., *The Fairy Faith in Celtic Countries*, 1911.
WILDE, LADY F. S., *Ancient Legends of Ireland*, 1888.
WILKIE, J., *Byegone Fife*, 1931.
WILLIAM OF NEWBURY, *Historia Rerum Anglicanum*, 1856.
WILSON, W., *Folklore and Genealogies of Uppermost Nithsdale, Dumfries and
    Sanquhar*, 1904.
WIMBERLEY, L. C., *Folklore in the English and Scottish Ballads*, 1928.
WOOD-MARTIN, W. G., *Pagan Ireland*, 1895.
WRIGHT, T., *Local Legends of Shropshire*.

YEARSLEY, MACLEOD, *The Folklore of Fairy Tale*, 1924.
Y Llyvyr Coch o Hergest (*The Red Book of Hergest*).   The text of the Mabino-
    gion and other Welsh tales (ed. by John Rhys and J. G. Evans), 1887.

INDEX

Gifts made by fairies, 37

Gods, possible derivation of some fairies from, 132 ff.; evidence of this from mediaeval literature, 133; derivation of fairies from the classical Fates, 133 f.; Tuscan fairies derived from, 141; Irish fairies "descended" from, 141 f.; fairies identified with goddesses of love, 147–8; conclusions respecting the theory, 154–5; Norse elves classed as, 162; sacrifices to these, 162

Gomme, L., on fairies as representatives of an aboriginal pigmy race, 117–18

" Green children," the legend of the, 8

Ground sacred to fairies, 187 f.

Gruagach, the, 4; offerings to, 5

Gwynn ap Nudd, as King of the Welsh fairies, 152

HADDON, A. C., 63

Hallowe'en, fairies and dead mingle at, 81

Hartland, E. S., 54–5

Hull, Miss E., 81, 103, 136, 143, 145, 179

Human beings, fairies as, 168

Hunting and riding in procession of fairies, 25–6

ILLUSION, fairy art of, 18

Initiation of people into fairy secrets, 190

Invisibility of fairies, 18–19

Ireland, fairies of, described, 3, 5–7, 11, 13, 17

Iron, fairy aversion to, 29–30

Iruntarinia, Australian spirits of the dead awaiting reincarnation, 158 f.; their resemblance to the Keltic *sidhe*, 158–9

KIDNAPPING by fairies compared with stories of return from otherworld, 75 ff.

Kings and queens, fairy, 15–17, 73

Kirk, Robert, 99, 100, 165

Krappe, A. H., 54

LAND of the gods (Keltic) not a sphere of the departed, 76

Lang, A., 59–60

Lar, the Roman domestic genius, 4–5; as ancestral fairy and origin of the belief, 91

Leechcraft, fairy, 28, 190

Leland, C. G., 98, 141

Loathly lady, the theme of the, 33 f.; explanation of the, 34–5

MAB, the " fairy queen," her origin, 136 f.; her possible association with the mythical Irish Queen Maeve, 136 f.; with the goddess Abundia, 136 f.

MacCulloch, Canon J. A., 62–3; his conclusions of relationship between fairies and the dead, 82–3; on the brownie, 88; his theories concerning the pechs or " Picts," 125 ff.; on natal influence of French fairies, 138

MacRitchie, D., 56–8; statement of his theory regarding fairies as aborigines, 115 f.; J. Jacobs on the same, 121–2; B. C. A. Windle on, 122; A. Lang on, 122–3; E. S. Hartland on, 123; A. Nutt on, 122–4; J. A. MacCulloch on, 125–8

Magic of the fairies, 17–21

Maury, A., 137

Merlin, 147

Mexico, grain-spirits in, 104 ff.

Morgan la Fée, 146; her myth discussed, 148 f.; her contest with other fairies, 148–9; confused with other figures of romance, 149; her resemblance to the Irish Morrigan, 149; possible derivation of her name, 149–50; Miss J. L. Weston on, 150–1; A. Nutt on, 151; her associations with Arthur, 151; conclusions respecting, 151–2

Morrigan, or Morrigu, an Irish fairy: her resemblance to Morgan la Fée, 149–51

" Mothers," the, ancient maternal deities: theory that fairies are derived from, 135 f.; in folk-lore, 140

Nanja, spots where Australian spirits await rebirth, 158, 159, 185, 187, 193

Neighbourly conduct of fairies, 30

Nereids of modern Greece, their resemblance to Keltic fairies, 140–1

Nimue, or Vivien, the fairy, 147

Nutt, A., 78, 101–4, 143–4, 151, 163, 175, 179

OFFERINGS made to fairies, 5, 89, 177–8; to Norse elves, 162

Ointment, magical, 19–20

Ossian, tale of, 72–3

PECHS, or " Picts," as aborigines or fairies, 3, 4; theories concerning, 115 ff.; J. A. MacCulloch on, 125 ff.; author's opinion respecting, 128 f.; peasant use of the term, 129; location of historical Picts and of traditions of the pechs compared, 129 f.

Phi, fairylike spirits of Siam, 108

Pigmies, Isle of the, 120–1

Pigmy races as fairies, theory of, 115 ff.; D. MacRitchie on, 115 f.; J. Jacobs on, 115 f.; B. C. A. Windle on, 122; A Lang on, 122–3; E. S. Hartland, A. Nutt, and J. A. MacCulloch on, 125–8; conclusions respecting the theory of, 130–1

Pilosi, spirits of ancient Gaul, 4, 107, 140

Pixies of south-western England, 188

9 782925 611288